GW00696551

NORTHAMPTON PUBLIC HOUSES & THEIR SIGNS

BY
JACK PLOWMAN

Happy Birthday.
Bill.
Jack Plowman.

AZLAN PUBLICATIONS
2010

Published in Northampton by Azlan Publications
2010
New Edition 2017

ISBN 978-0-9572480-0-7

Printed and bound by
MERLAND COPY & PRINT,
NORTHAMPTON.

CONTENTS

Illustrations.

Acknowledgements.

Introduction.

The Signs – Main Text.

Poem.

Tariffs.

New Pubs and Name Changes.

Sources.

Picture Credits.

Abbreviations and Conventions.

Future.

Maps.

ILLUSTRATIONS

There are quite a few old photographs of Northampton pubs, not the least the ones taken by the breweries at the beginning of the twentieth century. However, there is the problem of copyright and who owns them. I felt that rather than spend another year or so tracking down each picture it would be better to get the book in print. With this in mind I have used my photographs, a few photographs that are traceable and several drawings I have done based on some of the pictures I have seen over the years. I hope that in the future I will be able to produce another volume, perhaps just of old photographs, and/or combined with peoples' memories and anecdotes. To this end I would be pleased to hear from anyone with memories, stories, old pictures or anything else that they feel could be of interest to future readers. This book is primarily the result of *documentary* research and I would like to write, or *edit* another one that is made up of largely peoples' *own experiences*. The little pictures of pub signs in the text do not represent actual signs; they are largely my own creations.

PHOTOGRAPHS

Abington Park Hotel. 1
Admiral Nelson. 3
Admiral Rodney. 5
Angel. 11
Artizan. 14
Bantam Cock. 18
Bold Dragoon. 43
Boot Inn (College Street). 45
Britannia (Barrack Road). 48
Britannia (Bedford Road). 48
Castle. 59
Cock Hotel (as part of advt.). 70

Criterion. 80
Crown & Anchor. 88
Crown & Cushion. 89
Duke of Edinburgh. 97
Duke of York. 98
Fish. 106
Foundrymens' Arms. 115
Garibaldi. 121
Golden Horse. 130
Green Man. 135
Harbour Lights. 142
Jolly Crispin. 150
King William IV. 156
Longboat. 161
Malt Shovel. 167
New Town House. 174
Northampton Arms (sign). 175
Old House At Home. 179
Overstone Arms. 179
Plough Hotel. 189
Pomfret Arms. 192
Prince of Wales (Harborough Road). 194
Princess Alexandra. 195
Queen Adelaide. 197
Queen's Arms (Market Square). 199
Racehorse. 201
Railway Tavern [Hotel] (Cotton End). 201
Ram Hotel. 202
Rifle Butt(s). 208
Road To Morocco. 210
Romany Hotel. 213
Shipman's (& front cover). 223
Spade & Plough. 226
Spinney Hill Hotel. 227
Spread Eagle. 230
Sunnyside. Hotel 233
Swan (Derngate). 234

Swan & Helmet. 236
Trumpet. 249
Victoria (Poole Street). 253
White Hills Hotel. 262
White Horse (Kingsthorpe). 263
Windmill. 265

LINE DRAWINGS

Albion. 6
Bakers Arms. 15
Bear. 22
Bell[1]. 25
Bird in Hand. 27
Black Boy Hotel. 30
Black Lion (Old) [two]. 34
Black Lion (St. Giles' Street). 36
Boot Inn (College Street). 44
Bull Hotel (plus seal of Priory). 51-52
Bulls Head. 54
Cooks Arms[2]. 72
Golden Lion. 131
Green Dragon. 134
Jolly Smokers (Old). 151
Kings Head (Mayorhold). 154
North Western Hotel. 177
Peacock Hotel. 181
Princess Alexandria. 195
Quart Pot Inn. 196
Racehorse. 200
Red Lion (Horsemarket). 207
Riveters Arms (Scarletwell Street). 210
Roebuck. 212
Sportsman's Arms. 228
Twenty-Fives. 251
Welcome Inn. 256
Wheatsheaf (Regent Square). 258
White Elephant (& back cover). 259

---

[1] Based on an illustration in Victoria County History.
[2] From Northants Notes & Queries.

White Hart (Old). 261

ADVERTISEMENTS

Admiral Rodney. 5
Cock Hotel (with photograph). 70
Criterion (Fountain). 79
Five Bells (Old) [Harborough Road]. 108
Fleece Hotel. 110
Franklin's Hotel & Restaurant. 117
Half-Way House. 141
Lord Palmerston (Flying Horse) 162
Stags Head. 231
Swan (Derngate). 234
Swan & Helmet (Grove Road) 236

ACKNOWLEDGEMENTS

I am grateful to the following people, organisations, and their staff for their facilities and assistance whilst compiling this book.

- ❖ Northamptonshire Record Office.
- ❖ Northamptonshire Newspapers (Chronicle & Echo, Northampton Mercury &c.).
- ❖ Northamptonshire Libraries and Information Service, *especially Marian Arnold, Terry Bracher, Colin Eaton, Helen Grinter and Clare Trend.*

I would also like to thank for their help.

- ❖ Geoffrey Starmer for information.
- ❖ Merland Copy & Print, especially Robert Connelly.
- ❖ (From the 4th impression, 1st Edition) Chris Glazebrook, for corrections and new information about the Plough Hotel.
- ❖ And finally, and not least, my wife, Julie for putting up with all this.

ABBREVIATIONS AND CONVENTIONS
These can be found on page 275

INTRODUCTION

There is really nothing which has yet been contrived by man, by which so much happiness is produced as by a good tavern or inn.
Samuel Johnson 1709-1784

(How all this started)

Years ago, someone asked me which was the oldest pub in the town? The question got me thinking, and I came to the conclusion that there are three aspects of a pub's antiquity; **The Site, The Building** and **The Sign.**

These are independent of each other, there could have been a pub in one location for hundreds of years and it could have been demolished or destroyed and rebuilt over and over again. After all the majority of the pubs in the town would have been destroyed in the Great Fire of Northampton in 1675. At the time of demolition or destruction this was often taken as an opportunity to change the name, for example the Crown on Wood Hill becoming the Black Boy after the Great Fire. Another reason (especially in my lifetime it seems) to change a name is to attempt to change the clientele and improve the pub's image. The appellation 'Old' was often given to distinguish one pub from another of the same name, for example, the Black Lion in St. Giles' Street and the (Old) Black Lion on Black Lion Hill, *but* not always the oldest pub took the 'Old', it was often used as a ploy to give the impression that the pub was a 'Ye Olde Worlde' cosy pub. It is possible that certain favoured sites such as just inside or outside the town gates could have had a hostelry on them for hundreds of years, one example of this that *hadn't* changed its name for hundreds of years (from 15th cent.) until recently is the Bantam Cock.

The Bantam Cock also illustrates the second aspect, the building, until the early 1900s this pub was a completely different structure at right angles to its present orientation with a thatched roof and probably contained some of the original features from the 15th century. It escaped destruction from the Great Fire because it stood in an isolated position by the main road well outside the Town's East Gate. The title 'Oldest Pub' could present a problem from this aspect, as a building *could* be of great age, but not always having been a pub, however, this problem doesn't seem to have arisen in Northampton.

Of course, even if the building is of great age and has always been a pub it doesn't follow that it has always been called what it's called now. Likewise even if the site has always been a pub it doesn't follow that the site has always carried the same sign. Signs have proved to be very interesting and trying to discover the origins of some of them has led me down unusual paths. Because of this I am now better informed on such diverse subjects as Heraldry, Famous Warships, Racehorses and Stagecoaches, Boot and Shoe production and Sunday League Football! Some signs are of great age and often today have a different meaning as to their original. The Bull Hotel on Regent's Square is now no longer with us, thanks to the never-ending demands of the Motor Car. The sign that used to grace this establishment showed a bull and I'm sure that everyone who saw this sign, me included, thought that this is what the name meant. In fact, the original sign was almost certainly the sign of the *bulla* or seal. The pub was located just inside the North Gate, a prime site and opposite St. Andrew's Priory and almost certainly started as a medieval *hospice* and would have displayed the seal (or *bull*) of the Order.

LIMITS
(You have to stop sometime)

The main part of the book consists of an alphabetical series of entries, one for each of the Signs that I have discovered in the Town. I had to set some kind of limits as I started collecting information in 1982 and realised by 1995 that if I didn't draw a line somewhere I would be collecting forever and never get the book off the ground. The limits are: - **Time**, from as earliest as I can get (about 1200, but little proof) to 1993, a year when my favourite pub was 'revamped' and its name changed. **Area**, I decided that some old villages such as Abington and Kingsthorpe *are* part of what *I* regard as the town whereas Billing and Moulton are not. When I plotted what I thought of as 'The Town' on a map it proved to be the Borough boundary as it was before the New Towns Act, Designated Area 1968 – so this is what it is. Time, from early times to 1993 and Area, the Borough as it was pre 1968.

DEFINITIONS
(Ancient and Modern)

What is a pub, inn, hostelry, tavern, alehouse or beer-shop; what is the difference between Ale and Beer, if any – and which *is* the oldest pub in town? To answer any of these questions one has to resort to history and, in some cases, the law.

When did pubs first begin and what were they like? Earlier and simpler societies did, and in some parts of the world, still do, have a natural gathering of the people called by anthropologists a *sod*. This would probably take place in an informal way in the evenings after the days work had been done, when the gossip and news &c. would be chewed over and decisions made.

We don't have anything like this in our day and age; we are isolated from our fellows. We leave our houses, get into cars and go to work, speaking to no one. Many people today do not know their neighbours' names and 'community spirit' has to be worked at, rather than occurring naturally. However, the instinct is still there, it never went away; it survived in many forms over the ages. Here is a guess at a period in our past, Anglo-Saxon England.

The pub appears to be an Anglo-Saxon invention, a direct result of village life. With any small community, that is largely isolated from others, independent and its members interdependent, a habit of regular, informal gatherings will evolve. Probably in Anglo-Saxon communities one of the women would specialise in brewing, quite possibly the baker's wife and be known as the *Alewife*. Perhaps others brewed as well, but the term *Alewife* implies a specialist. I can imagine, of an evening, when the work was done and food eaten people would gather at her house (the bakery?) to drink and gossip. In the winter, what better place to spend your evening than in a warm bakehouse and in the summer to sit outside, like people do today? I see the Alewife's home as the precursor of the village pub, and later the 'home from home' local corner beer shop. Baking and brewing share much in common; grain, yeast and heat. An ideal place to brew ale would be the bakery.

When the land was enclosed and the Industrial Revolution came along many common people migrated to the fast growing towns like Northampton to work in the more lucrative trades such as Boot & Shoe production. To accommodate these workers speculators and Housing Associations built streets of terraced houses and, unlike the developers of the 1970s put in pavements, shops, churches and pubs.

I can remember the building of Thorplands and the announcement that Thorplands One was ready for occupation. There were no shops, one pub and most importantly no footpaths. The planners were all motorists and had no idea of what it would be like for a mother loaded with shopping and two kids, one in a pushchair and one in hand to alight from a bus and try to get to her new 'home' over muddy tracks or 'artistically' windy paths. Interestingly the developers were (and still are) building *'homes'* whilst the Borough Council were compulsorily purchasing peoples' *houses* at very low prices and knocking them down. In my book builders build *houses* and people make them into *homes* not the other way round! Enough of this, back to the plot.

The back street corner pub became the equivalent of the village inn and served much the same purpose. There were threats to its existence and not only from the Temperance and Teetotal movements - *movies* appeared as an alternative to 'going down the local', later we had radio and the final threat came with the mass interest in Television after the Coronation in 1953. Now people had a reason to stay in every night, so the local pub began to die out, but thousands of years of habit do not disappear in a few years, or even centuries. Today a good proportion of the population of this country are glued to their sets watching soap operas. Coronation Street and Eastenders are both very much centred around their respective pubs, the Rovers Return and the 'Vic. Even Emmerdale Farm has its Woolpack and the oldest soap in the world, The Archers had two pubs, the Bull and the Cat & Fiddle (which is now closed). Now instead of having real gossip (and a real life?) people can vicariously live the lives of fictional characters, even to the point of half believing them – remember the 'Free Deirdre' campaign?

So, what makes a pub an inn and an inn a tavern? Let's go back to some real history and the monasteries of the Middle Ages. In the 12th century the pilgrimage was popular. Monasteries and Friaries were, as part of their Christian duty supposed to care for the sick and the traveller, especially if that traveller was a pilgrim. To this end *Hospitals* came about, they not only cared for the sick, but for the traveller. The words *Hospital, Hospice, Hotel, Hostel and Hostelry* are all from the same source and sum up the function of the medieval hospitals. Monks have always been fond of brewing and wine making and would provide this for their guests, after a while they also provided drink and sustenance for locals as well as travellers. Later local lords realised the potential of this service and opened inns on roads passing through their lands (*Roadhouses*), hence the large number of inns and taverns called The *Somebody-or-Other Arms*, bearing the arms of their owners and probably starting the fashion of calling a pub *The Something-or-other Arms*. Northampton was an important market town and some sort of accommodation was essential for a town to function as a market as traders in those days would have to stay overnight if they came from any distance and would also require somewhere where business could be conducted, preferably over a drink.

Some idea of the economic importance of these establishments can be gauged from the State Papers of 1675 – the year of the Great Fire of Northampton when almost three quarters of the town was destroyed. By September 23rd, three days after the Fire it was reported that any surviving Inns were prepared to receive travellers and some gentlemen's' houses were converted into temporary inns. *Lest the want of these conveniences should discourage all persons from repairing thither, and thereby force the inhabitants to leave the place desolate, and in danger of being*

out of a possibility of ever being rebuilt.... An assurance was also given, *That all markets and fairs shall be kept there on the dates they used to be....*
Calendar of State Papers, Domestic Series, March 1675–Feb. 1676.

After the Dissolution of the Monasteries the *Hospitals* disappeared, many becoming secular houses of accommodation, sustenance and entertainment. We were then left with **Inns, Taverns** and **Ale-Houses.** The **Inn** was a large establishment, possibly once a *Hospital*, with plentiful accommodation for the traveller, his horse and his carriage or cart. It would often include *Market Rooms*, large rooms where displays of goods or auctions could be carried out. The **Tavern** was similar, less grand, but still able to care for the travelling public. Incidentally the Romans used to have **Tabernae** every few miles or so along their straight roads to provide refreshment for travellers and fresh horses for the military messengers that travelled along them. From this has come the idea that the Roman *Taberna* gave rise to the Tavern. However, it is more likely that this word was lost when the Romans left, and, being Latin in origin, returned with the French speaking Normans. *Ale-Houses* were at the bottom, catering only for food and as the name implies, ale. In the countryside a similar situation prevailed with Inns and Taverns beside the major thoroughfares and the Ale House being the village pub serving the locals. Of course, all these establishments would have served the casual drinker, no one turns away business, but regulations did crop up from time to time limiting certain establishments and times to the *bona fide* traveller, perhaps requiring a meal to be purchased as well as drink and closing to the public during the times of *"Common Prayer or Sermones upon the Sabothe"* (1568). These regulations appear to have been largely ignored. Interestingly the explanation I have been given for the laying down or flattening of the headstones in All Saints' churchyard was so that people who had been rousted out of their houses, pubs &c. to attend church (yes, they used to do that!) couldn't hide behind the stones until everyone else was in church and then return to their 'vices' in the nearby taverns and ale-houses!

From the **Mercury** February 10th 1752: -

On Sunday last the public Inns and Ale houses in this town were visited in time of Divine Service, by Order of the Mayor and Justices and several Landlords and people found tippling in their Houses were the next day obliged to pay the Penalties according to the Statute of Edwd. VI, Elizabeth and James I made for that purpose. Our Mayor also forbids Throwing at Cocks on Shrove Tuesday, or any other day in the Streets and Innes of this town.

In the past there was more legislation for drinking houses and the quality &c. of drink than any other trade. The ***Liber Custumarium*** is an ancient compilation of regulations and customs that was maintained for many centuries by Northampton's Town Clerks. A fifteenth century brewers' 'oath' is: -*Allso of all Brewers that thei brewe Good Ale and holsome for mannys body And they sell be mesur enseales. And yf thei sell be any Cuppe choppet or thryrndall p'sent them to vs. ffor the statute of the grete chartor.... One weight and one mesur through owte the realme of Englond.*

Cuppe choppet – a cup measure cut down to give short measure.

Thyrndall – thinned down.

***Records of the Borough of Northampton* 1898.**

I wonder how many of the popular lagers or fizz ales of today would measure up as being "holsome for mannys body"!

The reason for so much legislation is probably twofold. From the social point of view the two most important establishments of the past were the Church and the Pub. Before the advent of reliable, clean, water (as late as the second half of the nineteenth century!) ale was the one drink you could trust. Of course, after the seventeenth century tea and coffee appeared, but these were originally very expensive and out of the reach of most folks. The other reason is that as a *potable* drink was essential and was enjoyable it could and should be controlled unless people enjoyed themselves too much, and of course, it could be taxed.

The process of brewing eliminates unwanted microorganisms. Initially through the boiling of the water (liquor) to produce the *wort* to ferment, and secondly the actual process of fermentation involves a benign microorganism (yeast) that eliminates all competitors and maintains, at least for a time, its purity. Flemish weavers came to this country in the fourteenth century and introduced us to the hop with its preservative qualities thereby extending the ale's potable period. This new brew was called *beer* and the old word; *ale* retained for unhopped brews made in the old way. By about the eighteenth century the term *ale* was being used for the brew obtained from the first washings of the ingredients and was therefore the strongest. *Beer* and *small beer* were brewed from subsequent washings or *sparges*. Today the words are used interchangeably and have lost their distinctions. True ale is rarely brewed these days so strictly speaking almost all beer sold today *is* beer, but I think CAMRA should keep their "Ale" as CAMRB doesn't have quite the same impact.

Like *Ale* and *Beer* there are now no exact definitions of *Inns, Taverns, Ale Houses* or *Pubs*. Over the last two centuries or so all these terms have been applied to all sorts of products and establishments and now we have other terms such as 'lager', 'wine-bars', 'gastro-pubs' and 'bar-cafes' to contend with.

All drinking houses of the past I have found have been included in this book, but for the modern ones I have decided on the following definition. *An establishment that is open to the public, i.e. one does not have to be a member, pay an entrance fee or buy food to be served. That serves beer, but may also serve other alcoholic beverages.* This, of course, excludes clubs of all sorts, wine-bars, 'bar-cafés' and other modern 'concepts',

So, which is the oldest pub? Well to return to my original thoughts, there are three ways to look at it - the Site, the Building and the Sign. If it was still with us the Bull on Regent's Square would have qualified for its sign and the site, but alas, it is now lost under a road. Likewise the Peacock that stood on the Market Square would have fulfilled the same requirements as the Bull, and possibly some of the building could have escaped the Great Fire of 1675 thereby filling the third requirement.

A good proportion of the town was destroyed by the Great Fire so most buildings cannot be older than the seventeenth century. The George Hotel that once stood at the top of Bridge Street probably went back to the time of the First Crusade, being named after St. George. We know this was rebuilt after the Great Fire, so again it's a case of sign and site, but not the building and in any case all these venerable establishments are lost to us. The Bantam Cock on Abington Square can be traced back to at least the fifteenth century and escaped the Great Fire because it was outside the town walls – but it could be argued that it doesn't qualify, it being outside the town at the time. Even if we do admit it, it still won't qualify as the building, having survived the Fire was demolished and completely rebuilt at the beginning of the last century.

The buildings are the problem, so looking for the oldest surviving buildings would seem to be the key. There are one or two pubs on the outskirts of the borough that are Listed Buildings, but these, at the time were in villages that have been incorporated into the borough in recent times, so don't really count. Two pubs in town that are Listed are Shipman's on the Drapery and the Old Black Lion on Black Lion Hill.

Shipman's official name is the White Hart and was probably also called in earlier years the Crown and the Roebuck in the eighteenth century. The building is partly eighteenth century with some nineteenth century additions. I have no start date for this pub and as the *site* of a pub it could go back many centuries, but it didn't get called the White Hart until circa 1768.

The original building called the Old Black Lion is seventeenth century with nineteenth century additions and now has expanded into an eighteenth century cottage next door. Records of this pub are few, but its location, opposite the Castle and close to the West Gate of the medieval town would have been an ideal site for an inn or tavern. When a pub shares its name with the road it's on this means one of two things; it's on a Victorian estate and they called the pub after the street (e.g. the Overstone Arms in Overstone Road), or the road acquired its name because of a landmark i.e. the inn, that was on it. The latter case indicates an establishment of some age. I therefore declare the Old Black Lion as probably being the oldest pub in town. However as the sign of the Black Lion is explained under that heading the sign itself is probably no earlier than 1500.

ORGANISATION
(How the Book is set up)

The bulk of the book consists of alphabetical entries for each *sign*. If there is more than one pub with the same name the entry begins with an explanation of the meaning of that sign and then follows with each pub. A pub entry will include the pub's name, its address (if known) and any alternative names it may also have had. If an alternative name is looked up it will direct the reader to the main entry. I have tried to give start and finish dates for pubs where possible, but some pubs go back so far there are no records and others appear once in some document and are never referred to elsewhere. Many of these single references are derived from seventeenth and eighteenth century deeds where a piece of property would be defined by the properties around it, so you might get something like, *...and to the east a certain ale-howse commonly known or called by the Signe or name of the Lyon.* Most other dates come from Directories and the Magistrates' Licensing Records. The first Directory that includes Northampton is the **Universal Directory** of 1791. These directories were published at various intervals, sometimes two or three coming out more or less at the same time and perhaps a gap of several years before the next. None were published during the periods of the two World Wars. They are not entirely reliable either; they copied from each other, including the mistakes, often left out entries and, I believe, in some cases simply used the old set-up type to reprint a 'new' edition without any revision. This sometimes resulted in a pub being shown as trading by as much as seven years after it was demolished! Small insignificant establishments would often be omitted, either because they didn't pay for an entry (compilers didn't always charge), or were considered not 'smart' enough to be included. The *Universal Directory* for example only included those inns in Northampton that would have been of interest to travellers. So, allowances should be made for errors and omissions with directory dates.

Magistrates Licensing Records are, of course, entirely accurate *where they are available* we have none before 1903 and a few years around the 1950s are missing. One aspect of these records that confuses is that they record the name of the *licence holder* not necessarily the manager. People recall that "'ole 'arry Bloggs" had the pub in the 1960s, but the records show that Fred Smith held the licence. Fred may have been a shadowy figure in the background whilst Harry the barman was the real character everyone remembers. I felt that it wouldn't be a good idea to include all the known landlords' and ladies' names, as they would take up too much space. However, I have produced a database of all the names I have found and this is available for research (e.g. family history) at Northampton Central Library and Northamptonshire Record Office.

It has taken me somewhere in the region of ten years to actually put everything down on paper, check it and add new information as it came up. As a result some of the entries refer to situations &c. that no longer exist. As far as I know it is not inaccurate, only not up-to-date, in most cases I have left it, as it is with perhaps a comment in brackets [ ].

Of course, back in medieval times only priests and Jewish merchants could read and write, so everyone had a sign of some sort outside their premises or house. I remember when I first went to school (and of course couldn't read) we had our own peg and each had a picture over it; a teddy bear, locomotive, beach ball &c. Some signs denoted a particular trade and everyone is familiar with the barber/surgeon's red and white striped pole representing a bandaged, bloody limb or the three golden balls of the pawnbroker derived from the Arms of St Nicholas. (I understand that the *real* meaning of the three balls is; *Two to one, you won't get it back.*). These two along with pub signs appear to be the only survivors.

Something should be said about alternative names. Even relatively recently most people were illiterate and as a result they would describe a pub by what they saw on the sign, not the writing. A good example of this is the White Hart (Shipman's) it was first known as the Roebuck, the proprietor's name at the time being Roe. A white roebuck looks much like a white hart.

Probably the original sign for an inn, or *hospital* was the seal, or *bulla* of the religious order that ran it, but with the advent of lords setting up their own roadhouses with their Arms over the door and townspeople opening their own premises as drinking houses diversification set in. So by the time records were being kept drinking houses were using all sorts of signs (for example see the *Assembly Order* of 1585, p.XIV).

Signs not only cover all manner of subjects and themes, but also come in all sorts of shapes, sizes, materials and locations. Many were painted - directly onto walls or boards fixed to walls or hung from some sort of frame. This probably accounts for the popularity of the colour blue (Blue Boar, Bell, Anchor &c.) as blue is the most durable colour and painted signs were expensive. Look at any modern poster that has been exposed to daylight for a time and you will see that all the red colours have been bleached out with just the blues remaining. Having a sign carved in wood or stone would initially be more expensive, but it would be permanent and if it was painted it could be touched up by someone unskilled and cheap. The only downside would be the cost if one wanted to change the sign. Political and religious signs could fall into this trap. The Annunciation (showing the Archangel Gabriel visiting the Virgin Mary) was a popular sign before the Reformation, but quickly fell out of favour. One solution to the purchase of a new sign was simply to remove the Virgin and retain Gabriel, and call the inn the Angel.

HISTORY
(A bit of background)

Northampton probably started as an Anglo Saxon farmstead (Hamtune →*Ham Ton* → 'Home Farm') and perhaps one of my hypothetical bakery/proto-pubs was here!

The town probably first became defined when King Edward the Elder, son of Alfred the Great enclosed the Town with a bank, ditch and palisade.

When the Normans arrived they increased the size of the town considerably and moved the central crossroad from the bottom of Gold Street to the top, at the old Saxo Danish east *Portegate* and built a church (All Saints') right outside. In the west they constructed a castle. This meant that the Saxo-Danes were surrounded by a new town full of foreigners and overlooked by a huge castle. In the 1300s the town was expanded a short way to the east and northeast. Apart from the growth of suburbs to the north, south, east and west (St. Andrew's End, Cotton End, St. Edmund's End and St. James' End respectively) the town stayed more or less the same size until the second half of the nineteenth century. With the growth of the Boot & Shoe industry and the mechanisation of farming with such new tools as the Traction Engine and Steam Plough massive development took place and the town grew at a prodigious rate. Adjacent fields to the old town walls were swallowed up and covered in terraced houses, chapels and churches, corner shops, factories, garden workshops and *pubs*!

I have stated that this trade was the most regulated in the past and this is some of the material from the **Liber Custumarium** and other documents quoted in the **Records of the Borough of Northampton 1898.**

All ale brewers were ordered by the assembly, in 1575 to sell their ale for 2s.4d. (about 11½p.) *a dozen* (gallons), *and the 'typler' for 2s.8d.* (about 13½p.) *a dozen, by sealed measure.* All that sold strong ale were to sell a quart (2 pints) for a penny (less than ½p.), by sealed measure. To insure the carrying out of this, it was provided, *that every man that can and will present any defaulters shall have xijd (i.e. 12d = 1/- or 5p.) for his Labor and the pot.*

The Privy Council in 1577 issued orders that all counties in England should give full returns of the names of all those who were licensed as keepers of taverns, inns and alehouses in both towns and counties. Northampton, it seems, declined and when the lieutenant of the county sent in his certificate in November he gave a total of 8 taverns, 30 inns and 400 alehouses in the shire, *besides the Towne of Northampton wherewith we have not medled for that the maior of the same Town answereth that he by hymself will make certificate unto your honors of the true nomber thereof.* This return, if it was ever done, is not to be found but, the compilers of the **Records of the Borough of Northampton** estimate that the probable number of inns and alehouses to be about eighty. The nearest thing we have to a list of pubs at this time is the ***Assembly Order*** of 1585: - *That the Sygne of the harte nowe commonly called the hynde, the Lyon, the Bell, the Swanne, The George, the Bull, the Aungell, the Dolphyn, the Sallett, the harpe, the Katherene Wheele, the Talbott, and the one called the Greene Dragon be admytted as auncient Innes within this towne, and all other houses havinge sygnes at their dores, and useinge victualinge to be admytted as Ale howses and not as Innes, and yearely to put in Recognizances for keepinge of good Rule in their howses accordinge as herefore hath bene used, or ells to be demissed at Mr. Mayors and the Justices discretion which for the tyme shalbe.*

By 1606 the price of beer and ale had gone up (what's new?) and every brewer brewing beer or ale who sold by the dozen or half dozen was required to sell the best ale or beer for 3/- (15p.) a dozen. A dozen was to contain fourteen gallons at the vat side (this would have allowed for *ullage* – the loss of some liquid through evaporation, spillage and dregs). This regulation also reiterated the fifteenth century 'oath' that every brewer was to brew ale or beer *that was good and wholesome, under pain of three and fourpence (3/4d – 17p.), to be recovered by distress.* Of course, these regulations of the price of ale and beer were not to *raise* them, but to ensure that the breweries and alehouse keepers didn't charge too much – what a good idea, couldn't we do this today?

PERSONAL
(Drinking during my lifetime, c1961-?).

There is an account of Christmas at Watneys Brewery under the Malt Shovel, but nothing about the actual process that Watneys used to make their 'wonderful' beer. My job there was as a lowly tun cleaner in the North Brewery, we got into the fermentation vessels (FVs) after the brew had been run off and cleaned and sterilised them.

To make beer you need at least four ingredients, water, sugar, hops and yeast. It is often said that there is *no* water in a brewery, only *liquor,* however, you don't make tea, wash the floor or flush the toilets with liquor - you use water. Strictly speaking the term liquor only applies to the water used to brew the beer. The water used in the North Brewery came from a spring near Spring Gardens (hence the name). The pump-house still stands on the north side of Victoria Promenade. Generally speaking hard water is the best for making beer, in the past Burton-on-Trent made the best because of their particular kind of hard water. Other breweries such as ours would get the best they could, usually from a spring and 'Burtonise' it, i.e. add salts, usually gypsum to get it as close as possible to the 'ideal' Burton water.

Traditionally sugar is obtained from malt. There are two industries associated with brewing, malting and hop growing. To make malt you first start off by inducing barley to germinate through moisture and heat, this causes some of the starch in the seed to convert into sugar (maltose). The skill is to judge when the maximum conversion has taken place and then to kill off the process with heat. Maltings, whether attached to breweries or not, can be recognised by the distinctive steep pyramidal roof of the kiln used to kill the grain and often a half-storey high top floor with louvered windows where the malt was germinated. The grains, when needed, would be put through a *gristmill*, this would crack the grains to allow the water (sorry, *now* it's <u>liquor</u>!) to leach out the sugar. In days gone by this would be the only source of sugar, but in more modern times other sugars have been added.

Hops came, and still do, in huge sacks called pockets and in many different types. They would be weighed out in the correct proportions for each type of beer, and varied in colour from golden yellows to rich, dark greens. For those who remember the old money, I thought some of them looked like crumpled ten shilling notes (gold-brown ones) and others like pound notes (green) – the smell was wonderful, but not to be indulged for too long as hops make one drowsy.

If I remember correctly my day started at 6 o'clock, being a young man all those years ago, I and my young brewery colleagues often went out in the evening and drank quite a lot of our product. As a result I would often turn up for work with a hangover. Hangovers are caused by two factors, dehydration from the alcohol and something else from the plethora of strange, and often unknown, substances in our drinks. If one drank a mixture of alcohol and water of the same strength as beer (especially Watneys) one would be hard done to get merry, let alone drunk. The body can only metabolise so much alcohol at a time so there is an optimum strength for absorbing alcohol. This must have been worked out by rule of thumb years ago before the experiments of the 1960s, as the strength happens to be half the strength of 70% proof. This means that when one drinks a whisky and water you have a drink with the best chance of quickly getting affected. Tests showed that the more impurities in the drink the more potent it was, so vodka and water would take longer to get one drunk than, say a whisky and ginger. Of course, the vodka is reputed to leave you with a lighter, or no hangover in the morning. It seems the 'brown stuff' in a drink has a lot to do with its effects and beer always has plenty of 'brown stuff'! Cures are usually based on minimising the effects of dehydration (drinking a pint of water before retiring) and providing a fresh intake of alcohol – 'hair of the dog' in the morning (to counteract withdrawal symptoms) or a stimulant, coffee or coke.

When I arrived at work (with my hangover) the chaps who Burtonise the liquor and sparge the malt would have been at it since four o'clock. The malt would have been ground the day before, like the hops to a recipe, and shot into a large, circular *mash tun* the hot liquor would have been passed through a thing like a giant lawn sprinkler (actually the sparge) suspended in the top of the mash tun. The hot liquid would percolate through the malt dissolving out the sugar and would run out at the bottom. This process took place near the entrance on the way to the locker-room and if one felt under the weather one could borrow a beaker used to test the stuff and fill it with some of the steaming hot *wort*, this would be left on the side and one would go and change into your overalls, wellies &c. on your return the wort would have cooled to a drinkable temperature. It tasted and smelt of malt (surprise!) - very much like a sort of dark, nutty, Horlicks. Within half an hour or so the hangover would have gone – I conclude that the 'brown' substances from the malt were the elements that caused the hangover and imbibing them in the morning relieved the effects – the sugar would have helped as well.

Like hops, malt comes in different kinds and this has a lot to do with the process in the kiln. Some grains are heated just enough to kill them and others are burnt black, and everything between. Once the wort has been made it is sent to the *kettles*, which in my brewery were three giant stainless steel vessels, three storeys high. It's the tops of these sticking through the roof that often are the first clue that a building is a brewery. To the wort would be added the hops and any extra sugars that would have been dissolved in hot liquor upstairs in the sugar room. This lot would then be heated up – brewed - and finally drawn off, filtered, cooled and pumped through to my domain, the Fermentation Rooms.

It would arrive through a two-inch stainless steel pipe and be run into a Fermentation Vessel (FV). These things were huge, like giant, deep swimming pools and held thousands of gallons. Once the required amount (*gyle*) of wort had been run in we would take an oversize stainless 'dust-bin' with a measured quantity of yeast in the bottom, mix it with some of the wort into a slurry and tip it into the FV. The mixture would work for a few days generating lots of foamy yeast bubbles for a while and lots of sharp smelling gas (CO_2). Sometimes, especially in the summer, it would work too fast and the *attemporators* – sort of large copper radiators circulating cold water sunk in the FV would be brought into action to lower the temperature. Measurements were taken of the temperature and specific gravity at regular intervals.

Eventually the brew would be ready for running off. In the vaults under the FVs were outlets and pipes which would be connected up to the Conditioning Room pump. I can remember that a lot of what I did was undoing and coupling up pipes to run various liquids (wort, green beer, sugar solutions or even hot caustic soda cleaning solutions around). When all was ready we would open the valve under the FV and the beer would be pumped away to be conditioned in huge, chilled tanks prior to being put into kegs and sent out.

We would, with our kit lean on the side of the FV and watch the beer, or rather the rafts of dead yeast (which had multiplied greatly) slowly sink down to the bottom. Fixed into the outlet in the lowest corner of the vessel was a sort of filter, it was a circular, flat, container about 18" in diameter, 3" thick, made of copper. When the beer was very low a long metal rod with a hook was used to pull off the top and the beer could be seen streaming through the holes in its underside and down the outlet. The beer was being drawn off from *between* the surface yeast and the other, dead, yeast lying on the bottom of the vessel. As soon as 'strings' of yeast started to be drawn down the outlet a long wooden pole with a conical end was used from the top to plug the outlet and the Conditioning Room 'phoned and told to shut off the pumps.

More running about with spanners and the vessel was connected up to the Press Room. Ladders were thrown into the vessel and one or two of us would go down with squeegees and push the liquid and not so liquid yeast down the outlet which would be making loud, rude sucking noises. In the Press Room the very yeasty beer would be forced under pressure through large cast-iron presses fitted with cloths. The beer recovered would end up with the rest for conditioning. It always amazed me afterwards when opening up these presses just how much yeast was in them. We put, perhaps, a large bucket full in at the start and got about a cubic yard of the stuff out. The surplus I was told was sold to the people who make Marmite and ProPlus.

We now had a vessel with a skin of yeast all over it and a line of hard, crusted, dead yeast all around, near the top. A mixture of nitric acid and china clay was carefully mixed up to a consistency of thin white-wash and wearing protective gear and using ordinary yard brushes with handles about twelve feet or so long we would stand in the bottom of the vessel and brush the mixture up the walls. Once this was done we would climb out and go for a cup of tea, or a drop of our beer allowance. After about twenty minutes or so the acid had done its work and we would stand at the top with hoses and hose the stuff off the walls and eventually get in and squeegee the remnants down the plug hole. The acid would strip off even the hardest yeast deposits and sterilise the vessel at the same time, so it would be ready to repeat the whole process again.

I have seen many changes in the pub scene over the years. Pubs in the past, I mean long before I was born, all catered to some extent for food, but when I was a young lad this was not so. I suppose my drinking career started way back before I was a teenager, when I used to go out with my parents on Sunday afternoon walks. I believe this was a survival of the old custom that to get a drink on Sunday you had to be a *bone fide* traveller i.e. have journeyed more than one mile. Although this law had been long gone this seems to have established a custom of going on a walk to a distant and usually rural pub and sitting in the garden and having a drink – very healthy I'm sure!

Because I was only a boy I was not allowed to drink beer, I was allowed Tizer, or similar *or* cider or lager. Lager in those days came in only one form, Carlsberg, in bottles, and served in trumpet glasses made for the purpose (as in the film *Ice Cold in Alex*) along with the obligatory lime shot. Lager was considered a lady's drink and cider was for boys. As I often elected to drink one or two of these alternatives I must have often gone home with the equivalent of a pint of snakebite inside me!

Like my friends I started my solo-drinking career before the legal age of eighteen. I cannot recall when it was but probably when I was about fourteen. In the 1960s there used to be a jazz club at the top of Gold Street and I remember going into the Bell around the corner in Bridge Street (see Bell). One time I went in there to celebrate the coming of age of a friend only to have him denied service, "You're not eighteen – 'e is (pointing to me), but you ain't – so I ain't serving yer!" This really upset my friend as he was a couple of months older than I was, but I had to get the drinks because I was "old enough" to buy for someone under the legal age to buy, but over sixteen.

The 'pub crawl' was a regular feature of my early drinking days. We would go from one pub to the next having a pint in each and perhaps ending up in 'our' pub before closing time for the mad dash to sink as many pints as possible before getting thrown out at the allotted time (there were no 'lock ins' in those days- at least not for us youngsters). I believe the pub crawl was a left over from the days of war time restrictions and rationing when pubs often had very little to offer and one would (I'm told) be limited to perhaps only one half of beer. People therefore trooped from one pub to another getting what they could. Another reason for the pub-crawl could have been when pubs brewed their own beer; I have been told that people would inform each other when the good stuff was to be had. The Market Square on a Friday night in the 1940s

someone calls out, "Try Bill at the 'Tree, his beer's just come on."
(William Lay of the Tree of Liberty).

Although the breweries had more or less tied up the trade by
the early 1900s some pubs still brewed their own and it is
interesting to note that Kelly's Directory of 1940 has asterisks
against some of the pubs listed and, "* *Brewer of the Beer
Retailed.*" Evidently during the Second World War many pubs
brewed their own, probably as a result of rationing.

Anyway whatever the origins of the pub-crawl we carried on
the tradition although ours was a more organised affair. We didn't
just wander from pub to pub, but had a regular Friday night route.
The start and finish were usually the same; 'our' pub – this and the
other pubs varied, but would be stuck to for many months. I can
remember leaving home late on occasions and work out where we
would be at the time I would hit town, I would then go to the next
pub and wait and sure enough after a few minutes the gang would
arrive.

Pubs served beer- that was what they were for, beer,
relaxation and conversation. I don't know what a lot of them are
for now – apart from parting gullible people from their money for
inferior overpriced fizz and destroying any chance peace or an
intelligent chat with loud 'music'. If you wanted to eat you went
to a restaurant, pubs might have a little glass case on the bar with
small packets of chocolate biscuits a few sweets, peanuts and
crisps and, of course, there was the bloke on Fridays and Saturdays
with his basket of seafood (packets of prawns, mussels &c.). Some
pubs would do a roll with a wedge of cheese and some raw onion
at lunch times, but the concept of going ·to a pub to *eat* was
unthinkable.

Landlords tended to stay in one place, you could go away for
a year or so and still find the same bloke or lady behind the bar and
the chances were if you had been a regular they would remember
your order *and* if you were barred. Two examples of these
stalwarts are the aforementioned William Lay of the Tree of

Liberty 1932-c1964, c32 years and Edward Dunkley of the Black Lion, Giles' Street 1903-1940, *37 years*!

Another thing the returning prodigal son would have found was that the pub still retained its name. It would have not have changed in a year or so- not even in several decades. Pubs did in the past go in for name changes, but like the landlords they tended to stick for a long time, if not for ever.

One thing I could always rely on was the beer; surprisingly this was not an advantage. We used to live in 'Watneyland' – all our beer was brewed by Watneys in what had been the N.B.C. and Phipps' Breweries on the west side of Bridge Street, only a handful of pubs were free houses or of another brewery. There was the Saddler's Arms in Bridge Street (Davenports), Shipman's in the Drapery (Freehouse), that at one time only served bottled beer, the Garibaldi in Bailiff Street (Bass), Bear in Sheep Street (M&B), Headlands, Longland Road (Charles Wells) and the North Star, Welford Road (Ansells) – hardly much of a handful. This is one aspect of the past where (some) pubs have improved. Although many pubs now are serving fizz lagers (there are *some* decent lagers about) alcopops and pandering to the loud kids, lager louts and big screen 'sports fans', some pubs are serving some very decent real ales. Drinking in the local Weatherspoon's, Moon on the Square has been described by a friend, "Like drinking in Macdonald's." I find the atmosphere is not conducive to relaxed conversation, but it is quiet (no music) and the selection of beers is interesting, varied and *reasonably priced*. (Now Closed 2017).

Small independent breweries have sprung up all over the country in the last few.years, providing the intelligent beer drinker with a whole variety of new tastes. This turn around in brewing and beer retailing is probably due almost entirely to perhaps the most effective consumer group in the world, i.e. the Campaign for Real Ale (CAMRA). The local example is our own Frog Island Brewery at West Bridge. Started in 1994 with a five-barrel plant it was by 2003 using a ten-barrel plant, having doubled its output. However, as Bruce from Frog Island said at the time the independent breweries share of the market is only a minuscule *one-percent*! This state of affairs is reflected in the number of Northampton pubs now worthy of patronage. Some have staff who only know how to draw from a lager spigot, in some you have to shout to be heard, others seem to have been opened for the sole purpose of parting students from their loans with overpriced rubbish, others only open at night or weekends.

In my opinion the most dishonest are the ones that purport to have Real Ale, usually two 'guest ales' on tap. On arrival one finds the one of them is, "Off at the moment and we have no one to change the barrel." So one decides to have the other, only to find it has been so badly kept it has to be sent back. The policy seems to be to get you into the pub and sell you what they want you to drink, normally high profit, high priced lager or ghastly 'smooth' beers. They appear to only employ people who have little knowledge of cellarcraft and unskilled bar staff all on low wages.

In my lifetime the pub has changed so much, especially in the Town Centre, but there are pubs that are still somewhat like they were in the past. When these pubs were constructed they had at least two bars, called when I was a lad the Saloon Bar and the Lounge. They could also have a 'Snug' a small intimate bar often inhabited by old ladies and a 'Jug and Bottle' an even smaller room often the size of a telephone box. This tiny bar was furnished with a hatch to the serving area and a bench where one could sit whilst your order (a jug) was filled – it was only for off sales as people in those days would call into their local and buy beer for home consumption. We used to do this when we were first married, see the Grandby Arms, Vernon Street. After the War the price of beer was controlled, but as years went by it was decided that if you offered more facilities than the basics, one could put a bit on the price of a pint to pay for them. Thus was the lounge created, one bar was redecorated, perhaps with wallpaper, a few fancy lampshades, upholstered chairs and a bit of carpet and you could stick an halfpenny on a pint.

During my drinking career retail price control ended and the breweries started to charge the most they could get for their beer. It was realised that there was no longer a need to segregate the bar from the lounge and if they knocked the retail area into one large room with a central bar the number of staff, especially during quiet periods, could be greatly reduced - even to one. This, of course, saved on wages and made even more profit.

A while ago it was decided that smoking in public places like bars should be banned, not only for the comfort of the patrons, but for the staff. Pubs began to establish 'gazebos' outside where people could keep out of the weather and smoke. Then someone came up with the idea E-Cigarettes and 'vaping' which could be carried out in bars. Now people are objecting to the smell of e-cigarettes, it goes on (2017).

What of the future? I've been drinking now for over forty years and experienced at least the exteriors of pubs since I was a toddler (see Peacock). The changes have been prodigious, but to be fair other things have also changed. When I was a kid we had a radio, we got a television with a tiny screen for the Coronation in 1953. If my mum and dad were alive today they would be amazed by colour T.V., digital watches, computers, microwaves and all the bloody cars everywhere. If I could take my dad out for a pint now I don't think he would like many modern pubs, so what's it going to be for me when I get old (older!)? Fortunately I shall die sooner or later and pass on to that Great Pub in the Sky where the staff are friendly, know you and your order and the beer tastes like it should. Where there are no kids running about – in fact, *no kids*, and there is quiet or live music, convivial conversation and friendly faces.

In truth, I don't think I've ever been in a pub *completely* like that! Enjoy the book!

When you have lost your inns drown your empty selves for you will have lost the last of England.

Hilaire Belloc 1870-1953.

ABINGTON PARK HOTEL also **'A.P.H.'**, **The Abington,** and **Abington Park Brewery.** Wellingborough Road.

This pub was built in 1898. It is a Grade II listed building in the French Renaissance style designed by the architect Matthew Holding.

His work is well represented in Northampton. The most well known examples are the western third of the Guildhall and St. Matthew's Church on the Kettering Road. For a time Matthew Holding's portrait graced the sign outside this pub.

After Abington Manor House and twenty acres of land were offered to the town by Lord and Lady Wantage the Corporation purchased more land in 1895 and 1903 to make what is now Abington Park. The Park was opened in 1897, one year before the construction of the A.P.H. At this time the town was expanding rapidly in this direction and apart from the Park with its bands, other attractions grew up nearby. These were a skating-rink, which burnt down in 1914; a Wild West Rodeo in which spectators could join in and a Palais-de-Danse where the garage now stands. According to Mr. Hanson, *C&E* 30/9/95, in 1904 Mr. W. J. Bassett-Lowke formed the Miniature Railway of Great Britain Company. They were refused permission to run the track on the park, so it was sited on land adjoining, facing Manfield shoe factory. It opened on April 20th 1905, the fare being 2d; it closed sometime about 1914-5. All these attractions must have added to the trade at the hotel, it having a fine view of the bands in the park as well as having its own concert room for 80 persons, a fine billiard-room and extensive stabling.

Since its earliest days the A.P.H. has had strong sporting connections. William Rogers, ex-chief inspector of police and landlord (1908-25) had the Abington Park Bowling Club headquarters here and George Quennell (1925-39) after eight years at Franklin's Gardens succeeded him. Quennell was a player for the Star Cricket Club during their championship years and the pub has always retained connections with the County Cricket Ground nearby.

The exterior of this pub is largely intact, but the interior has gone through some pretty dramatic changes in the past. In the mid-1970s the Inn-Keepers' Associates *transformed the interior almost out of recognition.* They changed a Victorian interior into what they thought a Victorian interior looked like – totally destroying any atmosphere the pub may have had. False shop fronts were constructed, bird cages and trees installed – one felt embarrassed to be seen in there!

In 1984 Northampton's first microbrewery was installed here; a step in the right direction and much of the pseudo-Victorian rubbish had by now been removed. In 1988 the pub shut down completely for three months whilst it went through a complete refurbishment by the owners, Clifton Inns. An *extensive revamp* took place nine years later and the microbrewery was taken out.

ADAM & EVE Location unknown.

According to John Taylor, **Relations of Remarkable Fires in Northamptonshire** 1866, this is one of the inns that we lost in the Great Fire of Northampton in 1675.

Adam & Eve is a popular name for an inn and the arms of the Fruiterers' Company. Perhaps ours was once the premises of a fruiterer?

It is possible that the Adam & Eve *was* re-built after the Great Fire, or that the name was reused. I have seen documents at the Record Office that are post-Fire and refer to the Adam & Eve. From a Conveyance of 1679: -...*Knowne by the Name of Adam and Eve abutting upon the south side of a certain Churche there called or known by the name of All Saints a streete lying between and leading from one other streete there called the Gold streete to a certain place or house called the Sessions House.*

The *streete lying between* must be George Row and it seems that the inn is on the north side up against the church. This is possible and it would have been demolished several years later when the churchyard was tided up and railed. Certainly it had ceased to be an inn by 1718 as a second document has: - *A Messuage or Tenament situate in the Parish of All Saints in the Town of Northon formerly known by the name or sign of Adam & Eve....*

ADMIRAL NELSON The Green, 3 (1858), 5 (1906) and 50 (1910).

I don't think there is any problem with this sign, Viscount Horatio Nelson (1758 – 1805).

The earliest record I have of this pub is a W. Edwards (1824). With regard to the pub's name I think it unlikely that it pre-dates the Battle of Trafalgar in October 1805. From 1887 – 1904 this pub was in the hands of Mr. George Pickering, who appears to have run a 'tight ship'. He rarely, if ever, served a drink, leaving this task to his wife, daughters and barman. He was to be found in an armchair smoking a clay-pipe and discoursing on matters political. Mr. Pickering was a Bradlaugh supporter and no doubt spoke with a freethinker's forthrightness.

His predecessor, George Craddock was also a supporter of Charles Bradlaugh: - *Mr. Craddock of the 'Lord Nelson' we regret to hear has met with a serious accident by which his leg has been fractured. Mr. Craddock, with rare pluck, says, he does not so much regret the accident as his inability to work, as he did at the last election for Mr. Bradlaugh. This is the stuff Mr. Bradlaugh's supporters are made of.*

The Northampton Radical 3/10/1874

Charles Bradlaugh was a remarkable man; he chose this town to stand for Parliament because of our radical shoemakers. Northampton people were well known in the past for their 'revolutionary' attitudes towards religion and politics. Bradlaugh advocated, amongst other things, compulsory education, wealth taxes, and birth control. He was elected to Parliament by the people of Northampton in 1880. He refused to take the oath, *so help me G-D* as he was an atheist, and asked to Affirm instead, this was refused and he was thrown out. Another election was held in 1881, we returned Bradlaugh with an increased majority and once more he was thrown out. This process was repeated in 1882, 1884 and 1885 – finally, in January 1886 the Speaker gave in and Bradlaugh took his seat in the

House of Commons six years after being elected to it. No one told Northamptonians what to do in those days!!

In the first draft of this entry (one of the first I wrote) I put: *-I have often wondered why, apart from a statue in Abington Square, no places have been dedicated to this man, we have no Bradlaugh Road, Street or Square – no Bradlaugh Memorial Hall and no Bradlaugh Arms. Breweries these days seem fond of changing pub names, or opening new ones, so come on – here's a good name, let's at least have a pub named after the great man!*

Of course since then things have changed, we now have a Charles Bradlaugh pub on the Mounts; thanks to the Richardson Group and the Bradlaugh Fields along the Kettering Road. Bradlaugh might have been offended, he being against drinking and having a pub named after him, but I believe his objection to alcohol had a lot to do with *trucking*, paying off workers in the bosses own pub, thereby clawing back some of their pay.

To return to Mr. George Pickering and his 'tight ship'. There is an account of a farmer who had come to Northampton Market. He visited the Admiral Nelson and on taking out a well-stuffed bag of sovereigns to pay for his drink, dropped them all over the floor. George Pickering removed his pipe and shouted, "Stand up!" – everyone complied and stood like soldiers while the farmer retrieved his coins, Pickering then shouted, "Sit down!" which everyone did and continued drinking.

As a child one of our past mayors, Alderman W. A. Pickering used to stand on the skittle board and read the main news items of the day out to those that either could not afford a paper, or read one. Sometime before the Pickerings the Troup family held this pub as a free house, one of their descendants becoming the well-known local solicitor. It was also held in later years by Mr. William Hayes, referee and brother of Bob Hayes, the boxer. The Admiral Nelson finally closed its doors in 1953 with the transfer of its full licence to the Harbour Lights in Gas Street.

ADMIRAL RODNEY 48 The Drapery and 4 Market Square.
The earliest mention of this name that I have found is from a Vestry Book of St. Peter's Church: -

1781 Mar. 4 – Paide the Ringers for Adl. Rodney
taken St Eustatia.   *0..5..0.*

However, this does not refer to the pub, but to the man. It was customary in the past for the bells of churches to be rung for events of national importance and in February 1781 Admiral Rodney captured St. Eustatia and other West Indian islands from the Dutch. He was not only a hero, but had local connections, being the son-in-law of the Earl of Northampton, who supported him during the Spendthrift Election of 1768 when he was elected to the House of Commons as Member for Northampton. He was the hero of the naval battles of St. Vincent and Cadiz in 1780 and by these two victories Gibraltar was re-victualled when the garrison, starving, were on the point of surrendering to the Spanish. He was created Baron Rodney of Stoke Rodney. In later years he retired from public life and died suddenly on 23rd May 1792.

I have no earliest date for this pub *[1795]* but it could easily have started during his lifetime. Considering his close local connections it is possible that this is an example of a pub being opened by a veteran who served under him during his naval career. It is also possible that it had an earlier name which has not come down to us and was renamed in his honour because of one of his military or political achievements or at his death.

From the ***Chronicle*** October 17th 1891 we have: - *Mr. W. G. BRITTEN ADMIRAL RODNEY, DRAPERY, Will hold A SMOKING CONCERT In his NEW ROOM Every THURSDAY EVENING. At 8.0pm. When he will be pleased to see his old Friends.*

In the 1950s the Admiral Rodney hosted the "Muse Lounge Club". Started by Mr. Edwin Hargrave in 1955 it devoted itself to all aspects of art; music, painting (exhibited on the walls) and poetry. A founder member was the local artist Peter Berrisford.

In my school days I attended 'Ketts Kollege for Kool Kats' otherwise known as Kettering Road

STEPHEN GASCOIGNE,
ADMIRAL RODNEY,
DRAPERY, NORTHAMPTON.

FIRST-CLASS WINES AND SPIRITS,
CIGARS.

Taylor's Directory 1846.

School and later as John Clare Secondary Modern. My first art teacher at this august establishment was the above Edwin "Barney" Hargrave, who eventually moved to a barge in Little Venice, London. "Barney" was replaced by Peter Berrisford who caused a local sensation by organising Northampton's first exhibition of Modern Paintings at the Central Museum. Little did we suspect in those days of what our teachers were up to at night in the town's pubs!

The Rodney closed its doors in 1964, too early for me to really know the place. It stood empty for three years before an article in the *Chronicle & Echo* mooted the possibility of a bank opening on the premises.

ADMIRAL VERNON'S HEAD No location.

STOLEN or Stray'd, on Saturday the 3d of this instant December. A Large Black and White DOG. of the Danish Breed, with a long Tail, and his Ears cut very close. Whoever gives Notice of him to John Bolton, at Admiral Vernon's Head in Northampton, shall have five Shillings Reward, and no Questions asked:

N.B. He has very large black Spots.

Northampton Mercury 19th December 1743.

ALBION Corner of Regent Street and Square.

My memories of this pub are of the "Albion Club" a building I saw as a child when visiting the doctor's and in later years as a sad, boarded-up structure.

Albion is a poetic name for England. Albion was also the mythical son of Neptune and Amphitrite who discovered England and ruled here for about fifty years – or he was a Roman and the first Christian martyr in Britain. However, HMS Albion, a ninety-gun warship was launched at Plymouth in 1842 and I think this is the most likely candidate for the pub's name, even though we are about as far from the sea as you can get.

The Albion Club was an old people's club. In 1955 P. Phipps & Co. Ltd. gave five years free rent towards this project. The pub itself,

I understand closed shortly after the war. The deeds for this building went back to 1750 and it had been rebuilt since. In 1871 Ratcliffe & Jeffery purchased it and converted it from a private house into a pub. This is about thirty years after the launch of the warship and the vessel could have been in the news at this time. Around 1908 it was taken over by P. Phipps & Co. Ltd. who ran it until it closed, its last appearance in a directory is in 1940. The building stood empty then, except for a flat upstairs. Downstairs there was still a bar and smoke-room. The Albion was destroyed along with many other buildings when the roads were widened through Regent Square in the 1970s.

ALHAMBRA (and Music Hall) see Crow & Horseshoe.

ALLIES Inkerman Terrace, St. James' End.

Inkerman Terrace, according to the *Directory of Northampton* 1878-9 was: *Inkerman ter, St. James' end, is next Alma st.* and *Robert's Directory* of 1884 (one of the first to have street lists) has: *INKERMAN TERR, opposite CAFÉ* as a heading. The junction of Harlestone, Weedon and St. James' Roads, often erroneously called "St. James' Square" is in fact, Café Square, after a café that was here in the past. The bank on the corner of Althorpe Road was the café in question, so presumably Inkerman Terrace was the row of houses on the south side, fronting St. James' Road at this point.

The earliest record I have got is from *Taylor's* of 1858 with William Webb as the proprietor, the only other entry in a directory using the name Allies is again *Taylor* of 1864 and Joseph Ambidge is the proprietor. However under Beer-Retailers I have found other entries. It seems that William Webb by 1861 had moved to the Woolpack in Bridge Street and Joseph Ambidge is recorded as *Beer Retailer and Butcher* in Inkerman Terrace. The addresses are often ambiguous, e.g. *Duston, St. James' End* &c. Joseph Ambidge is recorded as being *in the area* until circa 1871, when he disappears. A Joseph Ambidge is recorded as a butcher at 63 Primrose Hill in 1876, so it looks like he gave up the sale of beer and settled to a life of a butcher.

As none of the directories have street lists before 1884 I cannot establish a link to a successor's name and without a full address I cannot pick the property up again in 1884. I conclude that it was a short-lived beer-house of the mid 19th century.

ALLIES 71 Melbourne Street.
A corner beer-shop. The first directory reference, in 1864 gives the proprietor as John Pratt and in 1878 Mrs. A. Pratt, probably his wife or widow. Benjamin Bryan was there in 1884 and a R. W. Wright occupied it from 1900 until at least 1929. One other entry, unnamed - 1932.

ALMA INN 7 Upper Priory Street.
This is one of the names that commemorate a battle, in this case the Crimean war. The Alma was a river that the British and French crossed when they won a victory over the Russians. Pubs with this type of name are called such to honour the victory, because they were run by a veteran of the battle, or there is some family connection with the battle and/or a regiment that fought in it. As the battle took place in 1854 and the earliest date I have is from *Taylor's Directory* of 1864, any of the above could be correct. However, there is a local connection. It seems that Captain Lindsay of Abington Manor was awarded the Victoria Cross for his part in the campaign and the pub could very well have been named in his honour

Wright's 1884 has, *Batson George, Alma, Upper Priory street* listed under *Beerhouse Keepers* and this must be, *G. Beetson* in *Lea* 1906 where the property is described as a, *A. House* (Ale House). It seems that James Beetson had it in 1864 and George Batson in 1884. I have also found references to both James and George Beeston in 1862 and 1878 respectively – however, George is a Beer-Retailer in Arundell Street. *Stevens* 1893 lists Smith, Thomas as a Beer-Retailer at 7 Upper Priory Street. So it seems James Beetson (or Batson) had the Alma in 1862 and 1864. Thomas Smith had it at least as early as 1893 and was still there in 1900. Sometime after this, but not later than 1906 George Beetson took it over for a time, but not later than 1907.

In the light of the fact that this pub stood on the northeast corner of Upper Priory Street and Arundell Street one wonders where George Beetson's beer-shop was in 1878 – perhaps it was an off-licence, or it could be the same premises with an alternative address. The *O/S* 2500 plans of 1901, 1938 and 1964 all show a larger than usual building on the corner as number 7.

ALTHORP ARMS 5 Sawpit Lane (1864) - 3 or 5 St. Andrew's Street.

This pub stood on the corner of St. Andrew's Street and Althorp Street so the name is easily explained. Not much is known about this pub except that it was a beer-shop and *Wright* 1884 gives 'bhs'. It seems to have been in possession of Bullock for most of its time. It disappears from the directories in 1933.

AMBUSH St. James' End.

Only *Taylor* 1864 lists this as the Ambush, proprietor Charles Frampton. My first thought was that this must have been in Ambush Street, but on the *O/S* 2500 plan 1901 this street is called Richmond Road – thirty-seven years later. Is it possible that the road was renamed after the pub? Perhaps there is a local significance in renaming the road that Charles Frampton recognised years before? However, *Northampton Alphabetical Postal and Street Guide* of 1876, the *Directory of Northampton* 1878-9 and *Robert's Directory* of 1884 all list this street as Ambush Street, so were the Ordnance Survey out of step with the locals?

Charles Frampton appears as a beer-retailer in St. James in various directories from 1861 to 1876. In 1889 a Charles George Frampton is running the Golden Horse in Bridge Street. *Robert's Directory* of 1884 has in the street lists, *Ambush st. 14 Wm. Allum. Beer-retailer* there is no proof that this is the Ambush pub. Because street lists do not start until 1884 there is no way of linking the earlier references to this one.

AMERICAN BANNER Bridge Street?

If this pub existed it was probably one of those small beer-shops that didn't survive for very long, for there is only one mention of it, in *Bennett's Directory* of 1901-2.

Bennett produced four directories; 1901-2, 1904-5, 1906-7 and 1910-11 and this is the only one to mention an American Banner in

Bridge Street – but the other three refer to an American Banner in Grafton Street; as does **Wright** in 1884 and **Lea** in 1900-1, 1906 and 1907. Unfortunately **Bennett** did not always list landlord's names; if he had it might have shown this entry to be an error. I have checked other directories to no avail, but I suspect that rather than this being yet another pub to add to the Bridge Street list it is an error on the part of **Bennett.**

AMERICAN BANNER 46 Grafton Street.

I have found little on the above pub and next to nothing about this one! The earliest directory entry is **Wright** 1884 ('bhs'), but according to a quote in the **Northampton Independent** Nov.1979 from CAMRA there was an American Banner in Grafton Street from 1865 to 1910.

AMERICAN FLAG IN 1865

The name of these two (?) pubs intrigued me and I suspected that they might have something to do with the American Civil war. The CAMRA start date of 1865 seems to confirm this for the war ended in 1865. In the same year President Lincoln was assassinated and on Dec. 18th Article XIII of the Constitution of the U.S.A. entitled, *Slavery* was adopted. The end of the civil war and the end of slavery (but not the assassination) would seem to be good reasons to commemorate with a pub sign in a liberal town like Northampton.

ANGEL 25 Bridge Street.

This inn is, or was, very old and considering its position on a main north-south route through medieval England, probably started off as a religious house for pilgrims. The sign is, of course, religious.

The sign could have originally been an angel probably the Archangel Michael or Saint Michael - patron saint of the military, such as the Knights Templar. Such signs were placed over inns to show that they were under G-D's protection. Some Angels started life as the Salutation - meaning the salutation of the Blessed Virgin Mary. At the time of the Reformation a sign showing the Archangel Gabriel

 visiting Mary would not have been popular and it is thought that many of these houses simply retained the angel and painted out the Virgin.

The Angel was one of those thirteen inns listed as Ancient Inns in the *Assembly Order* of 1585. Sadly, it is also the last surviving. It is closed at the time of writing and if it ever opens again I fear it will have some daft, meaningless name. [Written in 1998, it does have a daft name!]

The building itself is Listed, although it is a 19th century rebuild of a much older structure. This establishment was in the past both a coaching inn and a post house, as the large doors leading through to the inner yard at this moment attest. I am unaware as to whether these will survive the present work being carried out. [They did]. When the railway more or less wiped out the coach trade the Angel ran its own horse busses to the railway station to maintain its business.

The *Northampton Mercury* in 1753 ran a most curious advertisement concerning this inn. It seemed that there was exhibited at the inn a wondrous dog.

For he actually reads, writes and casts accounts, answers various questions on Ovid's metamorphoses, geography, the Roman, English and sacred history, knows the Greek alphabet, reckons the numbers of persons present, sets down any capital or surname, solves questions in the four rules of arithmitick, tells by looking on any watch of the company what is the hour and minute, knows foreign as well as English coins, shows the impenetrable secret (?), or tells any person's thoughts in company, and distinguishes all sorts of colours.

In 1927 a "Vat of the Ancient Order of Frothblowers" was started at the inn by the proprietor, P. C. Willams. This worthy Order organised dinners, smoking concerts, whist drives and dances to raise money for local charities. Mr. Williams went on to become a councillor, mayor and magistrate. There was some trouble in 1947 when the Lord Chancellor debarred him from the Bench because he was the licensee of the Angel. This caused trouble because of his local popularity and the fact that his trade did not debar him from the

Bench, only the licensing proceedings.

One of the little known claims to fame for Northampton is that James Sharpe, assistant manager of the gas-works, invented the gas-cooker here in 1826. For four years he tested it in his own kitchen, publicly announcing it in 1830. The first commercially made ones were brought by a hotel in Leamington Spa and the Angel, where a special dinner was cooked for 100 people.

In Feb. 1995 the Angel closed, initially for a 'revamp' and conversion to a 'fun pub'. In fact it had been closed due to falling trade, it seemed that young people didn't use it and there were too many hotels now on the town's outskirts taking guests. It was boarded up to protect it from vandals and plans were put forward to convert it into 23 flats and a bar. Plans began to go ahead but unfortunately the developers could not agree with the Council about noise protection.

The developers, Harmony Leisure finally gave up, and one year later in Feb. 1996 put the Angel on the market. By the end of the year it had been bought by Orchard Holdings and Elliott Charles Developments, they proposed a similar scheme to Harmony's. Similar problems concerning noise were encountered and the plan now seemed to be; a bar and restaurant on the ground floor with the upper two floors being offices. By 2008 the upper floors were empty and derelict. In 2012 the building was a shell, having been gutted by a fire and is still like this in 2017. However, the front page of the Chronicle & Echo August 2917 has:-

- *Fat Cat bar to be demolished.*
- *Angel Hotel to be rebuilt in original style.*

So we will see what happens, we need both the demolition *and* the rebuild.

ANGEL & STAR Drapery.

This looks like a case of an alehouse becoming a coffee house, the reverse of the Black Lion, Giles' Street.

To Be Lett,

And Enter'd upon at Michaelmas next, A Good and Well-accustomed PUBLICK-HOUSE, the sign of the ANGEL and STAR, known by the Name of the COFFEE-HOUSE, opposite the Womens Market, with a

Thoroughfare to the Corn-Hill in the Drapery in Northampton.
Enquiries James Maitland, Maltster, in Sheep-street, Northampton.

Northampton Mercury, 26th September 1748.

To be SOLD by AUCTION
By JASPER HAWORTH QUENRY

At his Room at the Angel and Star in the Drapery, Northampton, On Saturday the 3rd of February next, A Great Variety of Furniture of Beds, Bedsteads & Curtains, Tables, Chairs, Glasses, Chest-of-Drawers, Buroes, &c. Likewise a Quantity of superfine Black Broad Cloth.
N. B. The Sale will continue every Market-Day at the above-mentioned Place.

Northampton Mercury, 29th June 1759.

ARMY & NAVY see **Baker's Arms.**

ARTICHOKE Angel Street.

There is only one reference to this establishment, in **Burgess's Directory** of 1845: - *Carter - - Artichoke - - Angel-street*. This was **Burgess's** one and only attempt at compiling a directory *to the town of Northampton* and the Artichoke is listed under *Beer-Sellers*.

It appears that **Burgess**, like **Wright** in 1884, was being thorough and listed nearly everyone (we all miss a few!). This could account for they're being only one entry for this pub. If it was a small place, and beer-only places often were, it may not have attracted the attention of other compilers – or survived for very long.

There is a building on the corner of Guildhall Road and Angel Street (no. 28 Guildhall Road) that looks like it should have been a pub, so perhaps this is it [I'm told it *was* a pub, but not its name]. If not, could it be the Garibaldi Hotel that is only mentioned once, in the **Town & County Directory** of 1905-6? However, **Kelly's Directory** of 1906 has: - *28 Valentine, Mrs. Mary. Dng. Rms.* So, it may have been the Artichoke in 1845, but if it was, by the time of the Garibaldi it had become *Dng. Rms.* It is also shown on the **Fire Insurance Plan** of 1899 as a *Rest.*

ARTIZAN (INN) 51 Artizan Road.

A purpose-built pub and named after the road it stands in. Developers in the past were often more sensitive to the needs of their residents, making shops, pubs and even chapels an integral part of their development. Often today new estates have no amenities, sometimes not even pavements (for hasn't *everyone*  got a car?). However, those Victorian developers didn't do it out of a sense of altruism; it was speculation on possible profits. An early photograph of this pub shows it standing alone on the Artizan Road side and about three houses in Talbot Road.

This pub is still with us and based on a visit in late 1998 seems to be the place to go if you like playing crib. In 1878 a beer-house called the Prince Arthur, Leicester Road was closed and its licence transferred to this 'new' pub.

ARTIZAN LABOURERS Lady's Lane.

This pub only appeared twice, in 1928 and 1932. The proprietor's name (A. Tustin) appears only once and is untraceable through the Pub or Beer-Retailer lists, with no street number I cannot pursue this one any further.

BAKERS ARMS

This is a trade or occupation sign, but perhaps with a difference. As similar conditions are required for both brewing and baking it was not uncommon for the two trades to be carried on under the same roof. Both our Bakers Arms could fit, as could the Old Bakehouse in Bradshaw Street and The Old Grey Horse (later Phoenix) in Swan Street - the Phoenix was run for a long time by the Adams (of bakery fame) family.

BAKERS ARMS also **Army & Navy** (one entry, *Taylor's* 1864)
Barbers Arms (one entry, *Lea* 1900-1, obvious error). 31
Horsemarket.

This pub was on the west side of Horsemarket, just above St. Mary's
Street opposite what was the Girl Guides' Hall, now Northampton
Unitarians Meeting House. The earliest date, with a sign is 1864
when this address was called the Army & Navy, by the next entry in
1877 a John Curl was running it and it was called the Bakers Arms.
There was, however, a Beer-Retailer here from as early as 1847. The
last entry I have for this pub is in 1933.

BAKERS ARMS 37 & 39 Little Cross
Street – Castle Street.

The earliest entry under the sign of the
Bakers Arms is for William Munday in
1858. *Burgess* 1845 has a Munday in
Castle Street as a Beer-Retailer, but this
could be Thomas Munday who is at the
Blue Anchor, 3 Castle Street in 1858
when William is listed as at the Bakers
Arms, 37 & 39 Little Cross Street. As
can be seen from the drawing the pub is

on the corner of these two streets. William continues to be at 37 & 39
as a Beer-Retailer until 1864. *Wright* 1884 lists Jacob Bailey at this
address, as a Shopkeeper and Beer-Retailer. *Lea* 1900-1 has Harry
Andrew at this address listed under the heading Beer Retailers (off
license), but as can be seen from the drawing (which is based on a
photograph probably taken about 1910) it is anything but just an off-
license.

As far as listings under the sign there are four entries all
addressed as Little Cross Street, then there is a gap of over twenty
years (1907 – 1934) when there are four more references, all from
Aubrey's and all with Castle Street with no numbers. The **O/S 2500**
Plan of 1938 clearly shows the whole area cleared and St. Peter's
House nearing completion. As *Aubrey's* entries go on to 1941 there
are only two conclusions. <u>One</u>, in the twenty year gap the pub closed
– or not, but did move to somewhere on the south side of Castle

Street, perhaps reopening years later. <u>Two</u>, *Aubrey's* entries start in 1934 when the area had probably not been cleared and they simply continued to reprint the old type without bothering to check it. For now you take your pick.

<u>BANTAM COCK</u> 1 Abington Square also, St. Edmund's End

That this inn is of great antiquity there can be no doubt, although of course, being outside the town at the time it never became listed as an Ancient Inn in 1585. The building isn't original - only the sign.

As far as I can tell the sign is unique in England. There are plenty of Cocks and such as the Cock & ... Bottle, Dolphin, Trumpet &c., but only one Bantam Cock. One theory as to the name is that it was called thus to distinguish it from a popular Cock that stood at the bottom of Cock Lane (now Wood Street) off

Abington Street. The Cock has always been popular if for no other reason that in the past cock-fighting in pubs was as common as quiz nights are today. Another, more interesting theory relates to a local family. In the past a Lady Cockayne lived in a house on part of Gobion's Farm, a small farm that actually existed inside the town walls. Her crest was three bantam cock heads and she may have well owned the inn in the past, it was common for gentry to use their arms or crest as a sign for their inns.

There is a document dated 1486 that refers to a Gilbert Lyster, *holding ye inne just without Sainte Gyles on the road to Abingtone.* At the time the suburb of St. Edmund's End would have been well established and many houses would have grown up around the East Gate and the junction of the Wellingborough and Kettering Roads. Some of these properties would have definitely been inns. The document grants some very special privileges to Gilbert Lyster, so he must have been a man of influence. It is very likely that the document refers to this establishment and therefore puts it in the running as one of the oldest inns known in town. As far as I know only the Peacock, Catte &c. on Malt Row have earlier documentation. You could argue that the Bantam was outside the town at the time, but at least the sign is still flying, although it was changed to a pseudo-Irish name, but now is just "The Bantam". [Unfortunately it has been changed again (2008) into another stupid name!] [And again, the present landlord has changed the name back to "The Bantam".]

Being outside the town did have its advantages. Although it had a thatched roof at the time of the Great Fire of 1675 it was isolated from the blaze by Gobion's Farm and the town wall. It seems it was used for the shelter of some of the victims of the fire and the account written by a *Country Minister* of the fire shortly afterwards says: - *Fortunately, there were surviving inns, such as the Bantam Cock, which could absorb the numerous strangers come in to view them* (the ruins).

After the fire it was ordered that no more houses were to be built with thatched roofs in the town, so the Bantam Cock became one of the few thatched buildings in Northampton, it being *outside* the Town.

In the past the Bantam Cock would have been one of the last buildings on the Kettering Road before it gave way to open country. The Racecourse was common land and at the crossroads of the Kettering Road and the Kingsthorpe - Abington Lane (White Elephant junction) stood the town gibbet, where the public hangings took place. Tradition has it that as the Bantam was the last hostelry passed by the procession of the condemned it was here that the poor wretches took their last drink. No doubt, the hangman, sheriffs and the mob later returned to 'celebrate' the day's barbarity - so much for the good old days! Note that the gibbet stood on the south-east corner *not* where the Elephant is – the concrete ball recently installed (2008) on the Racecourse is in error.

I understand that this custom of having a drink on the way to an execution was common throughout the land. However, in some parts of the country, and perhaps here on occasions, the condemned prisoner wasn't given a drink. As it was usual to convey the prisoner in the back of a cart or wagon, when the innkeeper asked if he was to have a drink as well the guard would respond with, "No, he's *on the wagon.*" From where we are supposed to get that expression. On other occasions the prisoner would order drinks for himself and his guard and undertake to pay for them on the return trip!

I have in my possession a copy of an undated and anonymous booklet entitled, ***History of an Ancient Hostelry - the Bantam Cock***

Hotel, Northampton. I calculate from references in it that it must have been written between 1932 and 1938. Much of what is written below comes from this source and there are an excellent couple of pages on "Old Time Hosts".

The first is a George Barratt in the year 1748 and the reference is probably from the *Northampton Mercury*. The Bantam being an inn it had to offer refreshment for a man and beast and it seems from the advertisement it did this well.

> *Here at ye `Bantam 'George Barratt mine host*
> *Keeps a good table, bak'd, boyl'd and rost.*

The author gives no date, but I calculate circa 1845 it became tenanted by a Mr. James Peach a market gardener who fancied that he had the fastest donkey in town. In 1849 he was challenged by another market gardener, "Scorcher" Smith to a race from the Racecourse to the Bantam. It seems the crowds turned out, but despite the best efforts of the 'jockeys' the animals refused to run and merely ambled their way towards town. Apparently bets were taken and one of the punters knew that Peach's mount was in the habit of bolting when startled by a loud noise, so as they neared the Bantam he blew a blast on a tin trumpet. Peach's donkey promptly bolted and passed the winning line with a triumphant rider clinging desperately to its back!

The next landlord was Thomas Parker who took over in 1858. He was a local noted pugilist and many of his old pals used the Bantam as a gym. Political elections in the past were pretty lively occasions (see George and Red Lion) and it seems that during one of these he imported several of the old-time champions into the town as 'heavies' with the result that the

Bantam was besieged by rival mobs and had to be barricaded!

In 1899 Mr. Augustus Esbury Davis took over the licence of what was now a limited company. In July 1904 he bought up all the shares. The business flourished and it was during this period that the house was completely rebuilt and improved.

BARLEY MOW
A "mow" is a stack. Barley is used to make malt, so a stack of barley makes an apt sign for a pub.

BARLEY MOW 30 Green Street see **Labour In Vain.**

BARLEY MOW INN 11 or 13 Foundry Street.
There are only two entries for this pub under its name, one in 1864 and the other 42 years later. It does appear under Beer-Retailers quite often in the 1890s and 1910s. The only named entry with a street number gives 13, but all the Beer-Retailer entries give 11 – it is possible that the numbering of the streets changed at some time. The *Goad's Fire Insurance Plan* of 1899 show number 13 to be end of terrace and a dwelling, whereas number 11, two doors along is labelled PH. The pub stood three doors from the west end of the street on the north side, directly opposite a Sunday school. I wonder if they had any problems because of this?

BARRACKS CANTEEN Leicester Road (Barrack Road).
It is possible that this was part of the barracks, but I doubt it, I feel it is unlikely that a military mess would find itself in a commercial directory. It is only mentioned under its name twice, but it is given as an address for a Beer-Retailer once. The first entry has as the address Leicester Road. In 1847 Joseph Webb, the proprietor in the second entry of 1852, is given as, *Webb, Joseph, Tailor and Shopkeeper, Hope's Place.* Hope's Place was the side of the Barrack Road opposite the Barracks. The Webbs seem to have been a family of publicans, later Joseph turns up as a Grocer and Beer-Retailer in Lower Harding Street (this later became the Twenty-Fives) and still later at the Coach & Horses in George Row. Other Webbs at this time (1860s) were running the Old Chequers in Bath Street and the Rivetters Arms in Scarletwell Street.

The only other entry for the Canteen is in *Slater's* 1862, *Bolshaw, Joshua, Barrack Canteen* this is under Beer-Retailers. A Walter Bolshaw had the Green Tree in 1884 and the Kings Arms,

Horsemarket in 1889 (see entry) Mrs. Elizabeth Bolshaw (his widow?) ran the Kings Arms up to 1910. According to the **C&E** 1908 *Sgt-Major Bolshaw, late of the Death or Glory Boys (17th Lancers), now landlord of the Town Arms, Great Russell Street.* According to the **Magistrates' Records** Joshua William Bolshaw had the Town Arms until November 1909.

It looks like this was a short-lived establishment that perhaps became something else. There were several small pubs with patriotic or military names in the area about this time, no doubt catering for thirsty soldiers – and probably run by ex-soldiers. Sometimes the best address I can get is something vague like, Hope's Place and one example with this address; the Red, White and Blue, could easily have been its successor.

BAT & WICKETS 117 Bailiff Street.

This pub is still with us, on the corner of Louise Road and Bailiff Street. The name probably refers to cricket played on the Racecourse nearby, although these days it seems to be played more at the other end, closer to the White Elephant. Perhaps this is why, at the time of writing, the pub has a golfing club, but no cricket team. The earliest reference to this address, which can't be long after it was built, is 1878 when it is listed as a Beer-Retailers.

BATH TAVERN (OLD) 97 Bath Street (Row).

This pub stood on the eastern end of Bath Row on the corner, opposite what is now Compton House. It is first mentioned in 1858 when James Pointer is described as a Beer-Retailer. It first appears under the name of Bath Tavern in 1878. Although there seem to be no more references after 1910 this pub could have continued for many more years. It was a fairly small back-street beer-shop and probably chose not to advertise.

Of interest is a photograph from the Borough Architect's Department, which claims to have been taken in 1974 (probably 1964 see below) prior to the demolition of the area. It is a general shot of Bath Row and clearly shows a foreshortened view of the pub in a dilapidated condition. The painted sign is still there, but badly weathered and unreadable, even if it does have anything on it. It could by the time of this picture have been a private house. The *O/S* 2500 Plan of the area for 1964 shows the site of the pub as cleared of all buildings.

This is an obvious case of a pub getting its name from the street. In the 18th century a Cold Bath was constructed by the river and the street that led down to it became called Bath Street.

BAY HORSE Mounts and Upper Mount Street.

Only two entries for this one; *Burgess'* 1845, *Harvey – Mounts*, and *Hickman's, R. Harvey – Upper Mount street.* During this period the eastern end of Lady's Lane from Park Street to the Lower Mounts was known as Mount Street. As both this and the Mounts are given as addresses it seems reasonable to assume that this pub stood at the end of Mount Street on the Mounts, probably on the corner between these two. *Law's* map of 1847 shows no buildings on the southern corner.

A 'bay' is a horse colour, ranging from light brown to rich mahogany, but always with black points, i.e. mane and tail. This distinguishes it from any variety of chestnut. This Bay Horse was probably a Cleveland Bay, a breed of Coach Horse.

BEAR 11 Sheep Street.

There was a Bear in Bearward Street in the 16th and 17th centuries and this is probably it, although this piece of frontage is now called Sheep Street.

In the *Northampton Mercury* March 5th 1737 a "Bear and Ragged Staff" in Sheep Street was advertised for let. This, without doubt, is the Bear. It was common in the past, as it is today to contract pub names – when I was a lad I went, "down the Lion" not, "to the Black Lion". So this probably represents its 'official' name, the one used on deeds &c.

The Bear and Ragged Staff is a well known heraldic crest, Richard Neville, Earl of Warwick's consisted of a bear, muzzled with a collar and chained to a rugged (ragged) tree-stump. A more local connection is with the Bernards (or Barnards) of Abington, who owned the Estate from circa 1450 until they sold it to William Thursby in 1669 for £13,750.

However, it is more likely that the sign was chosen not because of its heraldic connections, but for the 'Bearward' – where bears were 'warded' or kept for the nasty purpose of bear-baiting. A despicable 'sport' (made illegal in 1835) where dogs were set on a chained bear and bets taken on the outcome.

The Bear appears in the *Universal Directory* of 1791, indicating its status at the time. It is also on *Law's* map of 1847, he only showed inns that were of importance to visitors to the town; this was the main motive for publishing it, so it was a substantial establishment at this time.

Sadly, as I write this (1997) the rather pleasant frontage of this pseudo-Tudor pub has been ripped out and a rather bland brick frontage inserted. Even worse, the name, for no good reason I can see but for the present fashion, has been changed to the Grogger's Rest, a name that has no connection with our town in any way. A few years ago, for a short while it was called The Tavern in the Town – but it reverted to the original name and I am sure it will again. [It did (2008)]. A little more under the **Carpenters Arms.**

BEARWARD ARMS also **Dun Cow** before 1869 **Burghley Arms** before 1898. 33 Bearward Street.
This pub stood three parts of the way along Bearward Street, tucked amongst the houses. This establishment seems to have a long career; the earliest entry I have found in the directories is 1830 and the last 1954. Even then it continued for a few more years as the "Northampton Electric Sports & Social Club".

The sign of the Bearward Arms obviously derives from street name, but the other two are potentially more interesting. Lord Burghley was a trusted advisor of Queen Elizabeth I and as is mentioned more than once elsewhere in this book, the 'Good Queen Bess' had more than a passing interest in the inns and taverns of her realm, perhaps Lord Burghley had some part in this?

The Dun Cow is mentioned in 12th century Irish legend and Guy of Warwick is supposed to have killed a Dun Cow of huge proportions and evil temperament (see entry for Guy of Warwick). Guy was a Saxon hero, son of Simon Baron of Wallingford and married Felicia; daughter of Roband, Earl of Warwick, a title he came to inherit. An old rhyme goes:-

By gallant Guy of Warwick slain
Was Colbrand, that gigantic Dane;
Nor could this desp'rate champion daunt
A Dun Cow bigger than an elephant:
But he, to prove his courage sterling,
His whyniard in her blood imbrued;
He cut from her enormous side a sirloin,
And in his porridge-pot her brisket stew'd:
Then butcher'd a wild Boar and ate him barbicu'd.

It is a pity that this interesting sign was superseded. According to *NN&Q* 1887 the Dun Cow at West Haddon had this rhyme on its signboard: -

I am the cow that ne'er did low.
My skin's as soft as silk
Come, gentlemen, return again
And taste of my sweet milk.

I wonder if our Dun Cow had a similar sign over its door?

BEEHIVE 50 Cow Lane (Swan Street).

This sign is a symbol of business and hard endeavour and has been used by banks and like institutions in the past. However, in this case I feel it is supposed to engender an image of a busy and thriving pub.

It was a beer shop, but I know little about this pub, or its exact location, but I do have a rhyme from the 18th century used on a sign in Cumbria: -

> *In this hive we are all alive*
> *Good liquor makes us funny,*
> *If you be dry, step in and try*
> *The virtue of our honey.*

BEES WING

Northampton has had two pubs of this name and there are two possible explanations for the name, racehorses and port. Beeswing was a mare that had a very successful career from 1835 to 1842 at Wellingborough and York, so there is a certain local connection. Another Beeswing won the Liverpool Autumn Cup in 1866.

On quality port you will find a 'beeswing' – a sort of optical effect. Calling pubs by this name would imply that good port, and presumably other drinks of quality, were obtainable on the premises. Traditionally port was drunk by Tories and punch by Whigs so it could also be an indication of the politics of the establishment.

BEES WING 2 St. Edmund's Row.

One entry under the name, *Taylor* 1864, Sarah A. Johnson, proprietor. I have also found her under beer-retailers in 1866 and 1871 listed as in Kettering Road. She may have moved a short distance, or it could be due to inaccuracies in the directories, for St. Edmund's Row is really the beginning of the Wellingborough Road. The pub would have been on the north side of the road, probably opposite the Volunteer. The properties here were very small and the Bees Wing either didn't last very long, or couldn't run to the expense of directory insertions.

BEES WING Todd's Lane (18 Grafton Street).

The reason why I have shown the name of these two pubs as Bees Wing and not Beeswing like the racehorses – or even Bee's Wing is that a photograph taken early in the 20th century has it thus. Although

I have records of this pub from directories for 65 years (1845 – 1910)I know little about it.

BELL

I have two inns of this name in Northampton, both of considerable

antiquity. There was also a Five Bells in Wellington Street and another Five Bells survives on the Harborough Road, but under another name. To add to these we have also had two Blue Bells.

In the past the sound of a bell was believed to protect those who heard it from lightening or storms, so this could be a possible explanation for the name. Even simpler is that the original proprietor's name was Bell. Handel said that the national musical instrument of England was the bell, we being so fond of it and it is a fairly common pub sign nationally. However, I think that most of the inns and pubs of any age with this name have it because of its religious connections and I would think this is true for both the Bells in this town.

BELL – ("LE BELL") Swinwel-strete (Derngate)

A rental of 1504 describes land next the postern called Derngate (Derngate was originally a gate, not a thoroughfare) and adjoining land belonging to the chapel of Blessed Mary the Virgin in All Saints' Church and the Fraternity of the Holy Trinity. It included four inns, le Crown, le Bell, le Tabard and le Bulle. (*VCH* Vol.III p.19). This is the only reference I have to these inns

BELL also **Birds Nest** and **Opus 2.** 18 Bridge Street.

This Bell is one of the Ancient Inns listed in the *Assembly Order* 1585. Undoubtedly this inn goes back a long way, being as it was on the main north-south route through the medieval town.

The building still stands although the pub closed in the 1960s. At the time of writing it is the premises of Woolwich Property Services and the ground floor is very different from when it was a pub. The building itself is 18th century, or earlier and from the outside the first floor looks very much as I remember it when I used to drink here in the 1960s. This was one of three pubs in the town that sold 'scrumpy' – I'm not sure how authentic this scrumpy was, but it was cloudy and very strong. The Bell was the worst place to buy it. The landlord would simply roll out a firkin behind the bar, whack in a peg and tap and start serving it at once! It was cheap and we Beatniks did not drink beer (I'm not sure why now, perhaps it was because we were living in 'Watneyland') We either drank cider or Merrydown wines, which were 'folksy' drinks such as elderberry and hedgerow. All these were available at the Bell and around the corner, in Gold Street, was the jazz club, so we regularly patronised the place.

LOST on Sat. 28th. May, between Daventry and Bugbrook, a new Suit of Headcloths and Ruffles, With a scallop'd Edging a work'd Handkerchief, a black hood, a blew silk Apron; a green Ribbon and a green Girdle. Whosever brings them to the Swan at Daventry, the Bell in Northampton, the Saracen's Head in Tocester, shall have ten Shillings Reward.

Northampton Mercury June 13, 1720.

These three inns above were all coaching inns and as can be seen the Bell was a place of local importance at the time. A marriage notice in the **Mercury**, May 2nd, 1789 tells of a Mr. John George, late master of the Bell Inn in this town, aged 52 to Mary Merryweather of the same place, aged 19.

The Bell is included in the **Universal British Directory** of 1791, emphasising its relative importance at the time. We know that it was called the Bell in 1585 from the **Assembly Order** and as it was an "Ancient Inn" it probably had that name for a long time before that. The religious connotations of the name indicate that it could have started life as a medieval Hospice as mentioned in the Introduction. In the 1970s its name changed to the Birds Nest, which is, or was, a pub-chain name. The pub was in decline and the change was to no avail and in the 1980s the conversion to the Opus 2 didn't succeed either – so after at least 400 years this inn vanished from Bridge Street.

BELVEDERE also Recruiting Serjeant and Boot & Shoe.
31 St. Giles' Street.

The name of this pub is unusual; a belvedere is a raised turret from which scenery could be viewed (from bel → 'beautiful' and vedere → 'see'). It could be that Joseph Barker, who changed the name, simply liked it. It is also possible that it is the name of a racehorse. The earlier name refers to a recruiting serjeant that probably used the pub for exactly that purpose; it is not a rare name. The Boot & Shoe, which it was called for a time after 1978, refers to the once staple trade of the town. This is a case, in my opinion, where a name change has been acceptable, however, we now have gone back to the Belvedere, and that's not bad either (and it's changed again, 2008).

This pub is still with us at the end of Fish Street. The earliest date I've got for it is 1824, but considering the site there could have been a pub here, perhaps under some other name, much earlier.

BICYCLE TAVERN 42 or 44 Wellingboro' Road. This pub was on the south side of the road about halfway between Victoria Road and St. Edmund's Terrace. The 1884 entry indicated a beer-shop. It closed sometime between 1934 and 1938.

About a century ago cycling was *the* past-time and many pubs in Northampton had their own cycling clubs (see the Bird-in-Hand). The other great hobby at the time was pedestrianism, see the Pedestrian

BIRD-IN-HAND 4 Regent Square.

This pub is still with us, but recently changed its name (2009). It is often thought that pubs with this name owe it to the proverb a bird in the hand is worth two in the bush – the Bush being a rival pub nearby! I have no evidence for a Bush being anywhere near this establishment and its name is the Bird in Hand, not the Bird in THE Hand. It probably refers to falconry (was there a mews nearby in the past?) or its heraldic, fists with falcons are quite common crests.

The earliest reference I have to it is in 1824, although considering its position on the main route through the medieval town and its proximity to the North Gate it could have been here for a long time before the directories began in 1791.

In the 19th century one of the great past-times was cycling. With the invention of the bicycle people of quite modest means suddenly had a means of travelling good distances in a day and all over the land during their holidays. Pubs and inns throughout the land responded to this new market by providing accommodation, teas, &c and often advertised such outside their premises. Cycling clubs sprang up and many of these based their headquarters in pubs. Around 1910 it had a sign above the door, *Head Quarters of the Northampton Rovers Bicycle Club*. This club originally was for riders of the new Rover chain-driven bicycles, as opposed to the 'ordinary' or 'penny-farthing', but later they admitted anybody. James Birt, one time safety cycling champion of the world, held the licence of this pub from at least 1889 – 1900.

Once a year this club held what they called the High Hat Run, when they dressed up in old-fashioned clothes and rode their most antiquated machines around town and then out to Franklin's Gardens. The Carnival Parade, once called the Cycle Parade which used to be on a Thursday in June and raised money for the hospital developed out of this jaunt.

BIRDS NEST see Bell.

BISHOP BLAIZE Market Square.
The only information I have on this inn is from pre-Great Fire (1675) documents - it was probably destroyed in that fire and never rebuilt.

Bishop Blaize or St. Blazius was a bishop in Cappadocia and became the patron saint of woolworkers and woolcombers. The reason for this was that his body was torn to pieces with iron combs - –not a nice way to go! Northampton was once an important wool town and this is just one of the many signs that allude to this trade.

BLACKAMORE'S HEAD No Location.
The Oxford Dictionary gives the meaning of *Blackamore* as, *Negro; dark-skinned person. –* it could have referred to a *Moor –* Northern African Arab, so it is possible that this is another version of the Saracen's Head.

The reference I have to this pub is from Peter Hayden's excellent book, ***The English Pub, A History:*** - *The Blackamoore's Head, in Northampton, would certainly have had a ballroom, for that was the 'seat' of Northamptonshire aristocracy, who could not be without their own inn but, of course, could not be associated with 'trade'. As such, the Blackamoore's Head was never one of the town's 'great' inns.* From this I guess that it must have been an 18th century inn. I have found no other references to it and considering its apparent importance, I wonder why?

<u>BLACK BOY</u> 55 Upper Mount Street, initially <u>**Labour in Vain.**</u>

A good example of the vernacular name superseding the original, has been referred to Washing the Blackamoor White in the past, this is explained under Labour in Vain, Green Street. Advertisement in ***Northampton Mercury*** Oct. 5th 1878: - *SALE Liquidation – Thos. Clarke, Baker and Beerseller…The Stock-in Trade includes a four-pull beer engine & piping, pewter beer measures, mugs, jugs, large & small sweet ale barrels, brewing plant, large balance weighing machine and weights, bakers' peels, hand truck, pony, cart, and nearly new set of harness, chaff cutter stable utensils &c. &c.*

It was two doors from the Town Arms, the first entry is 1845, became the Black Boy circa 1858 and the last entry is 1910.

<u>BLACK BOY HOTEL</u> 5 Wood Hill.

The Black Boy stood on Wood Hill on part of the site recently occupied by the Midland Bank (HSBC). I remember in the 1950s my mother telling me that this was a 'posh' place and I seem to recall boys liveried like American bellhops being about the place.

It closed its doors forever in January 1963 when I was 17. Although, like everyone else I drank underage I hadn't been into this place above once because of its then 'rough' reputation. My only visit wasn't a very long one and I recall American servicemen drinking in there, a lot of boisterous behaviour and gaudily dressed young ladies.

From descriptions it seems the cellars of this establishment were vaulted and extended under the road. There are many cellars like this in the town and are usually of the 17th or 18th centuries; however, if

this is real vaulting and I don't know if it is, then the cellars probably predated the Great Fire of 1675, which would have destroyed the building above. When the bank closed I was allowed into the vaults, however because of their secure construction there was no evidence of ancient cellars (2008). A Court was held after the Fire to decide claims, if cellars could be identified and cleared of debris a claim would be easy to prove, and if they were still sound a new building could be built straight on top of the old foundations. There was an inn called the Crown on Wood Hill before the Fire and these could have been its cellars.

There is more than one explanation for the origins of the name, Black Boy. It is unlikely that it is a colloquialism (see Black Boy, The Mounts); it could refer to the black servants who were once popular, or a 'blackamore' employed in the 18th century to advertise the new-fangled coffee shops. There is no record of it being called anything else and there is a notice of a stolen horse that mentions this inn in the *Northampton Mercury* of 1722 and again in 1731 when the *late widow Holloway (now Smith)* moved from the Chequer to here. My theory is that the inn was named in honour of King Charles II.

General Monk was one of Cromwell's men who became disenchanted with the Commonwealth and a supporter of the return of the Monarchy. As I understand it he considered that he owed fealty to England, not any individual, but to what was *best* for the country. Whilst Charles II was still in exile Monk made a point by drinking his health with, *"to my Bonnie **Black Boy**!"* Apparently Charles was very swarthy, having Moorish blood from his mother's side and this was his nickname.

King Charles II was not too impressed with Northampton as we had supported the Parliamentary cause during the Civil War. At the time the town was still heavily fortified and to prevent any possible resistance from this strategically important town he ordered that our Castle and walls be *'slighted'* – i.e. partly demolished so they could not be easily repaired. In 1675 the Great Fire of Northampton struck, completely destroying large parts of the town. A disaster fund was set up and contributions came from all over the land from £5,000 (a huge sum) from the City of London to 10 shillings (50p) from Shernford. The King gave 1,000 tunns of timber (a tunn is forty cubic feet) from the Royal forest of Whittlebury and remitted the duty of chimney-money for seven years. It seems the wood was for the rebuilding of All Saints Church, which had been largely destroyed, but for the tower (Burnt red stone can still be seen just inside the west door.) Legend has it that the surplus wood was used in the foundations of the new inn built on Wood Hill. I think that instead of calling the inn by its old name of the Crown they chose to honour Charles by using his nickname.

Although I have said that I recall the Black Boy having a 'reputation' in the 1960s, this certainly wasn't the case in earlier years. Through the whole of the 1920s this hotel was run first by William Bell and then by his widow, Edith. From all accounts it was a commodious building, hosting a number of organisations that made their headquarters here, including the Queen Eleanor Lodge of the R.A.O.B., the Managers and Foreman's Association, the Amalgamated Society of Engineers and the Railway Transport Workers. It had 14 bedrooms, 2 lounges, a large dining room big enough for 50 guests, smoke room and bars. An adjacent garage was purchased so cars could be 'put up' and repairs done on the spot. A back entrance meant guests didn't have to go through the bars to their rooms.

This state of affairs continued into the 1950s. The England v. Scotland Soccer International at Wembley on April 14th 1951 resulted in two bookings from Glasgow football 'enthusiasts' as the local paper called them. One party stayed overnight whilst another group of 70 stopped off for breakfast here. Cars by now were parked in a *spacious yard to the rear*. The back entrance to Dychurch lane was still in use and led into the remnants of an ancient foot-path that used to run from All Saints Church to Weston Favell village. Some of this path can still be traced. You could pass from Wood Hill through the old bank and out the rear door into Dychurch Lane, along the Riding and the north side of St. Giles' churchyard into St Edmund's Road.

Part of this used to be called Bird's Piece and the name can still be seen on the west corner at the top of Denmark Road. The path is blocked by St. Edmund's churchyard and disappears for a few streets beyond. Until recently it ran as a 'jitty' parallel to the Wellingborough Road from West Street to Wilby Street, only the eastern end of this now remains and it ends at the bottom of Collins Street near the Crown & Cushion pub.

BLACK BOY & STILL Bridge Street.

There are only two entries for this pub, both in *Pigot's Directories* – 1842 *Jno. Humfrey* and 1830 *Rbt. Butcher*. A Robert Butcher had the Plumber's Arms in Sheep Street according to *Kelly* 1847. There is no sign of either Humfrey or Butcher in any of the directories consulted under beer-retailers, but there is a Silvanus Humphry, Chemist and Druggist, Bridge Street in Kelly 1847. Although the spelling is different there is a connection in that the sign "Black Boy & Still" can be attributed to the arms of the Apothecaries. Much of our early medical knowledge came from the Arabs or Moors and the Apothecaries' arms included one of these gentlemen – easily mistaken for a 'Black Boy'.

BLACK HORSE

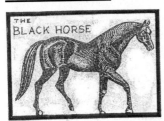

We have had two definite and one possible Black Horse in Northampton, one in Bailiff Street and another in Bridge Street. Whether either of these were heraldic in origin I cannot tell, but the horse, as common a sight in days gone by as the motorcar is today, often figured on pub signs. In Northampton we have had as many as twelve pubs with horse signs, from Bay, Black and Flying to the surviving Golden and Race-. There were also seven with either Horse & ----, or --- & Horse as well as three Horseshoes and others with specifically named (race) horses such as the Beeswing and Eclipse.

BLACK HORSE Bailiff Street.

Only *Burgess* 1845 lists this pub by name, *Allebone – Black Horse – Bailiff st.* *Hickman* 1847 lists, *Allebone J., Bailiff street, Beer-retailer.* Even by *Taylors* in 1864 there seem to be few properties in Bailiff Street, but without more information I have no certain way to locate it.

BLACK HORSE 148 & 150 Bridge Street.

Although this pub is mentioned in fourteen directories from 1845 to 1901 I have nothing more on it. As near as I can ascertain this pub stood on the west side of lower Bridge Street about opposite Navigation Row and probably disappeared when Phipps' Brewery was enlarged. A new fermenting house, cask washing yards, coopers' shops, boiler house, smithy and dray sheds were built in 1905 – along with a complete reconstruction of the brewhouse and rearrangement of the bottling stores. I am indebted to Mr. Geoffery Starmer for this information. According to information supplied by Mr. C. Glazebrook the building was in 1845 on the *east* side of the street (2017)

BLACK HORSE St. Gyles Streete.

We have from the *Great Fire Court 1675*, May 4th 1677: - *Toft or piece of ground situate on the north side of St. Gyles streete in the Towne of Northampton next adjoyning to a howse there called the black horse*....It is possible that this wasn't an inn as it is only referred to as a "howse".

We also have a Rental of 1504 that lists several inns in the area and a house: - *There were inns called 'le Crown', 'le 'bell', 'le Tabard & 'le Bulle' & a house called 'le Blakhall, in St. Giles st*.... Is 'le Blakhall' the Black Horse, and if so, was it ever an inn? As it was pre-Fire and doesn't seem to have been rebuilt we will probably never know.

BLACK LION.

This sign is not too common, but we have had two of them, both still with us. One with the prefix 'Old' and the other with a name change.

There can be little doubt that the sign is heraldic in origin and it is possible that it came from the arms of Queen Phillipa of Hainault, wife of Edward III (1327-1377) or it could be the ensign of Owain Glendower, the Welsh rebel who led a successful revolt against the English. He defeated Henry the Fourth in three campaigns (1405-1413) and styled himself Prince of Wales. Owain disappeared around 1416 after he had waged a guerrilla war on the English for several years. It is thought that Welshmen often set up the sign of the Black Lion.

If the above is correct then I cannot see any Welshman putting up such a sign until the English had forgotten its meaning. This would mean that it was unlikely that a Black Lion was called such until at least 1500.

BLACK LION (OLD) 1 Black Lion Hill.

There can be little doubt that this pub goes back a long way and it is one of the contenders for the oldest pub in town. The *RBN 1898* lists it as one of the 16th and 17th century inns, but I've not seen the documents. The *Good Beer Guide 1997, CAMRA,* describes this establishment as, ...*stone built in the 12th century.* – this is, of course, an error! The pub today consists

of two addresses, numbers 1 and 3, the pub having in the recent past expanded into the shop next door. Both these properties are Grade II Listed Buildings. The original inn is 17th century with some 19th century additions; whilst number 3 was an 18th century cottage. In the past Black Lion Hill ran right across what is now the end

of St. Peter's Way and joined up with Western Terrace. All that now remains is this pub at the east and another pub that was the Star, now a club, at the west. [The Star is now demolished (2010)]. The line of buildings curved back here giving a wide space opposite the entrance to the railway station. This predated the station and must have had something to do with the Castle. Chalk Lane is directly opposite the pub and its curve to the west outlines where the eastern ramparts of the Castle's inner bailey stood. Although I have no proof I am prepared to believe that some sort of drinking establishment has stood hereabouts from mediaeval times.

Surprisingly, this establishment does not appear in the directories until 1862, and all attempts to trace it back to an earlier date have proved fruitless. *[I have now found three references from the Mercury 1705-1754 (2017)].* There is an advertisement from the **Northampton Mercury,** 1735 about dogs stolen from the, Black Lyon in Northampton that could very well refer to this pub, although the other Black Lion probably appeared about 1720. No doubt it was the appearance of this new Black Lion in St. Giles' Street that prompted the prefix 'Old' to distinguish it from the 'upstart'.

An advertisement from the **Northampton Mercury** July 1729 has: - *At the BLACK LYON in Northampton is kept by Samuel Smith, the famous Stallion, late belonging to Sir Arthur Hesilrige, known by the Name of Red Rose: which will cover Mares this Season, at half a Guinea a Leap, and 6d. the Man.* Hesilrige House is near this pub.

John Roddis (1862) was the first proprietor in the directories and it could have been his son, another (?) John Roddis, who advertised the Black Lion in 1884. He styled it The Old Black Lion Hotel and offered, *Cabs, Flys, Wagonettes, Dog Carts, Etc. for hire, good horses, and careful and obliging drivers* he also advertised, *Good Loose Boxes. Livery & Bait Stables, Lock-up Coach Houses.*

The pub originally had an entrance or carriageway on the right that led through to a yard and extensive outbuildings as well as a long back wing. This entrance is now sealed up and is along with the shop next door now part of the lounge. Some of the outbuildings remain and must have been part of the facilities that John Roddis described. A few years ago I noticed several iron rings stapled to the wall of one of these buildings and was informed by an old boy that these were used to chain up the prisoners while they had their last drink before being taken over the road to the Castle to be executed! These rings are stapled to a brick wall, which cannot be older than 150 years. Anyone who is familiar with stables would recognise the significance of the size and position of these rings. This illustrates how easily stories can grow up and sometimes become accepted as fact.

BLACK LION 19 St. Giles' Street.

Black Lion July 1986

This pub is still with us, it was renamed after the cut-off date (1993) with a new (and inappropriate) name will be found in the Appendix.

I have it from someone who had sight of the deeds many years ago that this pub started life as a coffeehouse called the Plasterers' Arms and changed to the Black Lion in 1720. Through much of its past it had been associated with the theatre and variety halls. In those days this pub was the local headquarters of the Variety Hall Artists' Association. It seems that many towns had such a place. Performers were always on the move and their local headquarters would always put them up or find them accommodation as well as helping them out in times of trouble. There are references to the Black Lion as early as 1793.

I can remember as a child (what *was* I doing in there?) seeing lots of signed photographs of performers in frames on the walls of the back room. This room (men only) resembled a gentlemen's' club with a billiard table under the skylight (the skylight is still there, but covered over) and large comfortable leather chairs scattered around. By the time I was old enough to drink here the place had changed considerably although it never lost its connection with the world of entertainment. In the 1960s the back room became Northampton's equivalent of Liverpool's Cavern Club where local up and coming musicians started, or ended their careers.

It was during this time that the 'Lion acquired a new name, unlike the present one this was unofficial, a nickname. In 1957 a childrens' animated series appeared on television called *The Adventures of Captain Pugwash.* This pirate and his jolly crew had a ship called *The Black Pig.* The Black Lion Nutters Club, started for fun and charity fund raising, dubbed the pub with this name – even this name swiftly got shortened to just 'The Pig'!

Many pubs claim to be haunted, and this is one of them. The *C&E* 9/12/66 interviewed five ex-landlords who claimed to have experienced something uncanny on the premises. These were the usual pub type phenomena; lights on after being turned off, casks in the cellar moved, footsteps, doors opening on their own and shadowy figures glimpsed through glass doors and partitions. One theory offered was the murder of Annie Pritchard by Andrew McRae in 1892. He is supposed to have boiled her head, arms and baby in a bacon boiler on his brother's premises near the pub. The body, minus head and arms was found in a sack in a ditch near Althorp Station. He was sentenced to death on Christmas Eve 1892 and executed in January of the following year.

There is an 'undercroft' attached to this pub, a lower cellar going out under the street. These are quite common in the town in 18th century buildings. I examined it in the 1970s and found it to be typical of its kind. Unfortunately many of the regulars were having none of this and preferred to stick to the erroneous idea that it was part of the fabled 'Monk's Passages' that are supposed to honeycomb Northampton's underground. This has been put forward as a source of the supernatural events, but the ghosts reported are a heavily built man with a dog and a woman in a riding habit – not a monk's habit.

This ghost or ghosts do not seem to want to harm anyone, and although people have reported feeling cold and dogs are scared, it doesn't *seem* to be very scary. I believe, if there is a ghost, it's the ghost of 'Teddy' Dunkley. He was landlord for 40 years; by all accounts a great character and the one who really made the place a centre for the entertainment business. After what was done to his pub in 1993 I should think his spirit has departed, never to return!

I think that I should add that in the 1960s, one night after closing time whilst packing up my light-show I saw something I can't explain. Bob Brewer, the landlord saw it as well and he couldn't explain it either. I like to think it was 'Teddy' Dunkley locking up.

BLACK MAN 30 Green Street see **Labour in Vain.**

BLACK RAVEN Newland.

The Black Raven is a badge of the old Scottish kings, the House of Stuart and Jacobites, it figured in the arms of Mary I and the Macdonalds. So it looks like there may have been a Scottish connection to this sign. There is hearsay evidence that this establishment was adjoining Welsh House, so it would have been at the bottom of Newland, almost on the Market Square. This is borne out by the advertisement in the *Northampton Mercury*, November 1747 quoted below. In fact, the only evidence I have are three advertisements from the *Mercury*, two in 1747 and one in 1759. It gone by the 1880s as it is referred to as only a memory. It could be another name for the Black Spread Eagle.

> *To Be Lett. And Entered upon immediately.*
> *A Good Accustom'd Publick House, Known by the Name of the BLACK RAVEN in Newland, near the Market-Hill in Northampton standing well for a Market Trade.*
> *Enquire of Mr. Henry Peach, in Northampton aforesaid.*

The one that appeared before this in September informed the readers that Moses Tibbs was moving from the Black Raven to the Bell Inn. The only other advertisement appeared twelve years later; -

> *NOTICE is hereby given,*
> *THAT DOCTOR FISHER, from Onley, will be at the Black Raven in Newland, Northampton, on MARKET & Fair-Days, to be spoken with by any Person concerning his Business Of Sergeon and Man-Midwife.*
> *WILLIAM FISHER*

BLACK'S HEAD 38 Albert Street see **Wellington.**

BLACK SPREAD EAGLE Market Hill (Square).

This sign was on Market Hill in the first part of the eighteenth century and may never actually have been an inn. An advertisement from the *Northampton Mercury* of March 1720 is for a Dr. Walpole of Ecton, Rupture-Master – to be spoke with every Saturday at the Spread Eagle. This does imply an inn, as on market days various specialists would hire a room in an inn and to carry on their business with the market visitors.

A year later John Balderton at the Black Spread Eagle, same address, was making and selling the *New Italian Weather-Glass* – it appears to have been a combined barometer and thermometer. By 1722 John Balderton had become a seedsman and fruiterer and reverted in his advertisement to calling his premises the "Spread Eagle".

Heraldically the Black Spread Eagle is associated with Victoria Adelaide, daughter of Queen Victoria and Albert. As she was born in 1840 there can be no connection here. It may be, however, connected with Germany – but it also figures on the arms of Overstone.

It is not impossible that over the years the Eagle became a Raven and this establishment is the same as one of that name. There is also on record a 16-17th century inn whose location is unknown called the Spread Eagle – so it is possible that they are all the same place.

BLACK SWAN 17 or 33 Green Lane or Street.

There is some confusion as to this pub's location. Green Street according to the *O/S* 1901 ran into the Green and then onto Green Lane. If this pub was in the lane it had disappeared under the Gas Works by *O/S* 1938.

BLAST TAVON Newland?

This is an unusual name and I have no idea as to its origin. There is only one mention of it, in an indenture of 1677: - *ALL that Messuage or Tenement or Inne called or knowne by the name or Sign of the Blast Tavon- situate or being in or neere a street or lane called the Newland in the Parish of All Saints....*

BLUE ANCHOR (OLD) 1 or 3 Castle Street.

The anchor is a symbol of hope and blue is the colour of fidelity, so I am informed. The sign of the anchor is often interpreted as religious or nautical according to its location and antiquity.

This pub, according to *Wright* 1884 was a beer-house ('bhs') – so was probably not that ancient and we are about as far from the sea here as you can get. In the politics of the past blue was the colour of the Whigs, as opposed to the scarlet of the Royalists. This area would indicate that a Whig proprietor would have been a lot more popular than a Royalist one.

The *Fire Insurance Plan* 1899 shows houses and Public Houses in Castle Street and this establishment stood on the south side of the street, at the east end.

BLUE BALL Barrack Road.

There are several possible meanings to this sign, although this pub may never have existed. It can represent a crystal ball and be the sign of a fortune teller, it can represent the Globe and as such be the cognisance of Portugal implying the sale of Portuguese wines – not likely in a beer-shop or it can represent the South Sea Company, perhaps the landlord having lost most of his assets opened a humble ale house. Of course, it could be simply that he likes the sign.

The only reference to this pub is from the *C&E* 29/4/1959:

He remembers (3)

In its first days the Salvation Army was housed in a pub recalls 85-year old William Cox, of 36 Malcolm-rd. At the time of the take-over the licensed days of the Blue Ball – which was situated in Barrack-rd, opposite the Barracks were over and the Salvations turned it into a coffee house.

Unfortunately I came upon this reference forty years after it was written so it has not been possible to interview Mr. Cox! It is possible that this is a Blue Bell. William Marriott had a Blue Bell in St. Mary's Street between 1861 and 1867, but also a beer shop in the Barrack Road in 1866 (see entry below).

BLUE BELL.

There are three possibilities for the origin of this sign; that like the simple Bell in Bridge Street, it is a religious sign that it refers to the flower or the song *Bluebell of Scotland.*

Blue in the past was the cheapest colour and also the most hard wearing, it was also the colour that faded last - this is still true, look at any polychrome poster that's been up for a while. Inn signs are the art that takes the most battering, so a blue anything would be a good choice.

According to an old book I have on the language of flowers the Bluebell means True and Tender and although most landlords would like their customers to remain True and come back, Tender could only apply, I feel, to the Tendering of hard cash rather than asking for credit!

BLUE BELL 47 & 49 St. Mary's Street.

Only one entry as the Blue Bell, *Taylor's* 1864, William Marriott. He appears as a beer-retailer at this address in 1861, 62, 64 and 67; but he also appears in 1866 as a beer-retailer in Leicester Road and again in 1869 at Hope's Place (which was in Leicester, now Barrack, Road) at the Spread Eagle. The entries for St. Mary's street of 1861 and 1867 are both from *Melville* so it could be that they didn't update properly. This was probably another small beer-shop that survived from about 1861 to 1864. *Roberts* 1884 street list gives no beer-retailers or pubs for this address.

BLUE BELL Russell Terrace.

Burgess's Directory 1845: - *Lawrence - Blue Bell - Russell-terrace.* This is the only reference I can find to this establishment. *Burgess* appears to have been very thorough and listed many small beer-shops that don't appear elsewhere. Russell Terrace was a narrow dead-end running west off Cow-Lane (Swan Street) not far from Victoria Promenade. It was largely made up of tiny 'two-up two-down' properties, as can be seen from the *O/S* 2500 plan of 1901 – by the plan of 1938 they had all gone. The Blue Bell was probably one of these small houses operating as a shop with one room to drink in and just serving the immediate vicinity.

In the 1860s there was a beer-retailer, William Lawrence at 40 West Street (Good Intent).

BLUE BOAR

The explanation for this sign is well known. The badge of Richard III was a white boar. After his defeat and death inn signs that bore (no pun intended!) his badge were swiftly changed. No landlord wanted to be associated with the losing side; it was bad for business and a long life. Signs have always been expensive so the easiest and cheapest way to change the sign was to simply paint the boar blue.

The Blue Boar was also the crest of the Earl of Oxford who figured well in the placing of Henry VII on the throne. As the Tudors ruled this country until the death of Elizabeth I in 1603 this sign was a patriotic one for 120 years – long enough to become well established.

BLUE BOAR Gold Street & **BLUE BOAR** Market Hill (Sq.).
I have grouped these two together because they appear to be linked and the best way to explain this is to quote from *NN&Q*. Volume III 1889: The town may have boasted of two Blue Boars at the same time-the one on Market hill, and the other in Gold street; -unless the former was abandoned and its name or sign added to that of the Shoemaker's Arms, in Gold street. This theory is not improbable for according to Peter Peirce, the Blue Boar had but a poor reputation in 1764. His advertisement of April 16, 1764, ran as follows: -

> *As, I some time, since proposed to quit the Red-Lyon in the Horse-Market, Northampton, and, to that Purpose, had taken the Blue-Boar on the Market-Hill in the said Town, the Notion of which has been very detrimental; obliges me to take this Publick Method to assure all Gentlemen, Dealers, &c. that I have entirely quitted the Blue-Boar, and continue the Red-Lyon; where all such, who please to favour me with their Custom, may depend on the best Accommodations, and their Favours will be gratefully Acknowledged by Their obedient Servant, Peter Peirce.*

BOAT.
I have two Boats one of them an error, and a Boat & Horse.

BOAT 12 College Street.
This is only mentioned twice, by *Whellan* in 1874 and *Kelly* in 1877 *proprietor, James Lancaster*. I believe that this is an example of printers cribbing from each other – including their mistakes. As James Lancaster is listed as the proprietor of the *BOOT* at 12 College Street in both 1876 and 1878 I don't think there can be any doubt that this is an error.

BOAT Old Towcester Road, Cotton End.

This old building was still standing a few years ago, unfortunately it has been destroyed for a Carlsberg car park. Undoubtedly the boat referred to is a narrow boat as the pub stood on the west side of the little spur of the Old Towcester Road close to the canal lock.

BOAT & HORSE St. Peter's Street and Freeschool Street.
Possibly also **Odd Fellows' Arms** (see).

The reason why I think these two are the same pub, or at least, the same property is that the *O/S* 2500 Plan 1964 shows number 2 (Odd Fellows Arms number) St. Peter's Street to be on the north corner of St. Peter's and Freeschool Streets. The opposite corner on all three *O/S* Plans shows normal terraced dwellings whilst the north corner has a distinct and relatively large building with a good-sized yard.

In view of the horse in the name I feel the boat referred to here, like the Boat in Cotton End, is also a narrow boat. Perhaps Mr. James Jeffery once worked on the Navigation?

BODEGA VAULTS see **George Hotel.**

BOLD DRAGOON 48 High Street, Weston Favell.

A Dragoon is a soldier, the word being a corruption of the word *dragon* – a name given to their 'fire breathing' carbines – a kind of short musket.

The present building was constructed in the 1930s to replace another of the same name nearby. Originally a village pub it has, over the years, become swallowed up in housing and incorporated into the borough. This incorporation is probably why there is such a long gap in the directory entries. The earliest I have is in 1862, under beer-retailers, a Henry Clark of Weston Favell. As I know the names of the landlords of the other two pubs in the village (Horseshoe and Trumpet) at this time it is a fair guess that this beer house later became the Bold Dragoon.

The only other 19th century entry is for a *Henry Knight, farmer & bhs* (***Wright*** 1884).

BOOT.

There have been two Boots in Northampton's past, one, apparently very short-lived in Abbey Street and an older one in College Street.

Boots are usually attributed to St. Crispin, however, it seems that ten pubs in the past (I don't know which – or if they are still trading) in the neighbouring counties of Bucks., Beds. and Hunts, all were named because of a common legend. A certain monk from Monks Risborough became the vicar of the village of North Marston near Winslow (Bucks.), and is supposed to have conjured the Devil into a boot. *Sir* John Schorne Gentleman borne Conjured the Devil into a boot.* *Medieval courtesy for a vicar, John Schorne died in 1314.

I don't think that there is any doubt that *our* 'pair' of boots refers to the once staple trade of the town.

BOOT INN Abbey Street

There is only one entry for this pub under this name, in **White's** directory of 1896, *Mrs. A. E. Bailey, 1 Abbey st.* This address corresponds to the St. James W.M.C. site before redevelopment in the 70s. The pub, which seems to have been a beer-house, was there prior to 1896 and Mrs. Bailey must have been the widow of the previous proprietor as in those days as that was the only way a woman could get a licence. There is a J. Bailey, beer-retailer, listed in St. James' End in 1870 and 1871 and a John Bailey at Park Road, St. James in 1885. The present Park Road is nowhere near to Abbey Street. The Castle pub now stands in Park Road and is now the only address – a Walter Collins had the Castle in 1884.

BOOT INN 12 College Street.

This could be an ancient pub. There was a Boot in College Lane in the 16th and 17th century, which was, no doubt, rebuilt after the Great Fire of 1675. It is interesting that when I was working as an archaeologist for Northampton Development Corporation we rescued a hoard of medieval leather, preserved in the waterlogged silt at the bottom of the old Anglo-Danish town ditch. The leather evidently came from a shoemaker's workshop, as some of it was off-cuts. It was probably thrown into the ditch that stood open long after the Norman town had been built. This leather and old shoes was found only a short distance from where the Boot stood. If the Boot Inn went back far enough – to the 11th or 12th century, it would also be "in the ditch" as was, so it seems, the medieval leatherworker's shop. It stood in College Street, close to the end of Jeyes <u>Jitty</u> (<u>NOT</u> 'Jetty'!).

*Mr. Pryor was the last landlord and informed the **C&E** in 1952 that he had taken over the tenancy in 1905 from a Mr. Farey, who had emigrated to Canada. Mr. Pryor said that the licensee before Mr. Farey had been Mr. "Topper" Roddis. Mr. Roddis always wore a silk topper.*

The Boot Inn closed on April 11th 1907 and the licence along with three others were surrendered to obtain a licence for the new Clinton Arms in Far Cotton. Mr. Pryor became the first landlord of the Clinton Arms when it opened one week later on April 18th. This photograph was taken in January 2000 just before the building was demolished. The **Mercury** vol. 43 1762-3 has a **Boot** in Gold Street and could be the above (2017).

BOOT & SHOE see **Belvedere.**

BOOT & SLIPPER 10 Spring Lane.
The Boot & Slipper probably started out as a genuine trade sign of a shoemaker or cobbler, or because of the local employment.

I believe this pub stood on the west corner of Spring Lane and Compton Street. It first appears in the directories in 1858 under this name, not appearing earlier as a beer shop. I have been able to trace it as a beer-retailer up to 1907, then there is a gap, but the address appears again briefly in 1928-29, so it could have been going all that time. According to the **Mercury** vol.51 1770-1 there was a **Boot & Slipper** in Mercers Row (2017).

BOOTHVILLE see **Lumbertubs.**

BOUVERIE ARMS 1 Raglan Street.
This pub was on the west corner of Raglan Street and the Wellingborough Road and is clearly shown as "PH" on *O/S* 2500 Plan 1964. It disappeared when the Wellingborough Road was widened in the 1960s.

BREWERS ARMS see **Harbour Lights.**

BREWERS ARMS Cow Lane (Swan Street).
The first entry in a directory for this pub is in *Burgess* 1845 where it is listed under Beer-Sellers, so no doubt this was another small beer-shop. References are sparse and only one other directory, *Hickman's* 1847 gives it the name. *Pigot* 1824 has: -*Shaw, John, Gold st., Maltster.* Possibly a relative of the only name connected with the pub, i.e. Thomas Shaw. *Kelly's* directory of 1847 has: - *Shaw, Thomas, Agent for London & North Western Railway Co. & sole agent for the delivery of parcels. Angel Hotel, Bridge street.* **Slater** lists him in 1850 as a beer-retailer as does *Kelly* 1854, after this he and the address disappear.

BREWER'S ARMS Location unknown ('Northampton').
Brewer's-Arms, Northampton.
From the **Mercury** October 13th 1787
SAMUAL HADDON begs leave to inform his Friends and the Public in general, that he has laid in a great Quantity of all sorts of SPIRITUOUS LIQUORS, which he intends Selling by the following Prices, viz.

	s.	d.	
French Brandy at ..	2	0	per bottle.
Rum	2	0	Ditto.
Gin	1...	0	Ditto.
Peppermint	1...	6	Ditto.

Best Lemon Shrub* .. 2 0 Ditto.

*Shrub is a cordial made from sweetened fruit juice and a spirit, usually rum.

Gives some idea of prices in the 18th century. Could this be the same as above, not the sort of drinks one would expect from a beer-shop, but it could have changed over the years?

BRICKLAYERS ARMS.

We have had two of these 'occupation arms' and no doubt in both cases the proprietors were originally bricklayers who had retired to the more gentle trade of landlord, or who carried on two trades at the same time.

BRICKLAYERS ARMS 46 Kerr Street see **Silver Cornet.**

BRICKLAYERS ARMS 36 St. Mary's Street.

If the numbering on the *O/S* 2500 Plan of 1964 is the same as in the 19th century, then this could have been the large property with a side entrance just east and opposite the end of Pike Lane. There is another, more substantial building to the west.

BRICKMAKERS ARMS 59 Broad Lane (now Street).

A pub name with similar origins to the above. In 1847 Robert Butcher was at the Plumbers Arms in Sheep Street, by 1849 he was in Broad Lane. *Taylor's* 1858 is the only · entry with the name Brickmakers Arms and in 1864 and 1866 Mrs. Ann Butcher, probably his widow, is listed here. No more of it heard of until the street lists of 1884 when the address is described as a "Marine Stores" – i.e. junk shop.

BRIGG'S PUNCH-HOUSE see **Criterion.**

BRITANNIA.

This symbol of Britain has been used four times in Northampton that I've discovered; two of them are still flourishing.

Britannia is well known to all that remember our older currency. She used to appear on notes and the 50p piece and older readers will remember her image on the old penny and the even older halfpenny and farthing which both bore her image before the ship and wren. She first appeared on our coins in 1672 when Charles II struck the copper halfpenny and farthing. The pose, sitting with shield beside her and trident raised is very similar to an image of Pietas or Piety on some coins of Hadrian who ruled between 117 and 138 CE. This image in turn is supposed to have been taken from coinage struck by Lysimachus, King of Thrace from 313 to 281 BCE, which showed Athene in a similar pose. So our Britannia has come a long way!

BRITANNIA 51 Hope's Place (Barrack Road).

This pub lies on the east side of the Barrack Road, north of the site of the town's north gate.

The earliest reference is 1858, but considering its position it could have been there much longer. As things got a bit calmer in the late medieval period people began to build suburbs outside town gates. The importance of the north-south route through this town would have guaranteed that many of these houses would have been inns, so there could have been a hostelry of some description around here for ages. Its neighbour, the Gardeners Arms goes back to 1845, this establishment became absorbed into the Britannia in the 1940s – probably after the end of the war, when the Britannia was completely rebuilt and enlarged. [Another pub that's now changed its name to something irrelevant (2010)].

BRITANNIA Bedford Road (Rush Mills) also **Compass** and **Papermakers Arms?**

This one is also with us. According to an article in the *C&E* 25/11/94 this started life as the Compass Inn in 1827. The compass is probably magnetic, rather than a pair of. One pair of

compasses indicates Masonry, two Joiners and three, Carpenters. It can be the contraction of the word Compassion, a Hospice name. This pub served the river traffic in the past – as it still does, but leisure today rather than commercial.

The earliest I have for the Britannia is 1876 and we also have once listed in 1847 at *Cotton End, Hardingstone - the Papermakers Arms*. As country places, especially isolated ones like the Britannia, were described by the road they were on or the parish they were in Hardingstone is a fair description of the pub's location. The mill opposite was at one time a papermill, so it is possible that between 1827 and 1876 the pub was called the Papermakers Arms.

BRITANNIA Lady's Lane, 1 Victoria Street. also **Victoria.**

I can trace William Sykes as a beer-retailer back to 1858 and the sign first appears in the directories in 1864. *Kelly* 1940 gives this address as a pub called the Victoria, this is the same pub as the proprietor's name, William Cox carries over the name-change.

BRITANNIA 1 Lower Harding Street see **Earl Spencer's Arms.**

BRITISH BANNER.

A good patriotic sign! We've had two that I know of. This sign may date from the formation of the United Kingdom on January 1st 1801 with the union of Great Britain and Ireland, or from the Act of Union of 1707 when England and Scotland were united as the Kingdom of Great Britain.

Union flag 1707

BRITISH BANNER Grafton Street See **Twenty Fives.**

BRITISH BANNER 15 Market Square.

This must have been quite a famous pub in its time. It stood at the east end, on the south corner of Osborn's Jitty, just on the Market Square. In medieval times this jitty was known as Fleshmonger Lane, leading to where the meat was sold.

The earliest record I have is 1858 when a William Warren was the proprietor. The next is in 1864 when a Mark Warner had it. Mark

Warner is recorded as having the General Tom Thumb in 1858 and it is sometime between then and 1864 when he moved to the British Banner and founded a dynasty. A Warner held this pub thereon until the end when the licence was refused in February 1911. First Mark, then an A. M. Warner who seems to have been called by his middle name, Mark; and finally a Louis Warner, brother of A. M. Warner. I believe A. M. and Louis were Mark One's sons.

According to an article in the *Northampton Independent*, March 19th 1910 Mr. A. M. Warner was fond of collecting and displaying, curiosities. *It is not generally known, writes an 'Independent' representative, that there is in the bar of 'The British Banner' one of the most bizarre and gruesome collections of curiosities possessed by any publican.* The article goes on to list many of these including wooden legs, a giant clay pipe, relics of the Boer War such as cartridge belts and shells, horse pistols and rusty revolvers. A human skull, handcuffs and daggers were included, but one of the most interesting were a number of small black bread loaves hung on strings from the ceiling. These, it appears, were given to prisoners on their release from Northampton Gaol to sustain them in their new life, whereupon they would retire to the British Banner and Mr. A. M. Warner would exchange them for beer – which I am sure they felt a greater need for. Various artefacts were displayed on strings from the ceiling or on shelves behind the bar which included jars of freaks such as a pig with two bodies and a giant newt, on a high shelf were a number of, *waxen effigies with criminal countenances and distorted visages.*

An obituary of Mr. A. M. Warner is in the same edition of the *Independent* and says that the present licensee was Louis. The last directories to have entries for this pub are *Bennett* and *Kelly* both 1910.

BROADMEAD 61 Broadmead Avenue.
This pub, which closed in March 2016, no doubt got its name from the avenue. It was built in the late 1920s – although the earliest entry I have found for it is 1936. It is a purpose-built estate pub.

BROAD STREET TAVERN 49 & 51 Broad Street.
There are only two records of this pub, 1936 and 1940 and in both cases Henry Bonham is quoted as the proprietor. It was about halfway up Broad Street on the west side.

BRUNSWICK ARMS 75 Market Street, 2 Brunswick Street.
In the past the use of the name Brunswick has indicated allegiance to the Crown rather than to the Jacobites and many pubs in the country have carried it. The Methodists were suspected of having Jacobite sympathies and often titled themselves "Brunswick Methodists" so that there could be no misunderstanding. Another, more probable, possibility is the Duke of Brunswick who entered British Service and fought in the Peninsular War (1808) and was killed at Waterloo in 1815. The latter idea is nearer to the time of the pubs opening. Although *Law's* map of 1847 shows Market Street it does not show Brunswick Street, this appears on *Birdsall's* map of 1878, complete with shaded areas where the pub stood (NW corner). The earliest entry seems to be 1858 so the pub is probably contemporaneous, with the construction of Brunswick Street.

BUILDERS ARMS Kerr Street see **Bricklayers Arms**

BULL
This sign is not as straightforward as it would at first seem. All the signboards I have seen, including the one on Regents Square, have shown a bull, the beast. However, the sign is very ancient and of religious origin. One possible religious meaning could be that it is the emblem of St. Luke, but there is a far more interesting one. The Latin

Seal of St Andrew's Priory

for seal is *bulla* often shortened to *bull* as in *Papal Bull*. When the Monasteries began to set up their 'hospitals', they like everyone else put up a sign and this was often the seal of their Order – hence Bull.
A pilgrim in medieval times visiting Northampton could have been directed by a local to, "The sign of the Bull". If any of these seal/bulls still were up at the time of the Reformation I'm sure they were quickly converted into the beast.

A rhyme from an inn at Buckland, Kent: -
The Bull is tame so fear him not,
All the while you pay your shot,
When money's gone, and credit's bad,
It's that which (makes) the Bull run mad.

BULL George Row.

The Bull, George Row is listed in the *Assembly Order* of 1585 as one of the Ancient Inns. It stood next door but one to the famous George and must have been a precursor of the Coach & Horses, but whether these two were continuous I do not know. It seems that some sort of religious assemblies called *classis* were held by the Puritans in the 16th century and one of these was held at the Bull according to a document of July 1590. They were a board of Puritan clergy that sought to usurp the authority of the bishops. They were stamped out by the Queen and Archbishop in 1590, but revived for a while during the Commonwealth. The Bull crops up again in the *Great Court Book* in 1676, so I assume it was re-built after the Great Fire.

BULL Regent Square.

This Bull stood on the east side of the site of the North Gate of the Medieval Town. Most of it is under the road now, but part of the site is occupied by a Health Centre. Campbell Street used to be called Bull Lane, a clue to how long this establishment had been there. The inn could have been early medieval and perhaps the oldest **sign** in town. The building I recall was certainly not the original, but the site and sign could have been. The reasoning behind this is that directly opposite the inn, between Grafton and St. George's Streets lay, in days gone by, St. Andrew's Priory – one of the largest in the land. It is reasonable to suppose that they would not pass up such an opportunity, and would build a hostelry beside the town gate and adjacent to their Priory. So this pub could have been a good example of a medieval 'hospital' and the sign a *'bulla'* (see above).

BULLE (LE) Swinwel-Strete (Derngate).
A rental of 1504 mentions many properties around the town including some land near a postern (small gate) called Derngate one of these is called "le Bulle".

BULL & BUTCHER 94 Bridge Street also **Sun & Raven, Sun,** and **King's Arms.**
There was a Sun in Bridge Street as early as 1720 and the Sun & Raven could be an amalgamation of two adjacent inns. According to *The Local* Feb. 1982 it was called the Sun in 1730 and by 1780 it was the King's Arms, changing to the Bull & Butcher in 1830. The earliest directory that refers to it is *Pigot's* 1824 and that already calls it the Bull & Butcher. One story I was told for the origin of its name was the Cattle Market nearby with its attendant slaughterhouse. This can't be right as the Cattle Market didn't appear until 1873, so the reason given in the *Real Ale Guide* published by Northampton branch of CAMRA in 1983 is probably right: - *King's Arms before taking its present name from a butchers shop which used to stand next door.*

This would have been one of the prime sites for an inn in the past, being just inside the South Gate and on the main road. There are deeds for this property going back as far as 1720 and advertisements in the *Northampton Mercury* from 1731. The whole establishment was re-built and extended in 1912. It later bore the name O'Dwyers for no apparent reason.

BULL & BUTCHER 56 Horsemarket.
Taylor's directory 1864 has under the sign Bull & Butcher the name, Thomas Clayson and *Kelly's* of the same year lists *Thomas Clayson, Horsemarket* as a beer-retailer, this is all I can discover about this pub. *Roberts* of 1884 street list gives *56 H. Law, Mkt. Gdnr.*

BULL & GOAT Gold Street.
A reference I have to this establishment is from *NN&Q* Vol. III 1889 where the author refers to an advertisement dated 1725: - *William Atley, who kept the Tap at the Peacock Inn upon Market-hill in Northampton, now keeps The Bull and Goat in Gold street.*

This pub is probably the Goat, listed in the **Universal British Directory** of 1791 and is shown on **Law's Map** of 1847 and this is further indicated by an advertisement in the **Mercury** in 1739: -

To Be LETT

And Enter'd upon at Midsummer next. THE BULL and GOAT INN, a very good and accustom'd House at the Upper End of Gold-street near the Market-place in Northampton: with, Stalls & Stabling convient. Enquire of Mr. John Shortgrove, Ironmonger, In Northampton: or of Mr. John Griffin, Silk-weaver, in Coventry.

It is quite usual for people to shorten the name of a pub, although the Goat is referred to in the **RBN 1898** as a 16-17th. Century inn a *gift of Richard Massingberd 1680*.

BULL'S HEAD 33 Sheep Street.

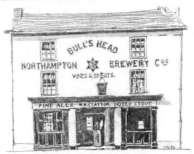

Although we have had several pubs with "Bull" in their name, this is one of only two, and they are connected, as it seems an early landlord took the sign with him to St. James' End. The name is supposed to date from the time of King Henry VIII (1509 – 1547), the bull's head being a badge of the monarch. There are indications that our Bull's Head is of some considerable antiquity. There was until the development of the nearby shopping centre a Bull Head Lane running close to the site of the pub and in well established parts of towns this usually means that the pub gave its name to the thoroughfare.

The **Northampton Mercury** carried three advertisements in the 18th Century for this inn that I have seen. The first in 1736 announcing the move of one, Matthew Morris (see below), the second in May 1754, a notice of the carrier service from the Bull's Head; and in November 1755, announcing the sale of an ass. In both the last cases the landlord is given as William Dodd.

Although the drawing doesn't show it, this inn must have been quite large internally and the **Northampton Directory** of 1878-9 carried an advertisement for the Bull's Head announcing, *Wines,*

Spirits, Ales & Stouts of the finest quality along with, Coale's & Allen's Sparkling Ales and, A large Concert Hall open to the Public Free. **Wright** of 1884 gives two landlords' names, one of them is in the Appendix, so there probably a change of ownership at this time, and both have the appellation "v" indicating, victualler. The pub was closed and compensated for in 1917.

BULL'S HEAD St. James' End.

There is an advertisement from the **Mercury** that is self-explanatory: -

MATTHEW MORRIS

Who lately kept the Bull's Head in Sheep-street, Northampton, Now keeps the Bull's Head in St. James' End near that Town: where all Gentlemen, Travellers &c., may meet with good Entertainment and civil Usage, and Grass for all sorts of Cattle in several Pasture Grounds. From their Humble Servant, Matthew Morris.

Northampton Mercury *19th June 1736.*

BUNCH OF GRAPES 6 Crispin Street.

Crispin Street is shown mostly demolished on *O/S* 1938 with only four or five houses left; it is, however, shown complete on the *O/S* 1901.

There are only two entries under the sign of the Bunch of Grapes, both in **Taylor's** directories of 1858 (James Allard) and 1864 (John Curl). It seems fish and fruit also figured in these two gentlemen's' lives. It is possible that the pub received its name from the fruit business that was at one time also carried out at number 6. In 1858 J. Allard appears under the pubs name so we have no indication of any other trades he may have also carried on, on the premises. The next appearance of number 6 I have found is 1861, *Curl, John & Co., beer-retailer, fishcurers, & fruitmerchants* – so he could have continued the original business. This type of entry continues until 1867. There is also one entry for 1864 from **Kelly's** of J. Curl in Compton Street. This could be explained by the next entry for this name in 1878 at 31 Horsemarket as a beer-retailer, but this is "jnr." and in 1896 there are two entries for J. Curl in Horsemarket, junior at 31 beer-retailing and senior at 33 as a fishmonger.

The pub probably ceased trading between 1867 and 1884 for the next reference to number 6 is ***Robert's*** 1884 street list, *6, James Allard, fishmonger*. By 1890 the premises were occupied by a W. J. Blandwell, horseslaughterer and fishmonger.

BURGHLEY ARMS see Bearward Arms

BUTT (The).
Error for the Bull, Regent St. (***Northampton Directory*** 1936).

CAMBRIDGE ARMS Barrack Road see Duke of Cambridge.

CARPENTERS ARMS 25 Adelaide Street.
The name is a good example of a 'tradesman's arms'. Although this pub has records up the 1963 there is little information on it. All that is now left of Adelaide Street now is the Duke of Edinburgh pub which in days gone by was on the corner and ten doors away from the Carpenters Arms.

The earliest record of it is ***Wright*** 1884 who records it as a "bhs"- a beer-shop as also does he for the Duke of Edinburgh.

CARPENTERS ARMS 'North-End'.
Bear Inn, NORTHAMPTON.
WILSON WILLIAM MOORES.
RETURNS his sincere Thanks to his Friends, and the Public in general, for Favours conferred on him at the above Inn; and begs leave to inform them, that he intends to quit the same Midsummer-Day next; at which time he proposes OPENING ANOTHER HOUSE, in NORTH-END,
(The CARPENTERS-ARMS;)
Where he hopes for a Continuance of the Favours of his Friends and the Public, which will be in his constant Study to deserve.
Mercury June 13th 1795

In times past 'North-End' referred to the northern part of Sheep Street so this Carpenters Arms could be the one above.

CASE IS ALTERED 25 Chapel Place.

The earliest record of this pub is from the *Northampton Directory* 1878-9 where a William Bannister is given as a beer-retailer. *Wright's* directory of 1884 gives. *J.H.Gibbs bhs.* – so it was, and probably remained, a simple beer-shop throughout its existence. There are only two other entries in directories, and that seems to bear out the idea, they are; 1907, J. H. Gibbs and 1929, Mrs. Ada Gibbs, probably J. H. Gibbs' widow.

This sign has probably generated more explanations of its meaning than any other sign in England. They range from banal to the ingenious and I believe that I have, after many years of collecting such material, finally found the original source of the name. I emphasise the word original because I believe that many landlords call their pubs with names they, or their wives, liked. Perhaps they had seen the name elsewhere and just liked it, or maybe it was the name of some famous or fashionable establishment that they wished to be identified with. I think they often had no idea of the original meaning of the sign, nor did the proprietor of the one they were copying!

These are a few of the theories I have come across.

The name is a corruption or "Casey's Altar". It seems that a Catholic priest during the Reformation had a secret altar and said Mass in the back room of a pub.

There are several that work on the idea of soldiers or navvies decamping leaving huge bar bills, causing a drastic alteration in the landlord's fortunes, so he alters his sign.

Probably the most complicated and convoluted ones are the ones dealing with the law. It seems one sign of the 19th century showed a lawyer sitting at a desk, in front of him was a farmer and through a window could be seen a bull in a field. The tale goes thus; a farmer visits the lawyer and informs him that the farmer's bull has fatally gored one of the lawyer's cows. "Then you must pay me the value of the cow." declares the lawyer. "Hah! No, I made a mistake," replies the farmer, "I got it the wrong way round – it was *your* bull that killed my cow – you must pay *me*!" To which the lawyer replied, "The case is altered." An interesting comment on the general idea of the honesty and fairness of lawyers, but proved to be closer to the truth than it at first seems.

For a long time I believed the one that was probably correct is the one that is based on the corruption of foreign words and phrases. One that is much quoted is the example of the "Infanta of Castille" becoming the "Elephant and Castle" – I now know this to be wrong, just a clever invention (see Elephant and Castle pub). The favoured ones in this case are also Spanish in 'origin' and are supposed to have come from soldiers returning from the Peninsular War (1808-14). The idea being that old soldiers who became publicans would put up such a sign, probably to attract other old soldiers to their pub. They are, Casa de Saltar → "Dancing House" and La Casa Alta →"House on the Hill" or "The High House".

This, to me, seemed a reasonable explanation at the time, but then I discovered examples of this sign dating from *before* the Peninsular War. The final straw came when I found out that Ben Johnson (1573?-1637) had written a play with this title. Research revealed that it was an extinct proverb or saying linked to a 16th century lawyer, Edmund Plowden.

Plowden was defending a man charged with hearing Mass. During the hearing Plowden discovered that the service had been performed by a layman, pretending to be a priest, who intended to inform on those attending. The astute Plowden is credited with stating, "The case is altered – no priest, no Mass." and thereby succeeded in getting an acquittal for his client.

So it seems, this is a pub name based on a proverb or popular saying. It is interesting that tenuous links exist between the Catholic "Casey's Altar" and the trial of an illegal Mass; the lawyer, farmer and the bull and the astute Plowden.

CASTLE
We have had two of these and they both referred to Northampton Castle.

CASTLE (OLD) 5 Phoenix Street also **Northampton Castle.**
It no doubt acquired the 'Old' appellation to distinguish it from the 'new' one just over the river. This pub stood on Castle Hill, sharing

it, along other buildings, with the Golden Lion, which is still with us. It probably stood where the yard of the Golden Lion is now. The Golden Lion is now gone and the site occupied by flats (2017).

CASTLE 1 St. James' Park Road.

This pub is a typical street corner Victorian pub, still sitting close to the river, just across from where the actual castle stood. Because of its proximity to the river it has been flooded out on several occasions. An early photograph shows a boat crossing the flooded Foot Meadow to the pub – they were keen on their drink in those days! Another pub gone! (2017).

CAT (LE CATTE) Malt Row (east side of the Market Square).

There is only one reference to this inn and that is from a sale document of the eighth of February 1456. It concerns the sale of the *Pecok* (Peacock) and says that the property is to the north of *Le Pecok* belonged to St. John's Hospital and was once called *Le Catte*. As this was once an inn before 1456 I think this must be the oldest record I have found of any pubs in the town.

CATHERINE WHEEL.

I've found two Catherine (or Katherine) Wheels in Northampton, one in Abington Street and the other in Gold Street. The device is the badge of the Worshipful Company of Turners, but it is also the badge of the Order of the Knights of St. Catherine of Mount Sinai. In medieval times the Abington Street site was part of the Greyfriars land and I wonder if there is any connection between them and this Order?

CATHERINE WHEEL Abington Street.

This seems to have been a well-established inn. The earliest reference I have to it is from the ***Northampton Mercury***, August 1753: - *A Very Good New-Milched Ass, and a Foal just five weeks old. Enquire at*

Mr. Whitticar's, at the Katherine-Wheel in Abington-Street, Northampton.

An announcement, also in the **Mercury** of June 1766 has: - *On Thursday Morning last the Wife of Mr. Collins, at the Catherine-Wheel in Abington-Street in this Town, died suddenly as she sat in a Chair in the Kitchen.* Another advertisement of 1757 also mentions Mr. Whitticar.

The inn stood on the north side of Abington Street almost opposite the end of Fish Street. It is shown on **Law's** map of 1847 and I calculate that if was still there it would be next door to Marks & Spencer.

St. Giles' Churchwardens' accounts of 1810 refer to the Catherine Wheel and a Briggs the Fiddler was paid 1/- (5p), it appears churchwardens had a pretty good time of it. In 1841 the license was transferred to the Little Bell in Augustine Street, however, I have found three references in directories after this date. **Burgess** 1845 has, unoccupied – which tallies, but both **Kelly** and **Hickman** 1847 give Richard Branston. Whatever the truth, part of it was pulled down in 1878.

CATHERINE WHEEL Gold Street.

The *Katherene Wheele* is one of the *Auncient Innes* listed in the **Assembly Order** of 1585 so it was of a good age and to have been included in the **Order** it must have been a well-established and substantial enterprise. The only other reference I have is from the **Northampton Mercury**, an advertisement of December 1773 has: - *All Parcels going to or coming from London, are to be left at the Catherine-Wheel in Gold-Street, Northampton.* I have no date for when it ceased to exist.

CATTLE MARKET RESTAURANT Cattle Market, Victoria Promenade.

The new Cattle Market opened on the 17th of July 1873 and the earliest mention we have of the establishment is 1878 in the **Northampton Directory**, under *Hotels, Inns and Taverns*: - *"Fleece", Bridge st., C. Konow; also refreshment rooms in Cattle Market.*

There is also a full-page advertisement for the Fleece with a footnote; *C. Konow is also the Proprietor of the Refreshment Saloons, Cattle Market*. According to the directories available Charles Konow was the proprietor of the Cross Keys from at least 1870 to 1876 so he moved to the Fleece in that year as he is shown as there in the 1876 directory. Within two years of arrival at the Fleece and five years after the Cattle Market opening Charles was running a refreshment saloon in the Market, presumably from his pub, which was nearby. It was probably quite easy to do this as I assume the saloon would only have been open on market days. A link between the Restaurant and the Fleece continued as Walter Francis East is shown as the proprietor of the Fleece in 1906 and 1910. There are no modern entries of this pub.

I cannot be sure that the establishment above was the same one as I used to visit in my youth. The one we used was on the western side of the market, near the auction shed. In the days of draconian drinking hours the pubs shut on Saturdays at two o'clock, but not on the Market. If you wished to continue drinking this was the place to go. One novelty, which is now no longer a novelty was the serving of 'proper' food, i.e. cooked. There was a kitchen at the back of the bar and every so often names would be called and plates of steaming food would be passed over to be eaten on the tables amongst the ashtrays and beer-glasses. More than once I availed myself of this, then, strange facility – the food was always good, plain fare and plenty of it – the sort farmers would appreciate. I suppose I was witnessing the last vestiges of the Market-Day Ordinaries of yesteryear.

CATTLE MARKET TAVERN 149 or 153 Bridge Street also 46 Cattle Market Road (after 1912).
George Ambridge was a beer-retailer at 153 Bridge Street in 1877. There are various similar entries for this man up to 1903 when he is described as a butcher and beer-retailer at 151 and 153. However, in 1884 he appears under the pub's name, this is eleven years after the Cattle Market opened.

The pub was at the north corner of the junction of Bridge Street and Navigation Row and Navigation Row led straight into the west entrance of the Market. I imagine that George, sometime between the opening of the Market in 1873 and 1884 seized the opportunity of attracting the market crowds by giving the beer-retailing side of his business a suitable name.

There are no entries between 1910 and 1928 and in 1928 the address had changed from Bridge Street to Cattle Market Road. In 1912 the license was shifted from number 153, *to a House and Premises to be erected and built on a Site adjoining the said Licensed Premises and being at the North-East corner of Navigation Row and Cattle Market Road.*

A precursor of this beer-house could have been the Horse & Jockey, which only appears twice, in 1858 and 1864 at numbers 153 and 155 respectively; there is no evidence of continuous occupation. The Cattle Market Tavern closed on March 17th 1959. The building opened as a restaurant called "Turrets" and this was succeeded by the "Stars & Stripes" – which itself became the Pelican Cove Rock Café in March 1994.

CENTRAL TAVERN 16 Newland.

This was a small beer-shop one door up from the corner of Princess Street; it also seems to have had a back entrance through a jitty that ran off Princess Street. It was one of those small retail outlets that were flattened by the Grosvenor Centre development. I can remember the place, just. I understand that at one time it was used as the headquarters of the Plumbing and Heating Trade Union.

CHEQUERS.

There is more than one explanation for this name. In the past the Great Earl Warenne was given the power to grant licenses and his Arms were: Checky, Or and Azure (chequered pattern of alternate gold, or yellow, and blue squares), his arms becoming the sign. Another is that the sign indicated that draughts or chess were played on the premises – it appears that this is the commonest sign to be found in the ruins of Herculaneum where it is believed to indicate just this. In medieval times it was the sign of a moneychanger – common in

seaports. We are far from the sea, but Northampton has been an important market town for most of its past, so money-changers or moneyiers would have been in evidence, especially near the Market Square. *Speed's Map* of 1610 calls the Market the "Checker".

The original Greek or Roman Abacus wasn't the bead-frame we think of, but a flat table marked out with lines on which small counters could be moved to make calculations. The Romans used little chalk hemispheres; the Latin for chalk is *chalx* from which we get such words as calculate and calculus. In medieval times the kingdom's finances were kept track of on a huge abacus in the Tower of London. The table had lines running both ways showing different aspects of the finances and resembled the board used for the game of chequers, so this department of government became called the Exchequer.

One of the four Chequers I have unearthed, the oldest, was on the Market Square. Was the pub named for its location, or the other way about? There is a possible connection with the Market being called the Chequer with the idea that the Mint was sited nearby, but I would have thought the King would have put such an important facility in the Castle. An idea that I have heard is that the Market was at one time paved with square stone slabs and resembled a chequer-board.

CHEQUERS (OLD) 54 Bath Street.
This is a good example of the old not being the oldest. The pub stood on the opposite corner of Lower Cross Street and Bath Street from the Sportsman's Arms. Although it was a beer-shop (1884 "bhs") it boasted a Quoits Ground and in an old photograph I have had sight of on the side wall can be seen "Founded...." In very faded paintwork, I think I can make out "184*" and this could be right. I can trace the address as a beer-retailer back to 1845 and the name first appears in 1864.

CHEQUERS 33 Upper Priory Street.
This pub was located on the northwest corner of Upper Priory Street and St. Patrick Street. A small beer-shop, the earliest I have for it is 1864.

CHEQUERS 56 Wellington Street.
This one, like the two previous ones, was a beer-shop built to serve the new factory workers in the 19th century. The earliest date I have is 1884 and the last 1910.

CHEQUER(S) Market Square.
I feel that this inn must have either been named because its location, or because it was used as a 'bank' for the Market in past times. It is definitely old and there are records going back at least as far as 1680. In the past inns were essential to a market town, not only for overnight accommodation, but to conduct business in and display and sell goods. Once agricultural seed was traded on the Market Square, at the Hind, turnip seed and at the Chequers, grass. The Chequers had 'corn chambers'; these were for farmers to sell their corn. I have an undated reference from a second party, which must have come from an advertisement, probably the Northampton Mercury, *Camels and Dromeday, which had much attention from the nobility.* In the spring and summer exhibitions were held at this inn, no doubt in the yard and perhaps in the corn chambers. From evidence from people wishing to register for the Great Election of 1768 we have: - *Said Voter lived in only one Room belonging to the Chequer Inn...That it was a place where they used to shew wild Beasts.*

It seems that the Three Tuns pub was originally part of this inn, confirming its size, however, the compilers of the ***RBN 1898*** claim to have seen "16-17th century" leases for both the Chequer and the Three Tuns. I have been unable to find anything for the Three Tuns of this date, but there was a Three Tuns in the Drapery up to 1750 according to ***NN&Q*** 1889. The author here also claims the Three Tuns, Market Square to be a portion of the Chequers. Possibly the Three Tuns, Drapery moved to the Market Square at some time. I have no end-date for the Chequer, but the earliest I have for the Three Tuns is 1824. We do however have an announcement from the ***Mercury*** 1731: - *The Late Widow HOLLOWAY (now SMITH) who kept the Chequer Inn on the Market-Hill in Northampton, is removed to the Black Boy Inn on the Wood-Hill in the said Town: where all Gentlemen, &c. will meet with good Entertainment.*

CHERRY TREE.

We have two pubs with this charming name, but I have no idea as to its meaning. I do remember as a child seeing the Cherry Tree sign on the Wellingborough Road which I think was etched on the glass in the door and wondering what it meant. The only theory I can come up with is that it comes from the same context as 'cherry picking' – taking the very best – the sign suggesting that the establishment that bore it was the very best.

CHERRY TREE 39 Bouverie Street.

There is one reference to a Cherry Tree at 39 Bearward Street (*Mark's* 1928) – this is almost certainly an error. The earliest I have for this one is 1858 and the latest 1929.

CHERRY TREE 89 Wellingborough Road.

This establishment was on the southwest corner of the Exeter and Wellingborough Roads. The earliest date I have is 1884 ("bhs") and it was lost during the widening of the Wellingborough Road in the 1960s.

CHINESE TAVERN 2 Green Street.

This pub was situated on the corner of Green Street and Narrow Toe Lane. The meaning of the name is a mystery to me, but the name could have come from the sign. There is, or was, a pub in Yeovil called the Goose which had a sign of a Chinese or Swan goose and the "Goose" became the "Chinese Goose" and later just the "Chinese" – finally developing into the Chinese Tavern. It's an idea, but I don't think I believe it! There are directory entries for this pub from 1858 to 1929, but the *Magistrates' Records* show that it was Compensated for in 1927.

CITY TAVERN 15 The Riding.

I thought I had solved the mystery of this pub name as the large office block on the corner with Fish Street is called City Buildings. However, City Buildings was built sometime around the turn of the 19th century and I have references to the City Tavern back as far as 1862. So, was the offices named after the pub? I think not as the pub, which survived to at least 1918, was halfway up the Riding on the north side and would be under the west corner of the Co-Op Arcade. It was very small and first appears in *Slater's* directory of 1862 under Retailers of Beer – *Hasler, John, Riding. Wright* 1884 has "bhs" i.e. 'beerhousekeeper'.

CLARENDON see **Two Brewers.**

CLEVELAND ARMS 78 Kettering Road.

This pub stood on the north-west corner of Cleveland Road. This whole area was cleared in the 1970s and redeveloped. The earliest reference for this address that I can trace is from the *Northampton Directory* of 1878-9, which has under Beer-Retailers, *Corby, Thos.* Thomas seems to have had a beershop in Brier Lane – the first part of the Wellingborough Road from just past the Volunteer pub to near Wilberforce Street. This beer shop is listed in 1845, 1847 & 1852. Thomas then seems to have moved to the Kettering Road and occupied the (new?) Cleveland Arms, although he doesn't seem to have named it such. The first entry under the name is in *Wright* 1884 - *Mrs. A. V. Corby* presumably, his widow.

CLICKER INN Silverdale Road, Weston Favell.

This pub opened on April 7th 1955 as a purpose-built estate pub. Described in the *Northampton Independent* of that date as, a new model inn for Weston Favell. It was built too late to have any of its proprietors listed in the directories. A visit in September 1999 showed that there had been much internal alteration and an extension, which includes an area for pool tables. After a period of closure planning permission was given in March 2011 for it to become a Muslim community centre.

CLICKERS ARMS 29 Upper Mounts also **Globe.**

There is no problem with the meaning of this name in a boot and shoe town like Northampton. The Clicker was the elite of the boot and shoe factory workers. Their job was to cut out the pieces of leather for the upper parts of the shoe. This leather was expensive and considerable skill was needed to get the maximum number of pieces from one skin or hide. Their name comes from the clicking sound their knives made as they cut out the pieces.

Using the *O/S* 1964 2500 Plan this pub must have been between the end of Earl Street and the property line of the Mounts Baths.

Therefore the Globe and later the Clicker were on the site presently occupied by the Charles Bradlaugh, probably where the garden is now. The dates for the two names are; Globe, 1845-1864 and the Clicker, 1884-1910.

CLINTON ARMS 1 Clinton Road, Far Cotton.

The *Northampton Daily Record* of Thursday 7th October 1897 carried the following advertisement: - *A Meeting will be held at the White House, Clinton Road. Towcester Road, Far Cotton, for the Formation of a Working Mens' Club On Monday, October 11th 1897 at 8.0, where Rules & Regulations for same will be made. All persons desiring to become members are invited to attend.*

The White House later became the Clinton Arms and the result of this meeting was the formation of Far Cotton W.M.C. It seems that the Clinton Arms, when first built was, for a time, used by the Club. A photograph shows a temporary sign over the door with the words "New Clinton Arms" obscuring the central part of another sign beneath. The words "Fa.." and "Club" can be seen.

An article about the Boot, College Street in the *C&E,* May 26th 1952: - *Mr. Pryor took over the tenancy of the Boot in 1905 from a Mr. Farey who emigrated to Canada. The Boot closed on April 11th 1907, its licence and three others were surrendered to obtain a licence for the Clinton Arms, Far Cotton. And Mr. Pryor opened the Clinton Arms on April 18th 1907.*

I visited this pub for the last drink on the night of its closing in January 1985. It was yet another victim of the Great God Car. The pub, Alton Street Garage and twenty-five other properties, all of which I believe were homes, were flattened to construct the Southern Approach Road. I use the word 'homes' advisedly, not 'houses'.

COACH & HORSES 3 George Row.

It is usually said that an inn of this name was a coaching inn, but this one could have derived its name from the substantial coaching inn one door away – the George.

It is interesting to note that *Kelly* 1847 lists Daniel Sellars jnr. as proprietor of the Coach & Horses and a Daniel Sellers for the White Hart (Shipman's) Drum Lane. They could have been father and son.

This inn stood about the same site as one of the Ancient Inns (1585) known as the Bull, next door but one to the famous George

Hotel. This may be why there is so little information about the pub – overshadowed by its neighbour. I have listed the Bull and the Coach and Horses separately as they don't occupy exactly the same site and I have no evidence that there was continuous occupation of the site as a pub. There is an advertisement in the **Mercury** Dec. 13th 1766 to an exhibition of needlework at this pub. The earliest date from the directories is 1824 and the last 1924. Hudson Bros. a polterer and butcher built a shop here during the General Strike of 1926 and opened it two years later. The **Mercury** 1766-7 has a mention of this pub (2017).

COBBLERS see **Lamb & Flag.**

COCK.

Northampton has had two Cocks in the past, one, in Kingsthorpe, is still with us. We also have had a Bantam Cock and a Cock Ale Inn.

There are several reasons why a pub should be thus named. Heraldic (the Bantam Cock is probably one) a pun on a name, or because of image a cock gives. It is colourful, loud and proud, 'cock-a-hoop' and 'cock of the walk' spring to mind – as well as its obvious masculine implications! It can stand for France (not likely, I feel), as a symbol for St. Peter, or most likely, that Cock-Fighting took place on the premises.

COCK Abington Street.

This inn stood on the east corner of Wood Street and Abington Street, where the Abington Street entrance to the Grosvenor Centre is. It seems to have ceased as an inn when the premises became Dryden's Freeschool, better known as the Orange Coat School, founded in 1707. In 1854 this school amalgamated with the Blue Coat School in Bridge Street. This school, the Corporation Charity Schools building, still stands at the bottom of Bridge Street and has, on the first floor two effigies of pupils in niches, one dressed in orange and the other blue.

The assessment records of St. Giles' Parish mention the Cock in 1658, 1688 and 1706 and Cock Lane is mentioned in the records of the Commissioners for the rebuilding of Northampton after the Great Fire.

Wood Street has been called at times both St. Michael's Lane and Cock Lane – presumably after a church and the inn respectively. None of the early maps of the town show it as St. Michael's Lane as this name died out with the Great Fire. *Nobel & Butlin* 1747 and *Roper & Cole* 1807 both show it as Cock Lane, but *Law* 1847 has Wood Street. This name change is thought by some to be because of the notoriety gained through the "Cock Lane Ghost" – but it could be for the same reason of 'propriety' that resulted in "Ditchers lane" becoming "Dychurch lane" and "Pissford" to change to "Pitsford". A deed of January 13th 1826 describes tenements as, *situate in White Friars lane, alias St. Michael's lane, alias Cock lane.*

There is an account of the Cock Lane Ghost in *NN&Q* 1891. The story runs thus; - *A saddler's apprentice was starved and ill-treated, as apprentices frequently were in those days. In this case the ill-treatment was more wanton and cruel than usual; and in the end the poor lad succumbed to his master's tyranny. The master got rid of the body, but the ghost remained to tell the tale. The ghost became known far and wide. At this time there were many sawpits in the vicinity of the lane. The land adjoining it was used for the deposit and sale of timber, and there, too, it was seen. The ghost story made it desirable to alter the name of the thoroughfare, and as the lane blossomed into a street, no one objected to Wood Street. Notwithstanding, the evil reputation long remained, and in the memory of persons still living he would have been a very courageous lad indeed who at night dared to go by the old houses opposite the present Princes' street.*

One version of this story has it that the victim was a tap-boy who haunted the cellars of the Cock itself. As a young man I was told of a ghost in Cleavers shop, which at the time occupied the site of the inn. It seems the story and the ghost lives on.

COCK Harborough Road, Kingsthorpe also **Hop House (Brewery).** Except for a short while (1995-96) this establishment has always been called the Cock. I understand this inn dates from 1622 when it was built as a coaching inn. It was a good site for this kind of establishment being on the junction of several roads, facing the Green and close to a tollgate.

The present building was erected in 1894. Built of Northampton Sandstone, it was designed by the architect George Stevenson of Duston. It is a Grade II listed building.

The Cock Hotel, Kingsthorpe.

The **Cock Hotel**

Kingsthorpe, :: ::
NORTHAMPTON.

Commercial & Family Hotel.

Proprietor - - HERBERT M. NIND.

GARAGE.
Good Accommodation for Motorists and Cyclists.
Trams pass the door.

This inn can claim the dubious distinction of being the first 'theme pub' in Northampton, being converted in 1970 to a "Schooner Inn" by Watneys. Later Berni Inns acquired it and it was reopened in June 1986. In late 1995 John Labutt Retail, a Canadian company bought it and spent half-a-million pounds on a 'face-lift' – installing a micro-brewery and a no smoking area (this, alas, was the eating area, not the bar). They also proposed a change of name to the "Hop House Brewery". By November a campaign had been launched and 300 people signed a petition to retain the old name, but to no avail as on the 4th of December the opening and renaming had been announced for the 12th. On the 8th the Council moved to rename the road junction outside the pub the "Cock Hotel Junction". The pub renaming took place as scheduled – and so did the junction, new road signs were erected outside the pub on the 12th January 1996.

By May the pub had been sold to Enterprise Inns who, although they were pleaded with, kept the unpopular name and by November it was once more on the market. McManus Taverns bought it and through the *C&E* invited opinions on the name. The response was overwhelmingly in favour of returning to the original name. McManus Taverns decided to call it the "Cock" rather than the old (but not so old) name "Cock Hotel". As Gary McManus explained, "We don't want punters from out of town calling and finding there are no rooms available." The renaming party took place on the 27th of April 1997.

COCK ALE HOUSE Location unknown.

I'm not too sure if this was the Cock – Alehouse, or the Cock ale - House. The reference is from a document dated 1780 and could refer to one of the Cocks already written about, probably the one in Abington Street. However, there was, or is a "cock ale". In Elizabethan times one would take an old rooster (presumably dead) and bash it until every bone in its body was broken. This cock (now definitely dead!) was put into a cloth bag with a quantity of raisins and boiled in ale – hence cock ale. I have drunk Cock Ale, but I was assured that it had been produced at the Cock Hotel microbrewery, Harborough Road, and not to the above recipe!

COCK'S HEAD Cotton End.
Cotton-End Statute.
WILL be held at the COCK'S-HEAD, on Wednesday the 26th of September instant.
⚜ Dinner at One o'Clock.
Mercury September 22nd 1798

A Statute would be held for the hiring of servants and workers, sometimes known as a Hiring Fair.

COMPASS INN Bedford Road. see **Britannia Inn.**

COMPTON ARMS 40 Compton Street.

Named after the street, Compton Street still exists, but it now runs east-west when it used to run north-south. The street is shown on the *O/S* 1901, 1938 and 1964 Plans although on the 1964 Plan the southern half is obliterated by a large building marked "depot" and all the houses have gone. The two earlier Plans show small terraced dwellings throughout its length with some rebuilding to the northern end on the 1938 Plan. Because there are no house plots on the 1964 Plan I have no way of knowing where this pub actually was, or which side of the road it was on. At the southern end there were two pubs, one on each corner, the Prince of Wales and the Boot & Slipper in all entries their addresses are given as in Spring Lane and therefore are of no help. Counting the plots on the 1910 Plan from every corner gives no clues in the form of a building that could be a pub (slightly wider, side entrance &c). All I can say is that in a street of 63 houses it was two-thirds of the way along one side or the other, from one end or the other! *Wright* 1884 (the earliest reference) gives "bhs" so it was, a beer-house. The last entry is 1910.

<u>COOKS ARMS</u> Market Square.

Between Mercers Row and the south side of the Market Square lies a double row of buildings. On the Mercers Row side, mainly shops, on the Market side, mainly estate agents, solicitors and a bank. Running between these two rows is a narrow jitty called "The Gutts". This runs from behind a wooden door next to the Rifle Drum pub through to Conduit Lane at the eastern end. It once carried on right through. This block, east of Conduit lane in 1831 had six properties on it – three of which were pubs! On part of this site stood the 'Conduit' or pump and water tank – so this small area of town was well supplied with drinking facilities. Two of these pubs faced onto Mercers Row, the Ship and the Duke of Clarence, whilst on the east corner of the Market frontage was the Cooks Arms.

THE COOKS ARMS. MARKET HILL.

The illustration clearly shows the name of the proprietor as "Wm. George" and this is the only name I've been able to find. The pub was lost during the erection of Waterloo House in 1833. It appears that the old buildings extended further into the Market Square and were put into line with the rest of the south side of the Square at this time. When Waterloo House was demolished I gained access to the site. It seemed to me at the time that Waterloo House had been built *inside* a larger cellar and to the north I discovered two fine 18th century sandstone, vaulted cellars running side-by-side out north under the Market Square. These were huge and I immediately thought that they would have made a fine jazz club (it *was* the 60s!). It is these sort of vaulted cellars which to the untrained eye look so like sealed up tunnels and give rise to tales of 'Monk's Passages'.

According to the article in *NN&Q: - the old vaulted cellars of the Cooks Arms, which extend some thirty feet under the Market Hill, still remain.* To my knowledge they still do.

Mercury Vol. 116 1836-7 : 'Proposal of Mr. Wright of Market Square to purchase the Cook's Arms and house adjacent for the purpose of pulling down and building at the back of them so as to improve the foot carriageway.' (2017).

COOPERS ARMS 53 Horsemarket.

This pub stood on the north corner of Castle Street and Horsemarket. I have been unable to find much about this establishment even though I have entries from 1845 until 1938 in the directories. I am yet to see a photograph of it. The *O/S* Plans show a property of some size but it still only rated a "bhs" in *Wright* 1884.

COTTAGE TAVERN 171 Bridge Street.

Only one reference from the *Northampton Mercury* May 1877: - *Free Beer-House known as "The Cottage Tavern" to be sold by Auction. Front Bar and Smoke Room, with Plate glass window: Sitting-room, pantry, and wash-house conveniently arranged behind the same: Large drawing-room, and w.c. over, with garden and appertances at the rear.*

Yet another small beer-house, the address doesn't link up with any other pub in this street for which I have a number.

COUNTY HOTEL 222 Abington Avenue.

The County Hotel, now called the Tavern, is owned by the trustees of the Northampton Cricket Club. In its early days it served as the cricket pavilion before the present one was built. The first reference in a directory is 1898 and the last 1970.

CRANE South Bridge.

This is one of the ones the compilers of the *RBN 1898* found in the 16th and 17th century leases and other records of the town. Like several others this is one that has not survived in any archives that I had examined.

CREAM OF THE VALLEY 31 Crispin Street.
This pub was on the west side of Crispin Street about three-quarters of the way up from Scarletwell Street. The name is rather unusual and I can only guess at its meaning. It may be an extinct expression for the very best, but "valley" makes me think of Wales. There is, or was, a pub in Churt in Surrey called the Pride of the Valley, its sign being a portrait of David Lloyd George (1863-1945). It seems he lived his last years at Churt, so it could be another pub honouring his memory – BUT to be so it would have had to named after him when, according to my earliest reference he was only 21! So this one is still a mystery.

CRICKETERS Broad Lane (now Street).
The name, 'Cricketers' is rather bald and suggests a full name something like Cricketers Arms' – or even 'Rest'. One entry, *Burgess'* exhaustive directory of 1845, gives the name Plumb. A Thomas Plumb is in *Kelly* 1847 at the Dun Cow in Bearward Street.

CRICKETERS ARMS 16 Bearward Street.
Again only one entry, *Taylor's* 1864, *Thomas Plumb sen.* so it looks as if there was a move from the above and the "sen." explains why *Melville* 1861 has a Thomas Plumb at the Dun Cow and another one at the Racehorse. There is only one more reference to 16 Bearward Street in *Royal* 1866, *Plumb, T. Bearward street., Beer-retailer.* Sometime after this I assume T. Plumb senior retired, although there is a *T. Plumb vict.* at the Halfway House in 1876 and again at the Bear in 1885 and 1889.

CRICKETERS' ARMS 43-7 Hervey Street.
This is a typical purpose-built Victorian artisans' pub. The earliest reference is *Wright* 1884 who lists the proprietor as "bhs". No doubt its name is a reference to the nearby Racecourse with similar reasons to the Bat & Wickets. In 1986 the pub went through some considerable changes, as well as celebrating the 21st. Year of a highly successful football team (what else would you expect from a pub called the Cricketers' Arms?). The pub's team were one of the founders of the Sunday League. The pub was once again in the news

in 1998 when locals protested at the proposed changes in the gents' toilets. This pub still had the old-fashioned wall and gutter and it was intended to install modern urinals. Public opinion prevailed and the toilets are still with us. This pub has now been converted into accommodation (2017).

CRICKETERS REST 46 Deal Street.
This pub seems to have been on the north corner of the junction between Deal Street and Maple Street. References are 1884 to 1910.

CRISPIN ARMS
There hasn't been a House of Crispin to possess Arms so this in one of those non-armorial signs referring to a trade. The term Crispin is an allusion to Crispinus or St. Crispin, the patron saint of shoemakers. Crispin Arms is another way of saying the Shoemakers Arms.

Considering our connection with the boot and shoe trade it is surprising that we do not seem to ever have had a church dedicated to this saint. However, we have had at least three pubs - two Crispin Arms and a Jolly Crispin as well as a Mental Hospital and we did have a street fair in October.

CRISPIN ARMS Bridge Street.
This establishment is only mentioned twice, **Burgess** 1845 has Baldwin, and **Slater** 1850 John Roddis. **Burgess** was the first compiler to really list all the pubs, beer-shops &c that he could find, so this place could have been about for quite a time before 1845 and just not got mentioned. A George Baldwin held the Magpie in Bridge Street and I have him dated from both sources from 1847 to 1877. A John Roddis was at the Crispin Arms Scarletwell Street in 1830 and seems to have returned there about 1852. There could be more than one as I have no record of him in Scarletwell Street after 1858, but I do have him at the Old Black Lion from 1861 to 1867. In 1876 there was a John Roddis at 10 Derngate as a confectioner and baker, which is his alternative trade given elsewhere. 10 Derngate could have been at the time the number for the Swan.

CRISPIN ARMS 53 Scarletwell Street.

This Crispin Arms seems to be connected with the one in Bridge Street, although John Roddis may have been two different people. *Taylor's* directory of 1864 has two John Roddis, one as the proprietor of the Black Lion, Black Lion Hill and one for the White lion, Kingsthorpe Road. Roddis is the earliest name for a proprietor of the White Lion, so if he opened it did he call it thus as a sort of reflection of his Black Lion – or, was this a relative of the same name?

The Crispin Arms first appears in 1830 with John Roddis as the proprietor, so perhaps he may have originally been a shoemaker. The last entry I have is for 1952 so it must have closed around then.

A unique custom used to be carried out in this pub in the past, the Election of the Mayor of Scarletwell. In medieval times the Town Hall stood at the end of Scarletwell Street on the Mayorhold probably on the site of the Old Jolly Smokers. In about 1300 it moved to the north-east corner of Wood Hill (where Burtons, the tailors recently stood) and remained here, surviving the Great Fire of 1675, until the Victorians built our present one around the corner in St. Giles' Square. In the distant past the Mayorhold area was the 'smart' part of town and one theory as to the origins of the Mayor of Scarletwell is that when the centre of local government moved from what is essentially the ancient Anglo-Danish part of town to the Norman 'New Borough' the locals resented this and just went on electing their own Mayor.

This idea may not be as far-fetched as it first seems. The Mayorhold was at the North *Portgate* of the pre-Norman *burgh* and as well as being a market place could well have been the administrative centre of the earlier town. It seems reasonable to assume that once all the shouting was over the Normans would have let things run very much as they had done before they took over.

The Mayorhold area is still called (at least by my generation!) the 'Boroughs' and has been since time out of mind. There are doubts as to both the origins and correct spellings of both 'Mayorhold' and 'Boroughs'. Is the Mayorhold where Mayors held office – or, where *Mares* were sold at the end of Horsemarket? Does the word Boroughs refer to the Borough, as in Town – or, *Burrows* as in rabbits after the so-called 'tunnels' and cellars (I've been down some) that are reputed to honeycomb this area? We don't know.

We had surviving in this town until quite recently two ancient offices that had long disappeared from almost all other ancient boroughs, to whit: *Thirdboroughs* and *Dozeners*. Thirdborough is a corruption of an Anglo-Saxon official one called a *Frith-Born* or *frank pledge*. He was a sort of headman of a small community bound to see the rest kept the peace – a sort of 'Community Watch'–Man, perhaps? Dozener is likewise a corruption, of *Decimer*. Edward the Confessor (1042-1066) brought out a law based on an enactment of Canute (1016-1035) ordering that households combine into associations of ten. Each of these had a Thirdborough over it and originally over ten of these was a Decinarius or Dozener. In Northampton the Thirdborough was dropped from the Assembly Orders in 1667 and the Dozener finally ceased in 1835.

Northampton, along with a handful of other towns seems to have kept many of its ancient Anglo-Saxon customs and terms well into modern times. True Northamptonians for example know what a *Jitty* is, the word may be Anglo-Norman, but you need a Saxo-Danish earthwork to have one! Why shouldn't the descendants of the Anglo-Saxon town fathers carry on electing their own Mayor? And if it assisted, like the offices of Thirdborough and Dozeners, in the smooth running of the town why shouldn't the Normans allow it? The Mayor of Scarletwell could well have been part of an unbroken line of Anglo-Saxon Mayors going back something like a thousand years!!

Below is a *verbatim* copy of a report from the **Chronicle**, November 14th 1899: -

ELECTION OF THE MAYOR OF SCARLETWELL
The election of the Mayor of Scarletwell took place at the Town Hall, Scarletwell, on Saturday evening, Nov. 11, nearly all the members of the Council being present.- The minutes of the last meeting were read and confirmed.- The Mayor then said that the next business was the election of the Mayor for the ensuing year.- Councillor Williams, on rising, was met with great applause. He said he had a gentleman to propose that had filled the office for 14 years, and he had carried out the duties honestly and faithfully. Although he had heard that there would be some opposition to the present Mayor, he had great

pleasure in proposing Sir Thomas Mawby, Knight of the Bristle, as Mayor for the coming year. (Applause) – Councillor Mallard briefly seconded. – Councillor Tarry said he had another gentleman to propose, and he felt sure that the gentleman would be elected, as he had lived amongst them for many years. He was a through good business man, and would be able to devote his time to the office of Mayor. He had great pleasure in proposing Alderman Blundell. (Applause.) – Councillor Page seconded.- After the voting had taken place, it was found that Sir Thomas Mawby, K.B., had a majority of one over Alderman Blundell,- The Mayor, on rising to reply, was greeted with great cheering. He thanked them very much for the honour they had conferred on him for the fifteenth year in succession. He had been over the course for 14 years, and he hardly expected the young one they brought against him would stay the distance, although he pressed him very close. He had won by a short head. (Applause.)- A smoking concert was held afterwards, when some excellent songs were sung.

The 'Town Hall' referred to is the Crispin Arms. 'Sir', Thomas Mawby, K.B. appears to have been the Mayor of Scarletwell for about 24 years. On April 17th 1909 the *Northampton Independent* carried his Obituary, *Death of the Mayor of Scarletwell*. I believe the Office ceased with his death.

It is interesting to speculate that this mock Mayor, an office I understand that was used to raise money for worthy causes and for the relief of the poverty-stricken inhabitants of the Boroughs may really be ancient – or perhaps it was created only a century or so ago. It is an area I shall continue to research into and any information my readers have would be very welcome. I would like the office to be resurrected, it is part of our local heritage and, sadly there still is a need to raise money for worthy causes.

CRITERION Bradshaw Street/Silver Street (pre 1938). College Street/King Street (post 1938).
Also: **Brigg's Punch-House** (1783 - c1805) **Fountain** (1824 - c1870). **Sultan** (c1874 - 1876) **Newt & Cucumber** (1992 - ?).

In my younger days this pub along with the one over the road, the Mitre and one around the corner, the Cross-Keys, shared a notorious reputation. It is interesting that this is the one whose name is not obviously religious, but *does* have two religious connections.

The earliest reference to this establishment is an advertisement in the **Northampton Mercury,** 22/12/1783 which informs us that *James Briggs begs leave to aquaint readers that he intends to open his WINE and PUNCH HOUSE at the corner of Silver-Street Northampton on Thursday the first of January next.*

Brigg's Punch-House appears again in the **Mercury** in 1805 when it seems to be run by James' widow – or perhaps his daughter.

BRIGG'S PUNCH-HOUSE

Wines, Brandies, Rums, Gins, and rich Cordials, of the finest flavour: Felix Calvert's Brown Stout and mild London Porter, rich Hereford Cyder, in any Quantity, barrelled or bottled. M. BRIGGS begs leave to inform her Friends and the Public in general, that she has laid in a large Quantity of the above Articles, of the first Quality, which she is determined to sell on the most moderate Terms. M.B. returns her sincere Acknowledgements to her numerous Friends for their very liberal Support, and hopes, from an unremitting Attention, to merit a Continuation of the same.

Silver-Street, Northampton, April 27, 1805.

By October 1815 William Dunkley is advertising in the **Mercury** that he has *entered into the above INN that is the FOUNTAIN INN (Formerly known by the Name of the Punch House).* He probably changed the name to the Fountain. A London sign bore the rhyme.

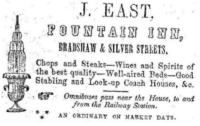

Hickman's Directory 1847.

Say what you will, when all is done or said,
The best of drinking's at the Fountain Head.

This inn is shown on **Law** 1847 as a substantial building with a fair sized yard to the rear at the *north east* corner of the junction of the four streets - this was its original position. An advertisement of the same year in **Hickman's** directory lists: - *Chops and Steaks - Wines and spirits of the best Quality-Well-aired Beds-Good Stabling and Lock-up Coach Houses, &c.* It also pointed out that Omnibuses pass the house from the Railway Station and an Ordinary was held on Market days.

It seems from other advertisements that the pub had a large room upstairs that was used for smoking concerts &c. In 1827 twelve members of the congregation of Castle Hill Church withdrew and formed themselves into a, *Society Professing Unitarian Principals* - this was the beginning of the Unitarian Church in Northampton. For the first few months until they acquired their own premises they

met in the room above the pub and I understand often ate Sunday lunch there. What a sensible arrangement! Unitarians are still alive and well in Northampton.

In the early 1870s it changed its name to the Sultan, only in the late 1870s to change it once more to the Criterion. This is a rather high sounding name for a pub, meaning a standard by which others can be judged – perhaps it was the name of a famous coach or racehorse?

As can be seen from the heading this pub had two addresses. In 1938 it along with several other buildings were demolished to make way for the new "Municipal Fish and Meat Market". However, a new pub had been constructed on the diagonally opposite corner, where it still stands. I understand that the old Criterion closed one night and the new opened for business the next day.

Unitarian meetings, but what of the second religious connection? In the past College Street was part of Silver Street. In medieval towns two streets adjoining called Gold and Silver Streets indicate the location of the Jewry and it seems possible that the Synagogue was located on, or close to, the old Criterion site. A will of William Raynsford 1630 has: - *all that messuage or tenement wherein she* (his daughter) *now dwells, sometymes now called the Synagogue of the Jews...in a certaine streete there called Silverstreete.* I wonder if any of the Synagogue survived in the structure of the old pub?

In 1992 the Criterion was changed its name to the ridiculous

Newt & Cucumber - later the Boston Clipper, now just The Clipper.

CROMWELL ARMS 38 Marefair.

This pub stood more or less opposite Hazlerigg House – or as it is sometimes known, Cromwell House. Cromwell is reputed to have stayed at Hazlerigg House prior to the Battle of Naseby.

The earliest mention of 38 Marefair as a drinking place is in the *Northampton Directory 1878-9*, when *Willson, Wm.* was quoted as a beer-retailer. *Stevens* 1889 has *Sanders, Charles* also a beer-retailer. By 1893 *Stevens* has changed *Sanders* to *Saunders*. The last entry, in 1932, has no name with it.

CROSS-KEYS 25 Sheep Street.

According to the *RBN 1898* there are, or were 16th and 17th century documents relating to this inn. I have located some from the 18th and 19th centuries, but not any earlier. A James York announced his transfer from the Cross Keys to the Hind in the *Northampton Mercury* in July 1749.

Because of the religious connections of the sign – the Cross Keys are the symbol of St. Peter and the Pope, and its location on the main north-south route through the medieval town of Northampton I feel that this inn could have very well started its life as a monastic hostelry. It could date back to the 13th century.

Thomas Bentley was the proprietor in the late 1870s and early 1880s. The *Northampton Directory* of 1878-9 has an advertisement for, *Bentley's Cross Keys Commercial Hotel – A Home from Home*. And a handbill of about the same date calls it a *Palace of Amusement* with dancing every Monday evening and a concert every Saturday night at eight p.m. There was stabling for sixty horses and 15 "lofty" bedrooms.

I can not only remember visiting the bars of this pub in the 1960s, but also supplying a light-show for a disco held upstairs and I have recollections of several smallish rooms off from the relatively large room we held the disco in. These rooms were probably the "lofty" rooms referred to and no doubt the disco was held in the room that once hosted concerts and dances in the 19th century. The reputation of the Cross Keys in the 1960s was such that I'm pretty certain those lofty rooms were also used for entertainment, but of a much different nature!

There is a rough, red, incised tombstone in the Museum collection, which had been used in the foundations of the Cross Keys and rediscovered in February 1878. From the design it is of a good age and probably ecclesiastical, adding weight to my theory of a medieval hospice or tavern being on the site. This stone came to light during Thomas Bentley's 'reign' and going on his advertising he was probably responsible for the last major alterations to be done to this building in its long life. It closed its doors for the last time in 1971.

An interesting recollection is from a friend of mine, Mr. Lynn Robinson. As a child he lived at number 27 Sheep Street, just across the other corner of Bull Head Lane. He used to play with Allan Parrott, the then landlord's son. It seems that his father, Frank Parrott was a big man in the cricket world with many important connections and Lynn can remember that Len Hutton, the famous cricketer, stayed as Mr. Parrott's guest at the Cross Keys on several occasions.

CROW & HORSESHOE 63 Gold Street also **Alhambra.**

I can understand why someone would call a pub the Horseshoe with its connotations of good luck, especially if it was at the top of a thoroughfare called Horseshoe Street, but the Crow & Horseshoe sounds an odd a combination as some of the modern daft ones. At first I thought it might indicate an amalgamation of two pubs. However, the Crow as a sign is very rare, probably because of the ominous reputation of this sombre black bird. Maybe, thought I, it indicated some sort of wry expression lost to modern humour, the Horseshoe being lucky, the Crow not.

Horseshoe Street was known in the past for its blacksmiths and at one time was called Crow & Horseshoe Lane, showing that one took its name from the other. Further research revealed that what we now call a crow-bar was once simply called a crow because the end was shaped into a 'beak'. This was not only used as a lever or prise, but as an agricultural tool: - *Get Crowe made of iron, deepe hole for to make.* (1578), *Oxford Dictionary*.

It also appears to have been a grapnel and an ancient kind of doorknocker! Considering Northampton's past status as a market-town the name of Crow & Horseshoe Lane, and that of the inn (which I feel derived its name from the lane) indicated to visitors that here was a thoroughfare where one could not only get your horse shod, but purchase agricultural tools &c. as well.

William Watson's will of 1802 left: - *to my friends John Vialls and Joseph Vialls bothe of Hardston aforesaid yeomen their heirs and Assigns All that Messuage or Tenement with the Stables Outbuildings And Appurtenances to the same belonging called or known by the Name of the Crow and Horseshoe Inn Situate on Gold Street aforesaid now in the tenure or occupation of my said sone Charles Watson.* **N.R.O.**
I wonder why he left it to his "friends" rather than his "sone"?

It seems to have been quite large and had its own brewery. The *Northampton Mercury* October 1851 carried the death of Joseph Steer, a brewer employed at the inn. The same publication carried an advertisement for the sale of the Freehold Inn and Market House in March 1860: - *With the large yard, brewhouse, ginger beer manufactory, stabling for 15 horses large malting, for 10 quarters.* It had a 24-foot frontage on Gold Street and a gateway from the yard into Horseshoe Street. (Information kindly supplied by Mr. G. Starmer).

It occupied the site that until recently was Bell's Hardware. The Crow & Horseshoe had its own entertainment facility, first called Thomas's Music Hall; this must have been when William Thomas became the proprietor circa 1855. It was later called the Alhambra and according to Lou Warwick (*Northampton Independent* April 1974) was of low repute. Eventually the license was transferred to the new Plough Hotel, built in 1879. The **Mercury** has various entries for this establishment from 1769-1846 (2017).

CROWN.

A ubiquitous sign found all over England and it is argued whether this sign or the Red Lion are the most common. I have discovered five or is it six Crowns in Northampton alone. Monson-Fitzjohn's

Quaint Signs of Olde Inns 1926 claims 1,008 Crowns to 921 Red Lions, but I understand things have changed since then; perhaps more Crowns have been demolished or changed to the Nutmeg & Weasel or some other stupid name.

Monson-Fitzjohn states that the origin of the Crown as a sign is due to the fact that the property has at some time been Crown property. This may be so in some cases, but I doubt if many were. The name Crown is a good safe name like the King's Arms or King's Head – easily adaptable to the reign of any monarch and unlike Arms and Heads a Crown is a crown and doesn't need repainting at every coronation. This alone could account for its popularity.

CROWN (S) Bridge Street, St. John's Street. also possibly **Wards Arms** and **Warwick Arms.**
There is only one real entry for this pub, *Pigot* 1840, *Edward Meacher, Bridge Street.* however, the building labelled "82" on *Law's* plan of the town 1847 is titled "Crowns" and seems to be it. Therefore it stood on the south corner of Bridge Street and St. John's Street. This property is numbered on the *O/S* 2500 1964 as 55 so with this is some confusion. The Three Crowns is listed in Bridge Street in 1830, 1845 and 1847, the proprietors being respectively *William Cherry, Morton and Joseph Robins boot ma. & clothier.* This property has no number, but it seems these two pubs are the probably the same. To add more confusion by 1858 the Warwick Arms was claiming number 55 as its address and it also goes back to 1840.

This is what I think happened. There was a pub called the Three Crowns standing on the corner of St. John's Street a long time before the earliest entry of 1830. This site by 1964 was numbered 55. On, or before 1840 there was also a pub next door (57) called the Warwick Arms. By 1858 the Warwick Arms had expanded and taken over number 55, extinguishing the Three Crowns. The Warwick Arms was called for a brief period the Wards Arms between 1901-1905 just to complicate things a little more.

The Crowns origins are not the same as the single Crown; in this case it is thought to refer to the three united kingdoms of England, Scotland and Wales. The three Crowns has the same meaning and often carries the portrait of James I of England (James VI of

Scotland), the first monarch to rule all three kingdoms. In medieval times the Three Crowns referred either to the Three Wise Men or to the Papal crown.

I could go on with these connections, but instead I will refer you to the entries, *Three Cups* and *Three Pigeons*.

CROWN (LE) Swinwel-strete (Derngate).
Only one reference, in a document dated 1504. Mentioned in *VCH*, not much is known about this pub – however the address is interesting as Swineswell Street is the old name for Derngate. The Derngate was once, of course, a gate – situated at the site of the junction of Cheyne Walk and Victoria Promenade which run approximately along the line of the old town wall.

It is thought that the word Derngate is derived from the Welsh word *dwr* which means 'water' – so Watergate, or it could mean 'the hidden gate'. This is a good name for not only was there a Swines' Well on the way to this gate, but just beyond a well dedicated to St. Thomas Becket, and further along the Vigo well and the river Nenn. Spring Gardens also joins Derngate close to where the gate must have been. It is fortunate that Swineswell Street did change its name for if it had not the Derngate Centre would be called the Swineswell Centre!

CROWN Dury (Drum) Lane also possibly **White Hart (Shipman's).**
In the 18th century people were fond of giving 'fashionable' London names to quite ordinary places. If you walk up Drum Lane into the Market Square today you will find the building to your right as you enter the Square is still called Dury Chambers but the lane has reverted to its more sensible, original name.

An advertisement in the *Northampton Mercury* 1766 gives the Crown in Dury Lane as being kept by a William Peck. I have no other reference to this sign, but suspect that it is another name for, or is part of, the White Hart- or Shipman's as it is now known.

CROWN Broad Lane (Street).
One entry, **Burgess** 1845, *Linnet-Crown-Broad-lane.* under Beer-Sellers.

CROWN Wood Hill.
From *RBN 1898*, this was probably the pre-Great Fire inn that was on the site of what became the Black Boy. See next entry.

CROWN St. Giles' Square.
Because of the close proximity of this inn to the one above I think there is a very real chance of a mix-up here. I cannot be certain that the deeds that I have looked at are the same as the ones viewed by the compilers of the Borough Records, but the ones I have seen could easily be misread and lead one to think the Crown referred to was on Wood Hill. A deed of Sale of 1650 (pre-Fire) has:- *near unto a Place called the Wood Hill next unto a Messuage or Tenement in the occupation of Joseph Hensman on the East side and a Messuage or Tenement or Inn called the Crown late in the Occupation of Peter Hanen on the West side.*

The will of Richard Benbow 1694 refers to a property on the site of the cake-shop on the corner of Wood Hill and makes the location of the Crown clearer: - *and in all that Messuage or Tenement with the appert. wherein Valentine Roberts pipemaker now liveth being the Corner house (facing?) upon Wood Hill on the West and the Inne called and known by the name or signe of the Crowne on the South side thereof in the towne of Northampton.*

There are eight deeds I have used from the Record Office that mention this Inn, but a Conveyance of 1859 finally clears up the location of *this* Crown: - *formerly the Crown Inn but now belonging to the County of Northampton and used for the accommodation of Her Majesty's Judges of Assize.*

There *was* a Crown before the Fire and it didn't stand on Wood Hill. However, although it is unlikely to have inns of the same name so close to each other there *could* have been another on the site of the Black Boy before the Fire. It is pretty certain that an inn of some name preceded the Black Boy, it is only legend that says it was called the Crown and this could simply be a mix-up of names of adjacent, but lost, inns.

The building that was this particular Crown appears to be still with us, now known as the Judges' Lodgings, standing next to the once hideously named Rat & Parrot!

CROWN AND ANCHOR.

 We have had two Crown & Anchors that I've discovered, one of which is still with us in Victoria Road. Although the Anchor is usually interpreted as a symbol of hope it can also mean the sea, especially ships and the navy. Combined with the Crown, a symbol of Royalty it can only mean The Royal Navy and this is the usual interpretation of this sign. Being so far from the sea could be why we have only had two pubs of this name. The surviving pub has at the time of writing an interesting and imaginative sign showing Neptune, god of the sea wearing a crown and holding an anchor.

There is also a dice based gambling game of this name much played by soldiers in the Great War and frowned upon by the Army brass. It is played with a board and three dice. The board has marked upon it the four suits of cards and a crown and an anchor. These six symbols are also marked on the sides of the dice. Players place stakes on one of the symbols and the banker throws the dice. If the symbol comes up on one of the dice the player gets their stake back, if two dice come up he gets twice his stake and three times if all three dice show the symbol. I can remember playing this game once in the school playground with marbles for stakes. I lost all my marbles (take that how you like!) and quickly learned why the Army didn't look kindly on this 'game'.

CROWN & ANCHOR 178 & 180 Bridge Street also Guy of Warwick.

It seems in days gone by this pub, or at least a previous one, was known as the Guy of Warwick. The Crown & Anchor stood on the west side of Bridge Street right on the north bank of the river at South Bridge. Although the pub survived until 1959 I have no recollection of it. In that year on the 13th of February the full-on licence of the

Crown & Anchor was transferred to a new, unnamed pub at the junction of the Headlands and Longland Road – later to be called The Headlands. **Mercury** vol.100 1820-1 John Grimshaw was the proprietor (2017).

CROWN & ANCHOR 6 St. Edmund's Road or 6 Victoria Road.

This one is still open. A typical street corner pub of the late 19th century, matching two similar pubs just down the road – the lost King of Denmark and the Princess Alexandra. Recently owned by McManus Taverns who sold it, along with six others to Mansfield brewery in

July 1997. A major renovation took place in 1994. It started life as a beer-only pub as the first entry, in *Wright's* 1884 Directory has "bhs".

E. Craddock was the proprietor, probably around 1910. Could this be the *Edwd. G. Craddock* listed for the Crown & Anchor, Bridge Street 1898-1900? If so, there may have been another name, or none for this establishment before the arrival of Edward who may have brought the name with him.

CROWN & CUSHION.

We have had three Crown & Cushions with one surviving. The name is thought to derive from the cushion on which the crown is conveyed to the throne during a coronation, perhaps indicating a pub opened in a coronation year.

CROWN & CUSHION 11 Fish Street.

This is a good example of where confusion can occur when using old data. A few years ago a map was produced of the 'old pubs' of the town. Unfortunately the man who produced it relied on the addresses supplied by the old street directories and fixed them onto an *O/S* 2500 Plan of 1964, the earliest that showed street numbers. In his haste to produce his map he did not realise that many of the streets had gone through number revisions between the late 19th century and the 1960s. As a result many street corner pubs found themselves half way up streets and others at the wrong end!

The Crown & Cushion caused me much trouble, as number 11 Fish Street is the present address of the Fish Inn. I was told by one local history fan that this had been its original name, but I knew this to be wrong, as the Fish is one of the old town's pubs. It was only through persistence and traditional stories I heard that there had been a pub on the opposite corner that I finally uncovered the truth. The street has been altered, widened and re-numbered – it was that simple. The pub stood on the opposite corner to the Fish, now occupied by City Buildings.

Before City Buildings was built in the early part of the 20th century there stood here, *an ancient ale-house and the old police station* (*C&E* 8/10/88). In 1790 it was decided to build a town gaol. This proved to be a grim structure, *where debtors got worse treatment than criminals, and lunatics suffered even more* (ibid.). It was enlarged in 1840 and later was used as a police station until a new one was opened up in Dychurch Lane in 1892. It was about this time that the street was widened.

CROWN & CUSHION Kingsthorpe.

I have not been able to locate this one exactly; it seems that Kingsthorpe had quite a number of pubs in the past. As until quite recently Kingsthorpe was a village on the outskirts of the town and not in the borough, so it, like many other places, got ignored. This quote however, is interesting: - *for not far from the Queen Adelaide Inn there are the King William IV on the Green, the Prince of Wales, the Crown & Cushion, and the Royal Oak. There are no fewer than eight public houses in Kingsthorpe in 1874.*

Northampton Independent 22-1-37.

This is five of them and I believe one of the others was called the Horseshoe, so I've still got two more to find.

CROWN & CUSHION 276 Wellingborough Road.

This pub is still with us, on the Wellingborough Road on the corner of Collins Street. The first entry for this pub is in *Taylor* 1858 and gives a Joseph Smith as the

proprietor and 212 as the number. On the *O/S* 2500 Plan 1964 this is a property two doors west of the Old House at Home and *Taylor* in 1864 gives this number as the address of that pub. *Law's* map of 1847 shows most of the Wellingborough Road undeveloped. Only Grundy's 'New Town' (West Street – East Street) exists on the south side of the road. In fact, no more development is shown east of East Street, even by a *Birdsall's* map of 1878. Therefore the Crown & Cushion that we now know could not have existed before this date. This is borne out by the fact that the sign does not reappear in the Wellingborough Road again until 1900.

Grundy's New Town was built between 1836 and 1850 and as there were no buildings between it and Abington Square it must have been a matter of guesswork as to the number of potential plots that lay between. Once the road had been developed west from the New Town, as is shown on *Birdsall's* map 1878 the plot numbers could be rationalised. This would account for the changes in numbers about this time. However, *Law* does not show any building where the Old House at Home subsequently appeared. There is a building halfway between New Town Road and Melbourne Street, and this oddly enough, corresponds to the present number 212.

The earliest date for the Old House at Home is 1864 and this is what I think happened. A Crown & Cushion appeared in the Wellingborough Road circa 1858 as part of the northern side of the New Town, i.e. the main road. For some reason it closed or at least, didn't appear in any more directories. Sometime around 1864 the Old House at Home opened on its present site; probably taking over from the Crown & Cushion (they both gave the number 212 at about the same time). Around 1900 a new Crown & Cushion was opened on its present site and was probably called such because of the previous one. A change of four numbers-two plots would be reasonable for a recalculation after the filling in of the road by developments. So, it looks like we may have had two Crown & Cushions in the Wellingborough Road, the earliest one being the predecessor of the Old House at Home. It has been observed that the Fish Inn and the Old House at Home are architecturally very similar, could the license and name of the pub adjacent to the Fish Inn been transferred from Fish Street to the Wellingborough Road, both being rebuilt by the same architect. The Crown & Cushion only later to be renamed the Old House at Home?

CURRIERS ARMS.

It is not surprising that I have found three pubs of this name in a shoe town like Northampton. Although not directly connected with the making of boots and shoes a currier is ancillary to the trade in that a currier is one who dresses and colours tanned leather. The sign itself is another example of a non-heraldic tradesman's arms.

CURRIERS ARMS 14 Freeschool Street.

This pub was on the west side of Freeschool Street opposite the end of St. Gregory's Street. I have little on this pub, *Wright* 1884 has "bhs" so it was a beer-shop and *Lea* 1907 has it twice, once as the "Carriers Arms" and once under its correct name.

CURRIERS ARMS 29, 30 Mayorhold.

As near as I can work out this was one door north of the corner of Bath Street and the Mayorhold. The *O/S* 2500 Plan 1901 shows a long property with a gateway through into a large yard behind.

CURRIERS ARMS 9 Raglan Street.

Only two entries under the sign, both in *Taylor's* Directories, 1858 *George Mason* and 1864 *Edward Roberts*. I have found Roberts mentioned as a beer-retailer in other directories. *Melville* 1861 also may explain why the pub was so called: - *Roberts, Edward & Son, curriers & shoe manufacturers, 9 Raglan st.* Beer-retailing was probably a secondary business. G. S Roberts, Raglan Street is listed in *Royal* 1866 as a beer-retailer and finally appears in *Melville* 1867 with the same description as in *Melville* 1861. This is true for all such entries and I do not trust the latter ones. *Melville* only produced two directories and I think the second one is a straight copy of the earlier one and as such cannot be relied upon.

O/S 2500 Plan 1964 shows number 9 as being a larger than usual house half way along the west side of the street with a side entrance leading to a building labelled *Works*.

DAIRYMAN 32 Vernon Street see **Freemasons Arms.**

DALLINGTON BROOK INN Aberdare Road see **Red Earl.**

DICK TURPIN Horsemarket.

The famous highwayman would make a suitable subject for an inn sign, implying the sort of hostelry of that period with its ample food, roaring fires and fine ale. I cannot confirm the reputation of this establishment as I only have one reference to it, from the *Northampton Independent* of November 1979 where the information given is only that above.

DICK TURPINS 134 Great Russell Street. see **Jolly Crispin.**

DOG Brier (Briar) Lane.

Only *Burgess* 1845 gives a name to this sign, both *Hickman* and *Kelly* 1847 have the landlord's name, T. Carver, to indicate that it still existed. There are only these three references and they all refer to T. Carver as a beer-retailer.

Brier Lane (correct spelling) is shown on *Law's* map 1847 and is in effect the start of the Wellingborough Road out of St. Edmund's Terrace. St Edmund's Terrace was a row of dwellings on the south side of the Wellingborough Road that ran from the junction of Wellingborough and Kettering Roads east to what is now called St. Edmund's Terrace (i.e. the alley-way by the public toilets) and appeared to include two rows of small dwellings either side of the present alley-way. Brier Lane came next and seems to have been the general name for the Wellingborough Road as far as Raglan Street. *Law* shows only buildings on the north side of the road, so this is where the Dog must have been. There were few buildings in the row so it is possible that the Dog and the Little Boat (*Taylor's* 1864, *George Parker, 78 Briar Lane*) are the same premises, however, *Taylor* lists a beer-retailer, George Bennett at number 44 Brier Lane.

DOLPHIN 15 Gold Street.

As a symbol the dolphin goes back a long way. The Minoan palace on Knossos which dates from about 1500 years BCE has (restored) paintings of dolphins on its plastered walls. The Greeks and Romans liked them too – they have been popular all through history. The dolphin is the badge of the Watermans' Company and was also used to indicate the French Dauphin or Crown Prince, I'm not sure of its significance here. This establishment went back a long way, as it was listed as one of the Ancient Inns in the *Assembly Order* of 1585 so it must have been well established by then. It is easy to see that it was a place of importance from the large number of advertisements and announcements appearing in the local press in the 18th century.

The building was demolished and the Grand Hotel built on the site between 1889 and 1892. Two articles in the *Northampton Mercury* in November and December 1889 describe evidence of the Great Fire of 1675 (burning), a number of cock-spurs and an Ancient British gold coin being discovered during the demolition.

During the Civil War on October 15th 1643 an attack was made on Northampton by Prince Rupert. They marched from Holdenby and attacked at midnight. As a result of this skirmish several soldiers were killed or wounded, the latter being put up at various addresses in the town. A burial recorded by All Saints' Church over a year later was probably due to this action: - *from the dolphin, a trooper unknone. October 26 1644.*

St. Peter's also mentioned the Dolphin in its records, from the Vestry Book of St. Peter's Church on the election of churchwardens – which seems to have been a jolly affair!

1769...........Spent att the Dollfin.........0..10..6.

The *Northampton Mercury* announced in 1737 that a *Richard Boswell from East Haddon now keeps the Dolphin* and in 1757 it told of the death of the landlady, Mrs. Aithy. About this time there were other announcements concerning lost or stolen property, sales of cheese and the letting of the inn as well as another announcement of a new landlord: -

CLARKE WILDING

Being removed from the Unicorn, in Bridge st. to the DOLPHIN INN, in Gold-street Northampton, takes this publick Manner of requesting a Continuance of the Favours of his Friends: and of assuring all Gentlemen, Tradesmen Chapmen & Others, (who will be pleased to honour him with their Commands) that they may depend upon receiving the Best Accommodation and most obliging behaviour.

N.B: The Sale of the entire stock, Household Goods Brewing-

Utensils; &c. at the UNICORN, will be on Tuesday the 13th. Day of August.

Northampton Mercury, July 29, August 5, 12. 1765.

A sale catalogue of 1827 describes the property: - *Coach and Commercial Inn called the Dolphin, now in the occupation of Mr. John Shaw....13 good bed chambers, large Market-Room. Three Parlours, Bar, roomy kitchen, Larder, Scullery, Four Cellars, large yard, surrounded with excellent Stabling for between 70 and 80 horses: Lofts & Graneries, Brewhouse, three saddlers' Rooms and pump of good water. The catalogue also describes the rest of the property – a Dwelling House used as a Coach office on the corner of Kingswell Street and Gold Street and a Tenement adjoining in Kingswell Street, Both of which can easily added to the Inn if required.*

By 1847 the properties were up for sale again. The auction catalogue details four lots of this, *extensive Freehold Estate.* This was because of the death of the landlord, Thomas Linnell.

It appears that by 1847 the Coach office had become a tobacconists and the tenement had become the 'Dolphin Tap'. The Inn was still the Inn, but now enlarged with a second bar, the Tap, with access from Kingswell Street. The fourth lot appears to have laid to the north of the Tap in Kingswell Street and probably occupied the corner of this street and Woolmonger Street and was another pub – the Rising Sun.

For many years its successor, the Grand Hotel had a bar called the Dolphin Bar in honour of this Ancient Inn. In the 1960s I would meet my friends here on Saturday lunch-times and perhaps learn of a party or two taking place that evening. Its entrance was in Kingswell Street at almost the same spot where the Dolphin Tap door must have been. Later this door gave access to a bar called the Kasbar.

DOVER CASTLE 26 Dover Street.

This pub was tucked away just off the Kettering Road and I can recall visiting this establishment in my youth, it seemed to be the haunt of 'Teddy-boys' – who by that time were becoming anachronisms. Based on the directory entries, this inn, as it was called in the first entries, opened at the beginning of the 20th century. **Bennett** 1901-2 has as well as "inn" – *Accommodation for cyclists &c. teas provided to order*, so it was at the time catering for the current craze. Sadly, along with other pubs of character it was destroyed in the 1970s – demolished as part of the Exeter Road Clearance.

DRAGON St. Mary's Street.

This is one of the pubs listed in the *RBN 1898* as being of the 16th or 17th centuries. Unfortunately the documents they used are not available today.

A dragon was the standard of the West Saxons and can be seen on the Bayeux Tapestry. However, I think in this case it is probably later, from the Tudor period. Dragons tend, in this part of the world, anyway, to come in two colours, red and green. We have a Green Dragon and when a dragon's colour is not specified it's usually a red one. Not only a symbol of Wales, but also one of the bearers of the Royal Arms of the Tudors. When you come across a King's or Queen's Head pub sign the usual sovereigns depicted are Henry VIII and his daughter, Elizabeth. Both, but especially Elizabeth are reputed to have been fond of inns and taverns and a red dragon would show one's allegiance to the Crown.

Alternatively, there was once a famous horse that belonged to Tregonwell Frampton – "The Father of the Turf" (1641-1727) called 'Dragon' – so perhaps the explanation is that simple.

DRAPERS ARMS 29 The Drapery.

A suitable name for a pub located in the Drapery, it seems to have been a short lived establishment at the turn of the 19th century. According to the numbering of properties in 1964 this pub was immediately north of Swan Yard.

There are only two listings as a pub of this name, both in *Lea's* directories of 1893 *Thomas L. Bates* and 1900 *H. Purser*. Thomas L. Bates is listed as a beer-retailer at this address from 1885. A Henry or Harry Purser was a beer-retailer at 44 Kettering Road and 21 Raglan Street (the Lord Raglan) in 1893 and 1894.

Incidentally the arms of the Company of Drapers bear three Imperial Crowns – this may account for some of the pubs of that name.

DRUMS Drum Lane.
This is another pub listed in the *RBN 1898* about which I can find nothing; however; it is probably the modern Rifle Drum.

DUCK & DRAKE Location Unknown.
This is another one from the *RBN 1898*. In this case we not only don't have the document, we don't even know where it was. An old name given to the game of skimming stones across a pond.

DUKE OF CAMBRIDGE 50 Barrack Road (Hope's Place) also **Gardeners Arms and Cambridge Arms.**
Hope or Hope's Place was the frontage onto the Barrack Road running from what became Louise Road to La Belle Alliance Cottages, now The Poplars. By comparing various plans and maps I have come to the conclusion that the piece of land between Nelson Street and Leicester Street once contained two or three properties, one of these being the Britannia Inn and another a beer-house called the Duke of Cambridge which disappeared around 1941. At some time about then the whole area was cleared and a new Britannia Inn constructed on the site.

The pub's proximity to the Barracks, which were built in 1796 probably accounts for its name. Frederick Adolphus, Duke of Cambridge was born at the Queen's Palace, now Buckingham Palace on 24th February 1774. He was the tenth child and seventh son of King George III and Queen Charlotte. He was a military man, and in 1805 he was made a colonel of the Coldstream Guards and in 1827 the Colonel-in-Chief of the 60th - or King's Royal Rifle Corps.

This pub appeared in an advertisement to be let in the *Northampton Mercury* August 1873 as the *Cambridge Arms doing a first-class business*, even allowing for advertising superlatives it must have been established for a while. The landlord appears to have been a John Dunkley.

DUKE OF CLARENCE (OLD) 11 Mercers Row also **Leg of Mutton** and **Queen's Dragoons.**
This pub used to stand on Mercers Row on the west side of the south-

west entrance to the Market Square, now occupied by a newsagent. The Duke of Clarence was a very popular man and on his accession to the throne became King William the Fourth and gave his new title to some more pubs.

It started life as the Queen's Dragoons, later, changing to the Leg of Mutton, no doubt indicating that food was available and stayed thus until 1814. In this year it acquired its last sign – the Duke of Clarence. Another duke of Clarence has a connection with Northampton, in October 1887 the Duke, a grand-child of Queen Victoria opened an extension of the General Hospital, however the pub is unlikely to have been named after this Duke for he would have had to have been at least 73 years old at the re-naming.

DUKE OF EDINBURGH 3 Adelaide Street also **Flower De Luce** and **Royal George.**

It is interesting that the first appearance of this Duke name (1884) coincides with the Duke of Cambridge's first appearance. Here we have two pubs on opposite sides of the Barrack Road changing their names to Dukes at possibly the same time, and no doubt, for the same

reason – the nearby Barracks.

The Duke of Edinburgh was the second son of Queen Victoria and Prince Albert, as well as being the Duke of Edinburgh he was also the Duke of Saxe-Coburg and Gotha. He was educated for the Navy and served in the Channel, North America, the West Indies and the Mediterranean. He became a Rear Admiral in 1878, Vice Admiral in 1882, Commander of the Channel Squadron in 1883-4, Commander-in-Chief in the Mediterranean 1886-9, an Admiral in 1887 and Admiral of the Fleet in 1893 – this may have had something to do with having influential parents.

The other rather short-lived names for this pub probably also refer to matters military, especially the Royal George, being, as it is, the name of a famous ship built at Woolwich in 1756. The Flower De

Luce could be the Fleur de Lis from the French arms and found on the arms of the sovereign of England, but could also refer to the badge of the Prince of Wales, or his regiment. The pub is now a pharmacy (2009).

DUKE OF YORK

We have had two of these; a short-lived early 19th century one in Bridge Street and another on St. Andrew's Road still with us.

There can be little doubt that both were named after Prince Frederick Agustus (1763 – 1827), the second son of George III and the subject of that well-known nursery rhyme about marching men up and down hills. Like all good rhymes of this ilk there is an element of fact behind it. It appears that when we were fighting the French in Holland in the 1790s the Duke of York was leading 40,000 men into the sunrise when he saw the entire French army of 150.000 men lined up for battle. Realising that he could not win against such odds, he led his men up a low hill, fooling the French into believing he planned a flank attack. The French manoeuvred their whole army to the other side of the hill whilst the Duke marched his men back down the same side as they had gone up. The resulting chaos enabled English fire and cavalry to force a French withdrawal and the Duke was able to get his troops out of Holland before the winter set in, saving many lives, perhaps including the chap who wrote the rhyme.

DUKE OF YORK St. Andrew's Road and 90 Salisbury Street.

Before WWII pigeon racing was a popular past time and at least two pubs in the town had clubs – this one and the Garibaldi, Wellingborough Road. These two clubs and the Northampton Town Flying Club bred homing pigeons as part of the war-effort.

Pigeons were taken on aircraft missions so in event of a catastrophe they could be released and inform base of the crew's fate.

DUKE OF YORK Bridge Street.

This pub is listed in three of *Pigot's* directories, 1824, 1830 and 1840. These directories do not contain as much information as later ones and do not include such useful details as street lists or property numbers. There are no references to this pub in later directories so I assume that it ceased as a Sign. Without any clues to its place in Bridge Street it is impossible to tell whether it changed its name or became extinct.

DULLEY'S ARMS see **Maple Tree.**

DUN COW see **Bearward Arms.**

DURHAM OX 1 Augustine Street.

This pub stood on the south-west corner of Augustine Street and Weston Place. Augustine Street on the south side disappeared during the construction of St. Peter's Way many years ago.

The Durham (or Ketton) Ox was a famous beast. In 1802 at the age of six years the animal weighed a staggering 34 cwt. and had a girth of over 11 feet. The Durham Ox was a popular sign in the past in rural areas – perhaps the original landlord brought the name with him?

EAGLE 53 Oxford Street.

I have come across three Eagles in the town, but two of them; the Eagle Tavern, Bridge Street and the Eagle, Wellingborough Road are short name versions of the Eagle and Child and the Spread Eagle respectively. This is the only lone Eagle.

In the Middle Ages this sign denoted St. John the Evangelist. Heraldically it is associated with the Dukes of Hamilton and the Earls of Cambridge, but it such a common charge it could be associated with anything – or perhaps the first landlord, John Albright, simply liked eagles?

The first entry I have is from *Slater* 1862 where a John Albright is listed as a *Retailer of Beer* in Oxford Street. *Taylor's* 1864 lists Albright under Beer Retailers, but also gives the sign. *Wright* 1884 gives the proprietor as *Edward Burrell v.* so it seems that the Eagle had risen in status from being a beer-shop to a place of victualling.

The building is shown on the *O/S* Plan 1964. *Kelly* 1940 gives Walter Morgan as a brewer of the beer retailed and there would have been plenty of space for such a venture, the pub was situated on the north-east corner of the Letts Road – Oxford Street junction. The area is now an industrial estate.

EAGLE & CHILD. .

The eagle and Child may seem an odd combination, but in fact, is derived from the arms of the Stanleys, Earls of Derby. The origins of this device are interesting and illustrate the value of a trusting wife – or maybe a very wise one.

An early Stanley, Sir Thomas Latham lived in the reign of Edward III (1327-77) and it seems he had an illegitimate child by a local woman. Sir Thomas arranged to have the child placed at the foot of a tree below an eagle's nest. He then took a walk with his wife and contrived to pass the tree, whereupon they 'discovered' the baby. Sir Thomas then persuaded his good wife that they should adopt this miraculously found baby – hence the device.

We have had two Eagle and Childs in the town, but why either of them should carry the device of the Stanleys is unknown to me. One possibility is that the Stanleys had at one time a regiment of their own and these establishments were opened by veterans of the same.

EAGLE & CHILD 9 Bridge Street also Eagle.

This inn stood at the top of Bridge Street on the eastern side, just below the George Hotel, now Lloyd's Bank. It must have been there for a considerable time, there are few records, but an advertisement from the *Northampton Mercury* of 1756 puts it back to that century: -
RODE away with from John Taylor's at the Eagle & Child In the Bridge street, a Bay GELDING, full-aged, about Fourteen hands and a half high, with a Star on his forehead, Blind of the near Eye, & Hath both his Huckle-Bones rubb'd With carrying Port manteaus, &c.

I have information from a Mr. David Hall, who held the Saracen in Abington Street around 1860 and converted it into a Temperance Hotel (what a crime!) that the property was originally named the Sign of Absolem Hanging in the Oak – the sign of a barber. The inference is that if Mr. Hall had the knowledge of the site's previous trade it was probably in the early part of the 18th century. Mr. Hall died in 1886 aged 81 so he was born in 1805. The **Mercury** vol. 51 1770-1 has reference to an Eagle & Child, Bridge St. (2017). It is possible that a parent or grand-parent gave him this information. It's also possible that it could have moved at some time.

EAGLE & CHILD St. Giles' Street.
This is one of the inns mentioned in the *RBN 1898* for which I have been unable to discover any documents.

EARL OF NORTHAMPTON'S ARMS see **Northampton Arms.**

EARL OF POMFRET see **Pomfret Arms.**

EARL RUSSELL see **Jolly Crispin.**

EARL SPENCER'S ARMS (INN) 1 Lower Harding Street, Crispin Street. Also **Britannia** and **Spencers Arms.**
This pub illustrates the care with which information from trade directories should be taken. There is one entry as the Britannia in 1858 and by 1864 it had become the Earl Spencer's Arms, it ceased as a pub on 6/1/1940.

Many publishers of directories simply kept the set type from one year to the next, altering the odd entry as· needed and often not checking the information. *Northants Hunts & Rutland Trade Directories* for 1948-9 and 1951-2 must have been one of these as they included this pub. I have an article from the *Northampton Independent* dated June 7th 1946 that includes a photograph of the remains of the pub with children playing in the rubble. There is no way that anyone in June 1946 could have ordered a drink here, or five years later in 1951!

EAST END TAVERN 27 Melbourne Street also **New Inn.**
This pub stood about halfway down the street on the east side, according to the *O/S* 1:2500 1964 Edition Plan street numbering. Both names refer to it being part of "Grundy's New Town". This was built between 1836 and the 1850s, so its first name, New Inn is appropriate and as the "New Town" was originally up the Wellingborough Road on its own in the fields so the East End Tavern is also fitting.

ECLIPSE 17 Grafton Street.
There are three possible meanings to this sign. There is, or was, an Eclipse in Tunbridge Wells named after a stagecoach that ran through that town, but it is unlikely that it also ran through

··THE ECLIPSE··

here, but it is possible that there were more than one coach of that name. Both coach and pub could be called this for the same reason – that it implied that they *eclipsed* all other competition. Finally, the reason that I favour is that like the Beeswing in Todd's Lane nearby it could have been the name of a racehorse. The pub stood on the northeast corner of Fitzroy Terrace and Grafton Street.

The only proprietor's name we have associated with this pub is a William Johnson. I have found a George Johnson, Confectioner and Baker in Todd's Lane in 1854 who could have been William's father. There is a Sarah A. Johnson at the Beeswing, St. Edmund's Row in 1864 – are the two Beeswings linked in some way? Finally, there was a William Johnston(e) in Bridge Street retailing beer from 1845-1850.

ELEPHANT & CASTLE Elephant Lane.

This is one of the *RBN 1898* 16th-17th century documents I have not seen. However there is a document dated 1757 in the **NRO**.

Elephant Lane is the old name for Western Terrace, just south of the east end of West Bridge. It is shown as such on the *O/S* 1:2500 Plan 1901.

There are complex theories about circuses and the like to explain the name of this lane, but the most likely is that in the past there was a pub called the Elephant and Castle here and it gave its name to the thoroughfare.

Then, we have to explain the name of the pub! The usual theory is that it is the English attempt to pronounce the *Infanta of Castile*. This could be right, but an elephant and castle is also an item of table silverware. In days gone by a person's status would be indicated by how close they had been sat to the Salt – this would have been a large silver container with the then valuable condiment in it. The further from it, the lower down the scale you rated. Salts were often made in

the form of an elephant with a howdah, or castle on their backs. This was in imitation of the Indian chess-piece that we call the rook or castle. To call your establishment after such a prestigious piece of tableware indicated a classy inn! An elephant with a howdah was also the crest of the Cutler's Company, on account of the ivory used for knife handles. The original owner could, therefore have been a cutler.

The 1757 document is a will of a Joseph Daniel, which refers to: - *and all that Messuage or tenement with the appurtances situate and being in the Parish of St. Peter in the said Town of Northampton known by the name or Sign of the Elephant and Castle and all that Close or parcell of meadow Ground Lying and being in the said parish of St. Peter within the said Town of Northampton near the West Bridge...*

ENGINEER

In the past Northampton had two pubs with this sign and as far as I know there are two explanations for the name. The Engineer in Rickard Street is probably named after the Railway Engineer ('Engine-Driver'), a job every right-minded boy when I was a lad aspired to, however, having come under the influence of the Eagle comic and Dan Dare, *we* all wanted to be space-men. The other pub, in Portland Street could have been opened by a retired engine driver, but just as equally he could have been a soldier in the Royal Engineers.

ENGINEER 2 Portland Street.

This pub stood on the south-east corner of Portland Street and the Wellingborough Road. The earliest record I have of it is the *Taylor's* directory 1864, under Beer-Retailers. *Wright's* 1884 gives "bhs" so it was a beer-shop. It must have closed between 1952 and early 1953 as the RAFA Club moved into the premises in March 1953. They moved out before the building's demolition when the Wellingborough Road was widened in March 1960.

ENGINEER 51 Rickard Street.

From the *Wright's* 1884 entry "bhs" we know that this was a beer-shop. From the directory entries it seems Widow Spokes remarried and became Mrs. Watts and it seems her son, Alfred, took over the license in circa 1953. 1906 *E. Spokes,* 1907 *Mrs. Spokes,* 1911 *E. M. Spokes (proprietorix),* 1927 *E. M. Watts (propr.ess),* 1928 *Emily Maria Watts,* 1952 *Emily Maria Watts,* 1954 *Alfred William Watts.*

The pub's identity as a beer-shop is confirmed by an advertisement in the *Northampton Mercûry* February 1868: -

TO LET IMMEDIATELY
THE "ENGINEER" BEER HOUSE, Far Cotton –
Apply to J. Willars, Lily of the Valley, St. Andrew's –Square,
Northampton.

The pub stood on the south-east corner of Rickard Street and Letts Road. All this area is now an industrial estate.

EVENING STAR 26 Upper Priory Street.
Wright describes this as a "bhs" and it has one earlier entry in the *Northampton Directory* 1878-9 under Beer-Retailers. It was on the south side of the street near the east end next to a factory. *Kelly's* directory 1940 does not award it a '*' showing that at the time, it was not brewing its own beer, unlike many other pubs in the town.

FAGIN'S see **Molly Malone's.**

FALCON
I have mentioned elsewhere that Queen Elizabeth was a popular subject for inn signs. There are several contenders for the meaning of this sign, one being the sport of falconry, but the most likely, especially for the earlier ones, is the badge of Queen Bess – "a falcon, argent, crowned or" (a silver, or white falcon with a gold crown). This was a common sign in her day – and probably a lot easier to paint than a reasonable rendering of the Queen herself. A proclamation of 1563 invoked penalties for poorly painted portraits of Her Majesty (see Queen's Head).
FALCON 23 Marefair.
This pub stood on the corner of Freeschool Street and Marefair. The earliest reference to this pub is in *Wright's* 1884, who gave it a "bhs". It closed in 1958, so I never drank in it, although the building continued for many years afterward as a shop, it was demolished in the 1980s.
FALCON Newland.
This is one of those from the *RBN 1898* that I cannot find any documents for, but see Fawkon (Le).

FANTASIA see **Morris Man.**
FAWKON (LE) Cornmonger's Row.
Cornhill, Corn Row or Cornmonger's Row are all names for what is now called the Parade, the north side of the Market Square. A Rental of 1504, much quoted here, describes an inn: - *'Le Fawkon' and an inn called 'Le Hart' in the tenure of William Crawme, notary, were in Cornmonger's Row.*

The Hart was probably on the site of the Corn Exchange (later the Exchange Cinema and now a 'Rock Café') and the Fawkon nearby. There is a Falcon recorded in Newland (see above). If this had been at the very bottom of Newland it could have been described as being on Cornmonger's Row.

FIG TREE see **Globe.**
FIREFLY see **Red Earl.**
FIREMAN'S ARMS 59, 59a or 61 Newland, 2 Inkerman Terrace.
This pub was situated on the north corner of Inkerman terrace where it joined Newland. It is clearly shown on the *O/S* 2500 1964 Plan titled "B. H." →Beer House.

I was not sure whether the fireman referred to is one that extinguishes conflagrations, or accompanied the Engineer on the footplate of a steam locomotive, but Mr. Lynn Robinson recalls a sign depicting a fireman in heroic pose with a hose in full spate extinguishing some blaze – so in its later years it was the former. The Fire Station is nearby, but the pub goes back to at least 1858 whereas the Mounts Fire Station was built in the 1930s.

For a while in the 1960s I worked for the C. W. S. and was told this story. I think it happened sometime in the 1940s or 50s. It seems a fire started in the Co-Op in Abington Street and the alarm was raised. Up at the Fire Station the engine was being cleaned and on the alarm being received the ladders &c. were speedily replaced and the engine sallied forth. The route to Abington Street in those days was down Newland (quite a hill) along the west side of the Market Square and left into Abington Street. As the engine reached the bottom of the Market the driver applied the brakes. In their haste no one had strapped the ladders on, so although the engine stopped, the ladders didn't and continued in a southerly direction through the windows of

Burton's, the Tailors opposite! It transpired that the fire had been quite a small one in a pile of coco-mats and had been dealt with by an employee with an extinguisher!

Although this pub survived until quite late into the 20th century, I have no recollection of it – probably because it was at the top of Newland, well away from my usual haunts. It is one of my regrets that I was not more catholic in my choice of pubs when I was younger, if I had been *I* might have known whether the Fireman travelled on an engine or a locomotive.

FISH 11 Fish Street, 1 Riding.

I can think of two good reasons why one would call a pub the Fish. This pub goes back a long way, although the building doesn't, if it did go back to before the Reformation it is possible that this is the Christian symbol of the *Ichthys*. It is a lot easier to paint a fish than the image of Christ.

According to an article in the *Northampton Post* of 3/12/86 the pub dates from 1750, but I suspect it is actually much older. The pub appears in one of the oldest directories, that of 1824. The street it is in is called Fish Street and this is always a good indication of a pub's antiquity, but this street could be named after its function – it could have in the past been the site of the fishmonger's stalls. Reginald Brown in his *Guide to Northampton* 1927 claims this is so, so possibly the pub got its name from a street. There is a third

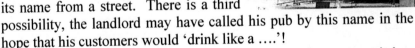

possibility, the landlord may have called his pub by this name in the hope that his customers would 'drink like a ....'!

In 1986 Hampden Hosts, the owners, proposed to convert it into a 14-bed hotel. This was met with great opposition and somewhere along the line it became a 'typical Victorian hostelry' with 12 beds. Lou Warwick got up a petition and secured 111 signatures and the owners got into trouble with the Council for starting work before permission had been given. Whilst all this was going on the landlord and lady, Colin and Tina Brownsell left (9/9/86) to take over the Gardener's Arms in Wellingborough Road. The pub reopened on the 5th of December of that year and despite people's misgivings proved to be quite tastefully converted. Lou is quoted as saying, "I wish the venture well, but I sigh for the old Fish." In February of the next year the Council gave permission for the hotel part to be completed.

FISHING BOAT TAVERN 15 Barrack Road.

Although this establishment is called a 'Tavern' this may be a bit of poetic licence as can be seen from the advertisement quoted below from the *Northampton Mercury* November 1863 (the only reference I have) it appears to be a fishmongers.

TO LET
With possession at Christmas next. "THE FISHING BOAT TAVERN" .
A BEER-HOUSE, situate at 15 BARRACK-ROAD NORTHAMPTON, suitable for a Butcher, Fishmonger, or Grocer, fitted with Marble Slab for Shop Front, and a good Curing house, with Large Yard attached, and every necessity suitable for the Fish Curing Business on the Premises. The Furniture, with Horse and Cart, at the option of the incoming tenant.

FIVE BELLS

Northampton has had three Five Bells, one is still with us albeit with a silly name, another one is known of through an advertisement and the third seems to have disappeared in the 1950s.

Three Bells and Eight Bells are common. However, five bells is a good time to call time and close the pub. It is just possible that it is a corruption of The Five Alls, a wry pub name that Northampton lacks. The sign usually depicts five men, the first, a King, has written beneath him "I rule all". The second is a Cleric with "I pray for all", the third a Lawyer, "I plead for all", then a Soldier, "I fight for all" – and lastly, a poor, downtrodden peasant, "I PAY for all!" Considering Northampton's radical past I would have thought such a sign would have been popular, especially if the peasant had been changed to a shoemaker.

However, it is possible that the sign refers to bell-ringing. Many continental travellers of yesteryear commented on England's church bells and it seems that we have been putting peals of bells in our churches since the 10th century and from at least the 15th century we've been ringing them in some sort of order. The practice was stimulated by the Reformation, becoming especially associated with the Anglican Church. By the 17th century intricate formulas (changes) had been worked out. It started as a gentleman's recreation practised by aristocrats and scholars, later, clerics and even labourers joined in. Women were not allowed. Participation was a mark of social status and so for an innkeeper to indicate on his signboard that he was part of this august company would imply high standards at his establishment.

FIVE BELLS (OLD) Harborough Road, Kingsthorpe.

I have traced this pub through the directories as far back as 1830 and no doubt it goes back a long way before then. It probably started as a coaching inn and acquired the appellation 'Old' because it *was* old.

TEA GARDENS,

Old Five Bells Inn, Kingsthorpe.

BRYAN LUCAS

Respectfully acquaints the public that the above Gardens are now open.—Tea, &c. for large or small parties on the shortest notice.

Hickman's Directory 1847.

Bryan Lucas, licensee in 1847, *Respectfully acquainted the public that the Tea Gardens were now open.* At the turn of the 19th century William Parberry was advertising "Pleasure Gardens" and we know quoits were played here at this time.

It seems that Quoits was a game that Northamptonshire was renowned for in the past and it was played in the gardens of most pubs that had one. The last pubs to host this game were the Five Bells and the Forge Hammer in St. James' End. In the 1960s the Nemo Poetry Group met in the back room and I, along with many others attended those meetings.

McManus Taverns acquired the Five Bells in 1993 and spent something in the region of half a million pounds on it. In October 1994 they announced its impending reopening in November and appealed for a new name, *a traditional name for the new-look venue which is linked to Kingsthorpe.* Garry McManus was quoted in the *C&E*, "We want to localise it and a name connected with the area's history would be great." They called it the Frog & Fiddler!

FIVE BELLS (OLD) Sheep Street.
> *To Be Lett. And Enter'd upon at Michaelmas next.*
> *A Good and Well-Accustomed PUBLICK-HOUSE, known by the*
> *name of the OLD FIVE BELLS, adjoining to St. Sepulcher's Church-*
> *Yard in the Sheep Street in Northampton: with very good Stables,*
> *Brew-house, and other Out-Offices thereto belonging, all in very good*
> *Repair: It stands well for Business, being in the Middle of the Beast*
> *Fairs. Enquire of Mr. Richards, Hosier, in the Drapery in*
> *Northampton aforesaid.*
> **Northampton Mercury** 1748

FIVE BELLS 26 Wellington Street.
This pub was on the east side of the street close to the Friend's
Meeting House.

There appears to have been three beer-shops in Wellington
Street in the 19th century – all traceable back to 1852, one of these
probably became the Five Bells. Unfortunately as there are no street
numbers in the earlier directories I cannot tell which is which. The
1852 names are, Julius Pearson, Sander Roberts and William Wilcox.
The latter is also shown in **Slater's** 1850 as being in this street, but
listed as Plumber, Painter and Glazier. Mrs. Wilcox is listed in 1878
as a Beer-Retailer at number 56 that is probably where her husband
carried on his trade as a Plumber and Beer-Retailer. Later years
(1884) 56 was known as the Chequers and 35 as the Talbot.

FLEECE.
We seem to have had two or three Fleeces in
Northampton in the past. I say this because there is a
16-17th century record of a Golden Fleece in Bridge
Street, however, this is probably the Fleece of later
records, it's name having become shortened as often
happens.

The Golden Fleece comes from Greek
mythology and was supposed to have been the hide of a fabulous ram
and made of pure gold. It was more likely to have been filled with
gold particles. Gold bearing ore is crushed and washed down a sluice
lined with corduroy. The heavy gold gets caught in the cloth whilst
the lighter silica is washed away. Every so often the corduroy is
changed and the gold extracted. In ancient times sheepskin was used

instead of corduroy.

The sign of the Fleece or Golden Fleece was always popular in towns where sheep and the wool trade were prominent like Northampton. It can also be the sign of a draper and the *Golden Fleece*, a ram hung up by a band around its middle is the badge of the Knightly Order of the Golden Fleece founded by the Duke of Burgundy in 1430. In Northampton I feel that both or three of our Fleeces were connected with sheep – there being several other inns on this theme, such as the Ram, Woolstapler's Arms &c.

FLEECE Abington Street.

This is another of those establishments listed in the *RBN 1898* as being mentioned in 16-17th century documents which I have been unable to find. However, the **NRO** does have two documents mentioning a Fleece, one from 1700 and the other 1824, neither of these documents say where the inn(s) are located.

FLEECE (GOLDEN) Bridge Street.

Another inn listed in the *RBN 1898* that I couldn't locate the original, although it is almost certainly the Fleece of later years.

FLEECE 115 Bridge Street.

This inn was on the east side of Bridge Street about 20 yards north of the Malt Shovel. It must have been of some importance as there are plenty of advertisements in the *Northampton Mercury*, the earliest of which I have found dating from July 1720. That this inn

C. KONOW,
Fleece Commercial Hotel,
BRIDGE STREET,
NORTHAMPTON.

Choice Wines & Spirits.
Burton & Home Brewed Ales.
Bottled & Draught Porter.

First Class Loose Boxes for Race Horses and Hunters, Lock-up Coach Houses.
EVERY ACCOMMODATION FOR COMMERCIAL GENTLEMEN.
Five Minutes Walk from either of the Railway Stations.

C. Konow is also Proprietor of the Refreshment Saloons, Cattle Market.

Northampton Directory 1878-9.

was at times known as the Golden Fleece is certain as the Mercury announces the arrival of Joseph Williams at the Fleece: - *Joseph Williams, who kept the Sun and lately the Sun and Raven, in the Bridge street in Northampton, now removed to the Fleece Inn in the said street. N. B. There is good Entertainment for Waggons, with the best of Stabling, and all other Conviences.*

Northampton Mercury 1739.

In October 1744 the paper informs us that Mr. Williams is moving from the Golden Fleece to the Old Goat Inn in Gold Street.

The Fleece was not the top of the range when it came to inns as another advertisement for the inn to be let of 1747 describes it as, *a Carriers' Inn...next to the Meadowes which lead to the countrie*.

The inn's age is unknown, but it could easily pre-date the Great Fire and would have probably been missed by it. By the 19th century and the advent of the railways, drovers and carriers were becoming scarce and the inn became a commercial hotel, serving both the Bridge Street and St. John's Street Stations.

The **Fleece** Cotton End was for 'Lett' advertised in the **Mercury** January 6th 1787.

FLEUR (FLOWER) DE LUCE.

 This is a corruption of *Fleur-de-lys* – iris flower or heraldic lily of the Royal arms of France. It became popular when the arms of France were quartered with those of England. However, there is another explanation, that it is the badge of the Prince of Wales which has a plume of what are believed to be ostrich feathers and in silhouette is about the same shape and became confused with the fleur de lys proper. So can this be another Prince of Wales pub that bore the badge as a sign and in the days of widespread illiteracy got called by the picture rather than the name? See Plume of Feathers for more. We have had two inns with this name, one of considerable antiquity.

FLEUR DE LUCE Location unknown.

There are two documents in the **NRO** that mentions a Fleur de Luce. In both cases the references are in connection with the White Hart (1579) and the Hind (1629). This is the same establishment located to the north of the Market Square so presumably the Fleur de Luce was somewhere around this area. As both documents are before the Great Fire it was probably destroyed and never re-built.

FLOWER DE LUCE 3 Adelaide Street also Duke of Edinburgh and: Royal George.

This was called the Duke of Edinburgh, but only this one entry in *Taylor's* 1858, by 1864 it was briefly called the Royal George and then by 1884 it had acquired its last name. See Duke of Edinburgh.

FLORENCE NIGHTINGALE 1 Devonshire Street.

This pub used to stand at the top of the road behind the Police Box and Public Toilets. The 'area was redeveloped in 1982.

Florence Nightingale was born in Florence in 1820, in 1854 she went to the Crimea to organise the nursing of the war wounded. She received the Order of Merit in 1907 and died in 1910.

The pub first appears as the Florence Nightingale in 1858, there is no sign of an unnamed beer-shop that I can find before this date. By 1858 she had been in the Crimea for four years and was already well known, so at the time this must have been a fitting name for a pub. Perhaps William Warwick, the first recorded proprietor, was a veteran of the Crimea and had seen this lady in action?

FLOWER IN HAND 1 West Street.

This establishment appears to have been directly behind the Princess Royal, which faces onto the Wellingborough Road and is number 176.

I know little about this pub and it seems to have succumbed to the Second World War. I do not have much idea as to the meaning of the name – perhaps it is heraldic?

FLOWING TANKARD 19 St. John's Terrace.

A picture from the *C&E* 01/12/61 shows what is by then a private house. It lay at the back of Albion Place. It seems that in 1961 some local residents remember quoits being played here – but where? *O/S* Plans show that the two houses, numbers 19 and 21 on the 1964 Plan were on earlier Plans a single building and of some size. There doesn't appear to ever have been a yard to speak of so was it played inside? I think the name is self explanatory – designed to raise a thirst!

FLYING HORSE see **Lord Palmerston.**

FORESTERS ARMS.

This name probably refers to the Friendly Society of that name rather than the occupation. Friendly Societies often met in pubs and the landlord was often the treasurer. We have had two Foresters in Town.

FORESTERS ARMS (HOTEL) 25 or 26 Gold Street also **Swan & Helmet, Gladstone's Arms (?)** and **Royal Hotel.**
This is a really confusing address. It appears that originally there was a hotel called the Swan & Helmet at this address; it first appears in the *Universal Directory* of 1791 and is shown as number 67 on *Law's* map of 1847. On the south side of Gold Street, a little way down was a group of properties numbered 23a, 23 and 25; the Swan & Helmet is given all these numbers by different directories. What I think happened is that there was originally an establishment called the Swan & Helmet that occupied all three sites. In 1864 *Taylor's* directory gives the Swan & Helmet the number 23a, and the only entry for the Gladstone's Arms as number 25, but it adds "and Woolmonger Street" to the address. So it seems to have gone right through the block and may have been a tap or vault. It continues as the Swan & Helmet until at least 1866. The Royal Hotel appears in 1869 at number 25 and continues until 1890, once being listed as at number 23a. In 1893 we get the first of two listings of the Foresters' Hotel at number 26 – this, I feel, must be an error. The last entry is in 1900 and the number is 25 and it is now called the Foresters' Arms. Well, I hope that's cleared that up!

FORESTERS' ARMS 226 Wellingborough Road.
This pub stood at the top of Earl Street on the west corner and no doubt was intended to serve the 'new' estate. I can remember as a child seeing the steel cellar flaps in the pavement and being intrigued by the idea of a cellar forgotten under the pavement. The dates are 1864 to 1959.

FOREST OAK 28 Lawrence St., 28 Oak St. (*Wright* 1884).
Wright must be an error, unusual for him, as 28 Lawrence Street is at the Northwest corner of Lawrence and Pine Streets. The earliest entry for this beer-shop is 1864 and *Law's* Map of 1847 shows only the first few houses built at the Barrack Road end. *Slater* 1862 mentions two beer-retailers in this street, at number 12 and the other unnumbered. No earlier directories list any for this street so I conclude that this street was largely built after this date and the pub probably opened in 1863 or 64.

FORGE St. Giles' Street or Market Square?
The authors of *RBN* 1898 said it was in St. Giles' Street means that they saw a different document than I have. This is an extract from the document I have seen: - *Of inns we find the following mentioned, which have ceased to exist. The Greyhound in Gold Street; The Swan in the Drapery; The Talbot in The Square; The Adam & Eve; The Hynde; The Forge.*

*From the **Book of Decree of the Court of Record.**_

There was a Talbot in the Market Square as well as the Hynde, we have no location for the Adam & Eve, but from the context it would seem that both the Adam & Eve and the Forge could have been in the Square.

FORGE HAMMER 47 Alma St., West End or St. James' End.
The addition of West End or St James' End to the address was to save confusion with Alma Street, Far Cotton (later Main Road). Both streets are undoubtedly named after the Battle of Alma in 1854. The pub's name is probably derived from the foundry that once stood on what is now part of the 'bus depot. The pub was at the far end of the street, last house on the north-west side by Palmerston Terrace. Blocks of flats now occupy this whole area.

FORGET ME NOT Bath Street see **Sportsman's Arms.**
FORGET ME NOT Wellingborough Road see **Volunteer.**
FOUNDRY ARMS (TAVERN) St. James' Road see **Foundrymens' Arms.**
FOUNDRYMENS' ARMS.
I have found two of these, one of which is still going in St. James' End, and is now called the Foundry Tavern. In both cases they were at one time in close proximity to a foundry.

FOUNDRYMENS' ARMS Bridge Street, variously, 176, 177 & 179 also **Iron Founders' Arms** (once 1858).
Using the only *O/S* 2500 Plan with street numbers (1965) this pub should be at the bottom of Bridge Street, near the river on the east side. Its location is on the north corner of the junction of Cattle Market Road and Bridge Street, it is still standing with external brown glazed tiles (recently demolished, 2009). The Eagle foundry was by the river on the opposite side of the road.

FOUNDRYMENS' ARMS St. James' Road also **Foundry Arms (Tavern).**

This pub is still on the corner of St. James' Rd. and Stenson St., once called Foundry St. and this name was still visible, painted on the brickwork of the house on the north-east corner in the 1990s. A foundry once stood on part of what was the red 'bus depot.

FOUNTAIN see **Criterion.**

FOX Location unknown.

A document in **NRO** Dated 1632 has: -*All the Messuage or Tenon$^{&}$ afformentioned called or Knowne by ye syne of ye ffoxe formly being two tenn^{s}*...This is all I know of this place and it may have not been an inn, it was probably not rebuilt after the Great Fire of 1675.

FOX & GOOSE Bridge Street.

A fox preaching to geese has been the subject of medieval misericord and pew end carvings and can be found on the oak panelling in Abington Park Museum. This work, circa 1500 shows a fox in a pulpit preaching to four geese; a lower panel shows the fox with a goose in its mouth. This is supposed to illustrate a European folk tale. Another possible origin is Aesop's fables. However I favour the idea that it was originally the Fox and *Geese,* a board game played in the past similar in layout to Nine Men Morris. Like Nine Men Morris, a Fox & Geese board could be scratched anywhere and anything could be pressed into service as gaming pieces, it could indicate that this game was played at this establishment.

I shall quote from an unpublished manuscript, part of a series of articles on signboards that appeared in the *NN&Q* in the 1880s: -*This Publick-House was situate in Bridge-street but on which side or end, and when opened or closed we cannot now say. All the information we have respecting it is in the three following advertisements. The*

Name of which we probably should have never heard of, had it not been for the defalcation of one George Oliver....

There follows three advertisements from the **Northampton Mercury**, the first warns that if George Oliver does not collect his Pad (an easy-paced horse) which he had left at the Black Lion it would be sold to defray expenses. This is dated April 1745 and going on the horse's description it was a pretty worn-out old nag. It seems he availed himself of a better horse for the **Mercury** of March 3rd of the following year carried this: -

WHEREAS George Oliver, on the 27th of December last, hired of Mr. William Clarke, at the Fox and Goose in Bridge-Street, Northampton, a grey Mare of the said Mr. Clarke's to go to Yorkshire, and when he hired her he promised to bring back in a Month or five Weeks at the farthest, but has not brought or sent her back as yet: This is therefore to give Notice to the said Oliver, that unless he brings or sends the said Mare to the said Mr. Clarke in a Fortnight from the publication thereof, the said Mr. Clarke will conclued the said Oliver has rode away with his Mare; and Mr. Clarke then proposes to put fresh Advertisement, with a particular Description of the said Oliver and of said Mare, with a Reward for apprehending and securing them or either of them.

An advertisement did appear, offering half a guinea reward, but not a fortnight later, but on January 4th and 11th of 1747, it doesn't seem that Mr. Clarke ever got his mare back.

FOX & HOUNDS 196 Harborough Road, Kingsthorpe.
The Fox & Hounds is probably an allusion to fox hunting. This pub is still with us. I understand that the pub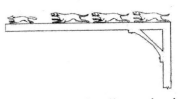
was first licensed in 1863, but the earliest entry in the directories is 1884 when **Wright** recorded, *George Brazier, Bricklayer and bhs.* It is common, especially with rural pubs, as this was at the time, for the landlord to have another occupation.

The **Mercury**, 1794-5 refers to a Fox & Hounds, Harlestone almost certainly the same pub (2017).

FRANKLIN'S GARDENS HOTEL Weedon Road, St. James also **Slipper** and **Melbourne Gardens Tavern.**
Franklin's Gardens were well known to children and adults of earlier years as a pleasure ground popular during weekends and Bank holidays. The Tavern was an integral part of the facilities, but as it faced the main road, it also functioned as a hotel.

The Gardens started life as the Melbourne Gardens in the 1860s, named after Lord Melbourne for much the same reasons as the Melbourne Arms. They were originally started by a Mr. John Collier and after his death were bought by John Campbell Franklin in 1886, who changed the name. Franklin brought in many improvements but after only two years sold it for £17,000. Even though he owned the Gardens for such a short time his name has stuck. The Jubilee Hall was built near the Hotel and in 1909 became a skating rink. This building later became the Salon-de-Danse, Cinderella-Rockerfella's, The Ritzy and Zone night-club – recently it was painted in the Saints Rugby Club colours. The Hotel itself was demolished and rebuilt in the 1930s, in the 1980s it was known as the Slipper and until recently was being used as a training centre by Ritzy's former owners, the Rank Corporation. The Saints owner, Keith Barwell bought both the Ritzy and the Hotel in 1998 and plans are being considered to reopen the Hotel as a bar and club shop. [It is now the Saints' club shop (2009)].

FRANKLIN'S RESTAURANT (HOTEL) 9 Guildhall Road.

This building is opposite the Central Museum and was built by John Campbell Franklin (of Franklin's Gardens fame) as a railway hotel mainly to service the passengers from St. John's Street Station at the bottom of the road. By all accounts it was popular not only with guests but the drinking public as well. It was constructed in the early 1870s and finally closed its doors in November 1954. There are two photographs of this hotel that both appeared in

FRANKLIN'S

HOTEL & RESTAURANT,

(Two Doors from the NEW THEATRE and OPERA HOUSE,)

GUILDHALL ROAD,

NORTHAMPTON.

The above Hotel is replete with every comfort, and comprises large and commodious Private, Commercial, Dining, and Bed Rooms; also Luncheon Bar and Buffet.

Hot Dinners in the Public Dining Room, From 12 to 3, at moderate charges.

Wedding Breakfasts and Ball Suppers by contract.

Plate, Glass, Linen, and every requisite for the table, lent on hire on reasonable terms.

Robert's Directory 1884.

the *Northampton Independent*; one in 1928, when Mr. John Cory took over from the "Misses Bird"; and one when it closed in 1954. The closure was blamed on the lack of parking for the customers. A 1928 photograph shows one car outside the hotel, whilst the 1954 one shows cars nose to tail all along the road. Even sixty years ago the car was dictating the quality of our lives.

FREE BROTHERS' ARMS Mayorhold.

There is only one mention of this place, *Burgess* 1845, under Beer-Sellers, *Jones Mayorhold* – no first name or house number. As no other directories record its existence I conclude that it was not too successful.

FREEHOLD ARMS Arthur St./Terr., Kingsthorpe Hollow.

This pub stood on the north-east corner of Arthur Street and Kingsthorpe Road, opposite the White Lion. First record in the directories is 1884 and the last in 1910, so it may have been a casualty of the First World War.

FREEMENS' (FREEMAN'S) ARMS 40 & 38-40 Bailiff St.

This was a corner beer-shop standing on the south corner of William Street and Bailiff Street – one corner up from the present Vocal Club.

FREEMASONS' ARMS 32 Vernon Street also **Mason's Arms and Dairyman.**

This pub started life as the Dairyman and its first, and only, reference under this name is in *Taylor's* 1858. In the 17th century the sign of the Dairy Maid or Man, Milkmaid or similar was used by cheesemongers.

This area was built up in the 1850s, by 1864 it had changed its name to the Mason's Arms and it is possible that William Threadgold, the landlord at the time, was, or had been a stonemason. After 1878 it became the Freemasons' Arms and stayed thus up to 1936, it's last entry. It doesn't seem likely that a Lodge of Freemasons met here, as it was a small back street beer-shop, the 'Free' was probably added to give a bit of class.

The pub was about halfway down the west side of the street and the *O/S* 2500 Plan 1965 shows a long extension down the garden. *Bennett's* directory 1901 records that it boasted a bagatelle board; the long extension was probably a brewhouse.

FRIAR TUCK 39 Lady's Lane.

Lot 1. ALL that MESSUAGE or Dwelling-House, used as a beer-house, and known as the "Friar Tuck" situate and being No. 39, Lady's-lane, in the town of NORTHAMPTON. Containing parlour, tap-room, scullery, two cellars, two rooms upstairs, used as a club-room, and two bedrooms, together with the warehouse, FRONT SHOP, and entrance to Mount-street, now in the occupation of Mr. Wm. Swann, at a yearly rent of £16.

Northampton Mercury *March 1867.*

FRIENDLY ARMS 96 Scarletwell Street.

Scarletwell Street, or Lane, derives its name from the famous Scarlet Well that was at the bottom of this thoroughfare. The remains of the 1837 superstructure, which resembled an ancient Greek tomb, can still be found if you know where to look. This well was mentioned in a charter of 1239 and was of great importance to the town. The well had some sort of property for dying cloth scarlet. However, the word 'scarlet' in medieval times did not always mean the colour, but a type of expensive cloth. Merchants came from all over England and even the Continent to avail themselves of its properties.

As to the origin of the pub's name I could speculate that it indicated a welcome, but I feel that it is more probable that it refers to a Friendly Society that was run from the premises, a normal thing in the past.

It was a beer-shop and in the earlier directories (1858-1878) is listed under Beer-Retailers. The sign first appears in 1884 and the last entry is in 1936. The pub must have been on the north side of the street and was probably lost when the school expanded.

GARDEN TAVERN Alliston Gardens.

There are only two references to this beer-shop (1906 and 1907). It doesn't seem to have survived for very long and as I have no street number I cannot be sure where it was.

There are two references to a Beer-Retailer, John Goosey or Goodsey in *Steven's* 1893 and 1889 at number 32 and this is shown on the *O/S* Plans as being a more substantial building than its neighbours, this was about in the centre of the north side and could have been the Garden Tavern.

GARDENERS' ARMS.
There have been three Gardeners' Arms in Northampton's past; one of which is still with us. It probably derives from a Friendly Society name.

GARDENERS' ARMS Barrack Road see **Duke of Cambridge.**

GARDENERS' ARMS 1 Bearward Street.
This property was probably right next to the opening that used to be at the end of Alley Yard, one of Northampton's original 'jitties', and just over the road from the Ram. The only landlord we know of is a W. A. Tanner in 1928. This name also occurs in another directory for 1927-8 at the Gardeners, Arms in Wellingborough Road. One of these is either a misprint, or Mr. Tanner owned two pubs with the same name. Entries run from 1927 to 1936, so it probably disappeared during the War.

GARDENERS' ARMS 1 Bouverie Street and 184 Wellingborough Road also **Milkmaid.**
This pub was originally called the Milkmaid and the earliest entry under this name is 1845. The pub is still with us and still called the Gardeners' Arms. Thomas Jeffs, who held it in 1845, was at the Princess Royal, up the road by 1862. The name changed sometime between 1864 and 1884.

The GARIBALDI

GARIBALDI.
Guiseppe Garibaldi (1807-1882), the Italian liberator was the inspiration for this sign and Northampton had five of them. Garibaldi visited England in April 1854 and was received with great enthusiasm by the masses. A nervous government quickly asked him to leave!

Garibaldi visited England in 1854 and died in 1882, so it looks like one, Bailiff Street, was named for his visit and the others after his death.

GARIBALDI 19 Bailiff Street.
There are conflicting accounts of this pubs origin, according to the *Real Ale Guide* 1983 there is a date stone on this building, high on the corner states that this was built in 1849 when it was named after the Italian partisan general Guiseppe Garibaldi. The date stone I've seen has "A.D. *1897*". An article

in the *C&E* 16/06/86 states that in, 1884 a mortgage document recites that *the 3 dwellinghouse 17, 19 and 21 Bailiff street had been through (?) together making one large building trading as a Beerhouse and Grocers shop known by the name of the 'Garibaldi* (sic). *It goes on to say that in 1905 it was known as the "Garibaldi Hotel".*

The first proprietor under the pub's present name was John Brown. I have been able to track this man, as a Beer-Retailer, back to 1852. Between 1845 and 1849 there was a pub called the Black Horse in Bailiff Street for which I have no number, so it is possible that this is a precursor. It certainly seems that sometime after 1884 ('bhs') it upgraded to a 'hotel' (1905). The pub is still going and was refurbished; that is, most of the internal walls were removed, in 1982.

GARIBALDI Guildhall Road and **GARIBALDI** St. Michael's Street?
I have grouped these two together because they both seem very short-lived and I have little information on them.

Guildhall Road has only one entry *Town & County* 1905-6, no proprietor's name and no street number. Likewise St. Michael's Road, one entry *Bennett* 1906, no name or number. They could be errors, or beer-shops that gave themselves a popular name for a while. St. Michael's Street is interesting, being the 14th century name for Wood Street! Did *Bennett* mean Road? I have checked directory street lists and *Goad's* Insurance Plans for both – all to no avail.

GARIBALDI 60 Cow Lane (Swan Street).
This pub stood on the west side of Swan Street two or three doors above the junction with St. John's Street. There are no records traceable before 1884 in the Beer-Retailer lists, but it does appear

sometimes in the lists after this date (up to 1906) indicating the status of the establishment.

GARIBALDI 1 St. Edmund's St. and 130 Wellingborough Rd.

The building still stands on the east corner of the junction with the Wellingborough Road. This pub, along with the Duke of York, St Andrew's Road and the Northampton Flying Club bred homing pigeons as part of the war effort during the Second World War (see Duke of York). It appears that this pub closed during the 1960s, but I do not recall it. I have managed to trace the address through the Beer-Retailers lists back to 1864, so the building probably started life as a pub

GASOMETER 25 & 27 Gas Street.

This pub used to stand at the end of Queen Street one door north of the north corner. I can just remember this pub; it was lost during the construction of St. Peter's Way. Of course, the Gasworks are nearby and a 'gasometer' (correctly called a 'gasholder') once stood by the roundabout, so the origin of the name presents no problem. All our gasholders have now gone (2017).

GATE INN or **THESE GATES HANG WELL** 60 Scarletwell Street, and 1 Crispin Street.

The dual address shows this pub stood on the corner of Scarletwell and Crispin Streets. The name Gate is often given an inn that stood by a tollgate. Although Scarletwell Street is ancient, it is shown on *Speed's Map* 1610 and could have been part of an extra-mural road around the Danish Burgh it is not in a position to ever have been a toll-road. This is probably a case of the landlord liking  the name, perhaps because of the rhyme that goes with it. It is a popular sign; I have references to two others in this County, at Greens Norton and Finedon. The signs all carry similar versions to this motto: -

This Gate hangs well and hinders none,
Refresh and pay, and travel on.

GENERAL TOM THUMB or **TOM THUMB** 101 Bridge St.
This was a small pub at the bottom of the Bridge Street hill, on the east side one door down from the junction of Bridge Street and Victoria Promenade, the corner property being the Grazier's Arms.

Tom Thumb is the tiny hero of an ancient nursery tale, popular since the 16th century. A famous American dwarf, named Stratton, was called General Tom Thumb. I understand that when Stratton was working for Phineas Barnum, the circus impresario, he stayed at the George Hotel at the top of Bridge Street. A fitting name for this pub as the pub itself was a tiny affair.

GEORGE INN (HOTEL) 1 George Row and Bridge Street.
Also **George Hotel Vaults, Bodega Vaults** and **Hole in the Wall.**
This venerable inn stood, until its demolition in 1921, at the top of Bridge Street and George Row on the site of what is now Lloyd's Bank.

The demolished building had been built after the Great Fire of 1675 to replace an earlier George. How far back that George went is unknown. Cosmo III, Grand Duke of Tuscany described it as the "Inn of St. George" when he visited the town in 1669. The *Assembly Order* of 1585 lists it as an "auncient inne" and George Row is obviously named after the inn, always a sign of a long-standing establishment. A clue lies in its name, it is, of course, not named after a king - the first George did not appear until 1714. St. George was the patron saint of the Crusaders and later, England. Is it possible that a soldier returning from the Crusades established an inn in celebration of his safe return, just as Simon de Senlis did when he had St. Sep's Church built? Perhaps it was called thus to honour such men – or to show patriotic support for England? We don't know. St. Sep's church was built circa 1100 and the Order of St. George established by Edward III on April 23rd 1344 – so it is possible that this inn went back as far as one of these two dates.

After the destruction wrought by the Great Fire it was imperative that accommodation was provided for travellers in as short as time as possible this being a Market Town. The owner, John Dryden of Cannons Ashby caused a purpose-designed inn to be immediately constructed on the site. This must have been a good design as a few years later it was being described as: - *the best and most commodious Inn for Noblemen, Gentlemen, & Travellers between London and West-Chester.*

A Brief History of the George Hotel, Northampton.
Henry Brown & Co., Northampton. 1897.

John Dryden died in 1707 and left the George to the Town for charitable purposes, it was used to endow the Blue Coat School.

Daniel Defoe in his travelogue, *A Tour Through the Whole Island of Great Britain* describes Northampton as, *the handsomest and best built town in all this part of England.* But also refers to the George, *The great inn at the George, the corner of the High Street, looks more like a palace than an inn, and cost above 2000l.* (£2000) *building; and so generous was the owner, that, as we were told, when he had it built, he gave it to the poor of the town.* As near as I can ascertain he visited the town in 1724.

Much of the Civil, Social and Political life of the town revolved about this inn, and many famous people stayed here, such as Paganini. In 1844 Queen Victoria and Prince Albert visited the County. The Royal carriage drew up at the George, an address was presented by the Mayor and Corporation, children sang and the horses were changed. From then on the Royal Arms graced the main entrance.

During the Great Election of 1768 three Earls opposed one another in Northampton; Lords Halifax and Northampton (Tory), and Lord Spencer (Whig). Polling went on for fourteen days and everyone was lavish with money. Wine and beer flowed like water and fights broke out continually. Lord Spencer's headquarters were at the George, whilst the Tories holed up at the Red Lyon in Sheep Street – two inns at each end of the Drapery. At one point 100 Whigs were forced to retreat into the George by 200 rioting Tories. Every window in the inn was smashed and Lord Spencer had to go out onto the balcony and promise to distribute £1,000 worth of bread and coal to secure peace. The election was known locally as the 'Spendthrift Election' and it appears to have cost a total of £400,000 – a staggering amount for the time! Lord Spencer spent £100,000 and the other two £150,000 each. It makes modern elections with our Swingometer on

T. V. seem rather tame! There was a similar incident again in 1826 (see Gunning Arms).

Other activities also took place; public auctions, hunt and race balls and the Town and County Justices. At the Restoration in 1649 Charles II in retribution for our Parliamentary support caused our town walls and castle to be 'slighted' – partly demolished: - *His Majesty is content y^t so much of it (the castle) should remaine as is necessary for ye Shelter of ye Justices in ye Bench.* Well, it seems that ye Shelter wasn't good enough and ye Justices often held Court in the George where they also stayed.

Other claims to fame was one of the finest Cock-Pits in the County (later becoming a skating rink) and on January 16th 1730 the first Masonic Lodge in Northampton was formed here, Sir Arthur Hesilrige becoming the first Worshipful Master.

There were several advertisements and announcements in the *Mercury* during the 18th century. In July 1732 John Stoughton from the Swan in Kettering announced that the *new repair'd* George had been taken by himself. In April 1739 it was *To be LET* and in November of the same year John Page announced his taking the inn. Once more in January 1759 it was *To be LETT – in present occupation of John Page to be entered upon Midsummer 1759.*

By the turn of the 18th century the structure was beginning to deteriorate and some rebuilding took place in the early 1800s. The trustees applied to Parliament for permission to sell it. In this they succeeded in 1806, selling it to a Tontine for £1,500. Ninety 'lives' were nominated at £50 each by 54 subscribers, raising £4,500 – the surplus was needed to upgrade the hotel. A Tontine was an early kind of life insurance; 'lives' would be sold to raise the finance and the number of 'survivors' nominated, in this case, five. When there were only that number of survivors left, the enterprise would be wound up and sold off, the proceeds being distributed amongst them. The George was sold in 1919 for £20,000 and I understand the buyers intended to build one of those new-fangled 'Kinemas' on the site. In this they were thwarted by the Corporation and in 1921 it was pulled down and Lloyd's Bank built.

George Hotel Vaults, Bodega Vaults and **The Hole in the Wall.** All refer to the same place, the vault or tap bar of the hotel.

The term vault implies the availability of wine, derived from wine vault. The first name is therefore self-explanatory. A Bodega is a cellar or shop selling wine, from the Spanish meaning 'apothecary'. So, some sort of wine-bar in Bridge Street - the first of so many?

The entrance to this place was on the Bridge Street side, right at the top, almost on the corner. Imagine my surprise several years ago when cash points were still a novelty and I was with some friends standing at the top of Bridge Street outside Michael Jones opposite the bank and one of the party said, "Hang on, I'm just going to the Hole in the Wall." Of course, what he did was cross the road to Lloyd's bank cash point, almost in the exact spot where the door to the Hole in the Wall bar must have been. This was the first time I had heard the expression.

GEORGE & DRAGON 61 St. George's Street.

It is easy to see why this pub got its name, however on the *N.B.C.* Plans it is labelled "Green Dragon" – this name occurs to my knowledge nowhere else. It is shown clearly as a larger building on the *O/S* 2500 Plans, on the south side of the street, about halfway between Arundel Street and Patrick Street. This building must have been demolished prior to the NDC Archaeological Unit excavation in the early 1970s.

A popular image of George and the Dragon is that found on the obverse of the gold sovereign. It is said that this sign did not become popular until it was used as the insignia of the 'Garter', but I don't think this pub goes back that far.

GLADSTONE'S ARMS see Forester's Arms.

GLAZIER'S ARMS see Grazier's Arms.

GLOBE.

There have been five pubs called the Globe at times in this town. All seem to have flourished in the last half of the 19th century. The meaning of this sign is often given that it is a symbol of Portugal and informed the public that Portuguese wines were available. However, all these pubs are in locations (except Bridge Street) that indicate beer-shops and/or show other evidence of being so. As beer-shops didn't sell wine it seems that this sign implied that the 'whole world' drank here.

GLOBE 141 Bridge Street.

This pub appears to have been on the east side of the lower part of Bridge Street, about halfway between the Malt Shovel and Navigation Row. The buildings in the area are small and this establishment gets more mentions as a Beer-Retailer than under its own sign. Dates from 1845 to 1893.

GLOBE 25 Castle Street also **Star?**

The address given in the one entry that has one (1864) is the same for the Star; however, in 1864 there is no mention of the Star. In 1901 and 1904 *Bennett* records both names as being in Castle Street, but gives no numbers or publicans' names. As five other directories record the Star as being at number 25 between 1884 and 1907 I conclude that the premises may have been taken over sometime between 1864 and 1884 and the name changed. From studying the Plans of the period (*Law* 1847, *O/S* 1901 &c.) it seems that many changes took place with the buildings over this period, so it is possible that the street numbers also changed and the number is a coincidence – I do not think this is likely. Julian Roelands, the only name associated with this pub, first appears in *Melville* 1861 as, *Currier & B/R 29 Up. Mount st.*, in *Slater* 1862 he is a Beer-Retailer at number 25 Castle Street. The Globe is then not recorded for 37 years, so I think the second appearance of this name in Castle Street (1901 and 1904) is a resurrection, unfortunately thanks to *Bennett's* brevity we have no publican's name to work with.

GLOBE 14 College Street.

This was next door to the Boot. Dates are, 1864 and 1933.

GLOBE 10 Kettering Rd. & St. Edmund's Row also **Fig Tree.**

The reason for linking these two pubs is the carry through of William Powell. Working from *O/S* 2500 1964 Plan I calculate that number 10 would have been on the south side of the Kettering Road where the Garden of Rest is now. A row of houses shown here on *O/S* 1901 includes a larger one where number 10 would have been. *Burgess* 1845 gives the address as St. Edmund's Row, an old name for the

very start of the Kettering Road. It is shown as a "PH" on *Goad's Insurance* Plan of 1899. William Powell is recorded as being at the Fig Tree in 1845 and 1852 and at the Globe in 1858.
GLOBE see **Clicker's Arms.**

GOAT Gold Street also **Bull & Goat.**

Three goats' heads between a chevron is the arms of the Worshipful Company of Cordwainers and is considered to be one of the explanations of the Goat & Compass pub sign. A white goat is part of the arms of Russell, Earls and Dukes of Bedford. The Bull and Goat may refer to some ancient story or may be from someone's name – or it could represent the amalgamation of two inns. Whatever the truth is it was of considerable antiquity and at least in its latter years, of some importance.

The earliest document dates from 1635, so it predates the Great Fire of 1675 in which it was almost certainly destroyed. It may have come to prominence if it had been swiftly built after the Fire when accommodation was in great demand. It was important all through the 18th century, mentioned in the 17th century, but not listed as an Ancient Inn in the *Assembly Order*. The Bull & Goat was 'taken and entered in ...by Stephen Gauden' on March 3rd 1783 (**Mercury**) later advertised for let in the *Northampton Mercury* in April 1739 and this is probably the same inn.

Law's Map of 1847 numbers it 65. I have references to an entrance in St. Katherine's Street that runs parallel to the north side of Gold Street and *Law's* Map clearly shows a building with a large yard, surrounded by outbuildings and with a wide entrance. The original frontage onto Gold Street was taken down and shops built at the front, whilst the rear yard became a Coach Manufactory.

Near the end of 1885 some correspondence was instigated in the *Northampton Mercury* by the discovery of a lead plate near the bottom of Wood Street. On this plate was the inscription *Ye Goat Inn, 1681. TM*. According to one contributor there are deeds that are written in, Old English style, and date as far back as the sixteenth century. Advertisements in the 18th century from the *Northampton*

Mercury are mainly concerning the letting of the inn, or coaches – for it was a coaching inn. We are informed that Joseph Williams had taken the Old Goat Inn in 1744 and a will of 1731 refers to the place as the Bull & Goat. A will of Joseph Daniel 1757 has: - *known by the name or Sign of the Old Goat situate and being within the parish of All Saints in said Town of Northampton on the north side of a certain street there called the Gold street....*

According to the *Northampton Independent* of April 12th 1957 the yard was still there. An arch with a carved stone goat head and an inscription Site of old Goat Inn had also survived. We did have on the eastern side of what was Brierley's store a small plate that said, *"SITE OF THE GOAT INN DEMOLISHED CIRCA 1860."*

GOLDEN BALL 13 Market-Hill (Square).
The Golden Ball is mentioned as a sign in *NN&Q* 1889 and the author quotes an advertisement from the *Northampton Mercury* of March 17th 1739 when one Jos. Satchwell offered paperhangings for sale by the square yard. The author then quotes from another advertisement of "seventeen years later": - Whereas Joseph Satchwell, at the Golden Ball on the Market-Hill in Northampton, finds *his keeping a Publick-House has been detrimental to his other Business; begs leave to acquaint His Friends, that he has now laid down the Publick Business, and only carries on his private-Trade, as before: where all Persons will be kindly used, and their Favours gratefully acknowledg'd by Their humble Servants, Joseph and Eliz. Satchwell. N. B. I carry on the Millinery Business, with Mounting of Fans, and Furnishing Funerals; and take in Boarders, &c. as usual.*

The Golden Ball was an old sign for a silk mercer so would have been appropriate for Joseph's main business. A later note in *NN&Q* states that *the sign of the Golden Ball was where Messers. Howes, Percival & Ellen's offices now are.* *Steven's* 1889 gives the number 13.

GOLDEN CROSS St. Martin's Street.
One of those listed in the *RBN 1898* of which I can find no trace. St. Martin's Street ran along the line of the present Broad Street and was named after St.

Martin's Chapel that became a ruin as early as 1254. The exact location of this chapel and the Golden Cross are unknown.

After the capture of Jerusalem in 1099 the arms adopted by the Crusader Kings of Jerusalem were five gold crosses on a silver shield, a cross-potent between four Greek crosses.

GOLDEN FLEECE see **Fleece.**

GOLDEN HIND see **Hind.**

GOLDEN HORSE.

The Golden Horse is probably heraldic, but as both pubs that have borne this name are linked the theory below could be right.

GOLDEN HORSE 138 Bridge Street.

This pub was near the brewery on the west side of Bridge Street and seems to have had good trade with the boats off the River Nenn. I believe it was eventually swallowed up by brewery extensions. As to the name, the Black Horse was only five doors away, so perhaps this sign, or the Black Horse's is an example of rivalry? Vol. 123 1843-4 mentions this pub (2017).

GOLDEN HORSE 59 Southampton Road.

This pub was built to cater to the new residents moving into Far Cotton at the time and the licence for the original Golden Horse was transferred – along with the landlord. Until a few years ago there were five pubs in this area, three were swallowed up in the Main Road Industrial  Estate and the fourth, the Clinton Arms, a victim of the Motor Car (road widening).

GOLDEN LION.

Like the Golden Horse this could be heraldic. There were probably three pubs with this sign. The oldest is from the *RBN* 1889, I have no location, nor have the documents been found. Taylor's unpublished material refers to a Golden Lion in Bridge Street and this could have been it, or another one. The surviving Golden Lion, in Castle Street cannot be the 16th-18th century one from the *RBN* 1898 as Castle Hill, is clearly shown as undeveloped on all the early maps of the town. **GOLDEN LION (two?)** Both, Location Unknown (see above).

GOLDEN LION 49-51 Castle Street.
Law's Map 1847 seems to show the original premises and the *O/S* 2500 Plan 1901 shows something similar, by the 1938 *O/S* Plan the whole site had been cleared and only two buildings are shown, the pub and the

hall. The pub no longer exists and the site id flats (2017).

GOLDSMITH'S ARMS Drapery.
The only directory to list this pub is *Pigot's* 1824 who is the first compiler to list more than just coaching inns. *Pigot's* 1830 does not list it so presumably it had ceased to trade. Unpublished material from *NN&Q* says that the Goldsmith's Arms was given up 63 years ago i.e. circa 1830. The **Mercury** vol. 54 1763-4 refers to this pub (2017).

GOOD INTENT.
This name could be from a Friendly Society or a Lodge. A schooner of this name was smuggling around the 1830s and a stagecoach from Kent also bore this name.
GOOD INTENT 38 Cloutsham Street.
There is only one entry under this name, but the landlord's name appears in other directories under Beer-Retailers (1885-1900). Shown as an ordinary terraced house on the *O/S* Plans.
GOOD INTENT 40 West Street.
West Street is part of Thomas Grundy's 'New Town', built between 1836 and the 1850s. This pub was on the west side halfway down and had a side alley. This whole area went in the Bouverie Street Clearance of the 1970s.

It must have been a jolly place at times, judging from an advertisement in the *Northampton Daily Reporter* 6th October 1897: -

GOOD INTENT, West Street. Proprietor J. Knightly.
Saturday Night Concerts commence next Saturday, Oct. 9ᵗʰ.
Chairman Mr. G. Marlow.
Phipps & Co's Sparkling Ales & Stouts. & Choice Cigars.

GRANBY ARMS 77 Vernon Street/Stockley Street also **Marquis of Granby.**
John Manners, Marquis of Granby (1721-1770) was a brilliant soldier, during the Seven Years War he was colonel of the Blues and very popular with the troops. There are signs all over the country due to the Marquis having set up many of his wounded senior non-commissioned officers in their own inns. This could be the reason that when he died at the age of 49 he left debts of £37,000! This pub may be an example of the name taking someone's fancy as this part of Northampton wasn't built up until at least a century after the Marquis died.

This was a typical 19ᵗʰ century street corner pub. In the early 1970s my wife and I purchased our first house, almost opposite – so it became our local.

It had its regulars and in fact, it had little more and needed no more as I cannot recall it ever being empty. It was a small place and started life in the 19ᵗʰ century as a beer-shop (1884 "bhs"). It has all the characteristics (and characters!) associated with the old 'Home from Home' local. The atmosphere, especially on a cold night, was warm and welcoming and although it sold Watney's beer, at that age I knew no better. There were seats that were 'somebody's' – and although no one minded you sitting in them, when 'somebody' came in you were expected to give them up. Every night there were the same faces and all the local gossip was aired.

We had draconian licensing laws in those days, so on Sundays (Noon-2am.) we would take a jug with us and get it filled just before closing time, to return home having had a couple of hours in the Granby while the Sunday joint was cooking over the road – Happy Days! After a couple of years or so we were compulsorily purchased, the area flattened, and redeveloped.

It may appear that I have eulogised excessively over a small back street pub, but this pub was in my personal sphere of experience and I am well aware that all over Northampton - indeed all over England there were thousands of such pubs like this one, pubs that sold most of their beer to perhaps 30 to 50 families within a couple of streets of the place. They were the backbone of English pubs and drinking and sadly, at least in the south, largely gone forever, as have the communities that used them.

GRANDVILLE ARMS 32-34 Grove Road.
This pub is still with us, but not as a pub. The earliest entry is 1884 and it closed in November 1959, in March of the next year the RAFA Club moved from their old premises in the Wellingborough Road (the former Engineer pub) into the former Granville Arms. They left here in October 2011 and closed citing the main reason being the ban on smoking, however they now appear to be at the Kingsley Park W.M.C. Their old neon sign can be seen at the Old Bakehouse Antiques, Abington Avenue (2017).

GRAFTON ARMS see **King William the Fourth.**

GRAZIERS' ARMS 99 Bridge Street and **Glaziers' Arms** (1893, error).
This pub stood on the south east corner of the junction between Bridge Street and Victoria Promenade. A sign from this pub is displayed in the bar of the Malt Shovel.

GREEN DRAGON.
We have had two of these - one is a contraction of the George & Dragon in St. George's Street, the other one is much older. One of the supporters of Queen Elizabeth the First's Arms was a red dragon and considering her popularity and interest in inns one would expect more red than green dragons, but this is not so. When an innkeeper wanted to honour 'Good Queen Bess' it was either the Queen's head or the Queen's Arms that were displayed. The Green Dragon on the Mayorhold was almost certainly there before the reign of Queen Elizabeth I (1558-1603). The one in St. George's Street is a contraction of George & Dragon and would have been called the Green Dragon because that is what was on the sign, interestingly the

George in George Row seems to have contracted from the other end and lost the Dragon instead of George.

GREEN DRAGON St. George's Street see **George & Dragon.**

GREEN DRAGON Mayorhold and 54 Bearward Street.

This inn stood at the end of Bearward Street facing onto the ancient Mayorhold which has been sacrificed to the car and is now merely a road junction and traffic lights.

In the Middle Ages this was an important part of town and the Guildhall or Town hall stood opposite the Green Dragon at the end of Scarletwell Street. This is probably why it was called the Mayorhold (see Crispin Arms).

In 1970 the NDC Archaeological Unit excavated the site of this pub and found the remains of a fine medieval house. A few weeks after the end of the excavation we were called back. A hole had been dug in the road in front of the pub site to cut off some of the services and the workmen had broken through into a barrel-vaulted stone cellar. This proved to be circa 18th century and part of the pub. This was one of the "Ancuient Innes" in the *Assembly Order* of 1585; it was demolished in August 1970. It most certainly was not part of the fabled 'monk's passages'!

GREEN MAN 52 St. James' Road also **Thomas A Becket.**

This pub stands on the bend of the road a few hundred yards past West Bridge and once next door stood the Harborough Arms, which was demolished for road widening.

There are records of a Green Man in St. James as far back as the 17th century and considering its position it had probably been a coaching inn. The present building is not old.

In 1970 Mick McManus took over the pub and changed the name to the Thomas A Becket. I do not usually approve of name changes; however there are two good reasons for this one. Firstly there are the connections between Thomas Becket and the town; the barons attempted to try him at Northampton Castle, just across the river from the pub, and it was from here that he fled to the continent in 1164. The second reason is not so obvious. Many years ago a friend, now sadly passed on, was working as a commercial artist for Watney-Mann painting pub signs. He was commissioned to produce a Green Man for a village pub. Apart from being an artist Tom was also a Witch and knew full well what a Green Man was. He produced a sign showing a shaman type character, dressed in greenery and performing some sort of fertility dance. I never saw the sign, but I gather it was pretty explicit. The sign was hung and everything was fine until the so-called architectural staff from headquarters in Mortlake came to view the improvements. Tom told me this "young squirt in his 20s and a bad suit" tried to tell him that the Green Man is always Robin Hood in Lincoln Green. The sign was taken down and Tom, under protest, but knowing where his bread was coming from, painted another. The landlord kept the original because he, and most of the village, liked it! The locals got up a petition that was even signed by the vicar, but all to no avail and the sign was never replaced. Tom later painted one for this pub – *not* a Robin Hood, but a Medieval Jack-in-the-Green, a sort of Morris Dancer type holding two torches.

In prehistoric times the Green Man was the sacrifice or Divine Victim made to maintain the fertility of the soil. The film *The Wicker Man* is a modern (and unlikely!) version of the idea. In some cultures this sacrifice was also the king who ruled for only a set number of years before being killed. The anthropologist, Margaret Murray in her book *The God of the Witches* suggests that Thomas

Becket substituted himself for King Henry II as this sacrifice. Therefore Thomas Becket could be seen as the Green Man!

GREEN MOUNT St. Edmund's Road.
This is one of those listed in the *RBN* 1898 of which I can find no trace. Like many towns in the Middle Ages Northampton expanded outside its walls, forming suburbs along the roads leading to its gates. It must have been somewhere along the Wellingborough Road, near Abington Square.

GREEN TREE.
We have had two Green Trees. What the sign means I have been unable to discover, it could be a symbol of fecundity, or heraldic.

GREEN TREE 26 The Green (1864 & 84), 56 Green St. (1907-56).
Probably chosen because of the address. The earliest entry is 1858 and *Wright's* 1884 gives 'bhs', a beer-house, the last entry is 1956.

GREEN TREE Malt Row (Market Square).
Malt Row is the old name for the east side of the Market Square. In a Charter of Sale 1456 some of the properties are described. The Peacock in Malt Row (where Peacock Place is now) had to the north a pub called the Cat and next above the Green Tree. There is a Green Tree in the lists from *RBN* 1898 without a location and this is probably it. This pub along with the Cat probably perished in the Great Fire 1675 and unlike the Peacock, were never rebuilt.

The Rental of 1504 referred to elsewhere also lists this inn: - There was a tenement called *'le Grenetree'* near the Friars Minor. The Friars Minor are otherwise known as the Greyfriars and their Friary occupied the land to the east of the Market confirming the location of *le Grenetree*.

GREYHOUND.
The Greyhound was one of the badges of the Tudor kings and appeared on the arms of both Henry VII and VIII. Until the end of the  18th century a silver greyhound was worn on the sleeve of the king's messengers and still is the sign of a British Diplomatic Messenger. This goes back to King Charles who broke a number of silver

greyhounds off a piece of tableware and gave them to trusted men as signs of recognition when they acted as his messengers. We have five of these pubs and it is possible that some of the later ones were simply named because the landlord liked greyhound racing, or the breed of dog.

GREYHOUND Woolmonger Street.

The only reference is from the *RBN* 1898 where it is listed as one of the 16th or 17th century inns, but see below, Greyhound, Gold Street, did this pub go right through the block?

GREYHOUND 14 Gas Street.

There is a junction between Gas Street and Woolmonger Street, but if the numbering in the 19th century is the same as the *O/S* 1964 this pub must have been on the opposite (west) side of the road, probably under the large traffic-island. The first proprietor listed is a Mrs. Mary Norris in 1864. The next entry, the Greyhound in Market Street has for its first proprietor, listed in 1858 a Thomas Norris – there must be a connection. The last entry I have for this pub is 1907.

GREYHOUND 104-106 Market Street.

This pub was at the Kettering Road end on the north east side next to a factory.

GREYHOUND Alma Street, Far Cotton.

One entry, *Taylor's* 1864, George Smith. This was probably just a small beer-shop. There is some confusion, however, *Melville* 1861 has G. Smith at the Rose & Crown, Alma Street and he is recorded as being a Beer-Retailer in 1862 and 1869. *Taylor's* 1864 has George Smith at the Greyhound and an Edward Seal at the Rose & Crown, so they are not the same pub.

GREYHOUND Gold Street.

Referred to in the *Great Fire Court 1675* 22/06/1676. Presumably destroyed in the Great Fire and not rebuilt, at least under this name.

GRIFFIN Gold Street.

One of those in the *RBN* 1898 list which is now lost to us.

GUNNINGS ARMS 71 Bridge Street.
The Gunnings Arms stood three doors below the church of St. John at the bottom of the hill according to the *O/S* 1964 numeration.

The Gunnings were local aristocracy from Little Horton who seem to have loomed large in local politics on the side of the Tories over the last two centuries. In 1826 there was a scandal concerning Sir Robert Gunning when the Corporation voted £1,000 out of Borough funds for his election expenses to try to make both Borough seats Tory.

They failed, the result of the poll was; Sir George Robertson, Bart. 1,348 (Whig), Major Maberly 1,137 (Tory) and Sir R. H. Gunning, Bart. 1,005 (Tory) - Robertson and Maberly were elected.

This is from the *Northampton Daily Reporter*, March 23rd 1904, which is a quote from the *Northampton Mercury*, June 17th 1826: -
This town has been in a feverish state of excitement during the whole of the present week. Several outrages have been committed, but last night a scene of tumult and confusion prevailed before the George inn which has not been equalled during the election. As one of the friends of Sir Rob. Gunning was addressing his electors after the polling, a party of his opponents' friends were excited by some persons, who immediately commenced breaking the windows of the inn by throwing pebbles, the destruction of which would have been much greater had not Lord Althorpe promptly presented himself at the balcony. His Lordship requested them to desist from these measures as by such conduct they were injuring the cause of Reform. There were a considerable number of panes broken; and we understand that some persons were struck by the pebbles, though we believe that no one was seriously injured.

GUY OF WARWICK (South Gate) also **Crown & Anchor** (178 & 180 Bridge Street).
This inn must have been of some age as it is mentioned in the *RBN* 1898 as one of the 16th and 17th century inns; however, I have not seen any documents this old. The author of *Glimpses of Old Northampton: Its Signs NN&Q* 1889 says it was known under that name at least 160 years ago. There are advertisements and articles in the *Northampton Mercury* going back at least to the 1720s. A

marriage settlement of 1772 gives us some clues and confirms what the author of the above article said, that it became the Crown & Anchor. One interesting part of this settlement may, if it is not an error, give us a clue as to why it was called the Guy of Warwick: - *near to the South Bridge and High River there formerly in the several Occupations of Guy Warwick* (!) *and Joseph Brooks.* Perhaps the originator of this sign was actually called Guy Warwick or the clerk got it wrong. Guy of Warwick was supposed to have been a valiant Saxon Earl and many stories were written about him in the 17th and 18th centuries – so he would have been a good subject of a sign about that time (see the Bearward Arms for more on this hero).

The marriage settlement mentions several messuages or tenements either as property in the settlement or adjacent properties used to define the former. There are also pencilled additions written above the main script. I have no date for these but one above the properties which are marked as one building on *Law's* Map 1847 (number 84, Crown & Anchor) has, *called the Crown & Anchor* – the rest of the definition gives to the north a certain messuage or tenement which according to the pencilled additions is, now an alehouse occupied by Amy Dray (or Jay – unclear). To date I do not have any more information about this alehouse and it may end up being unnamed forever (see entry-under 'X').

HALF MOON.

The Half-Moon is probably the heraldic Crescent. It seems that this symbol has connections with the crusades and the Knights Templar, probably derived from the Saracens. Possibly some of these signs have the same sort of meaning as the Saracen's Head, it would be a lot easier to paint a crescent than a portrait of a Saracen.

Properly a crescent moon should always be shown in the form of a reversed letter 'C' – the new or waxing moon. Like a 'C' is the waning moon, considered unlucky. Interestingly in heraldry there are three forms of the crescent that exemplify this idea.

DECRESCENT   CRESCENT   INCRESCENT

The Moon's crescent is often shown in medieval paintings of the Blessed Virgin Mary at her feet with its points upwards. This is also true for many Tarot cards where the High Priestess or Lady Pope is shown in the same pose, often with a triple crown illustrating the triple nature of the Moon. This indicates the link between the BVM, the High Priestess and the ancient triple Moon Goddess of Selene, Diana and Hecate.

After the Reformation 'Popish' signs were not welcome and as the sign of the Annunciation lost the BMV and became the Angel so this sign may have lost the Virgin and retained the Crescent.

HALF MOON 163 Bridge Street.

Plans from the turn of the 19th century show this inn to be on the east side of Bridge Street just below Navigation Row. In the past there were public baths on Cattle Market Road that more or less backed onto this inn; they were heated by the waste heat from the brewery opposite.

The compilers of *RBN* 1898 saw a 16th or 17th century document of this establishment, which described it as between south gate and bridge. The earliest record I have found is 1816.

HALF MOON Gold Street.

TO BE SOLD by Auction

...Messuage or Tenement...in Gold Street...well accustomed Publick-House, Known by the Name or Sign of the Half Moon.
Advertisement in the **Mercury** April 5th 1762.
Also 'to be let or sold...enquire of Mr Wm. Gibson.' **Mercury** March 21 1774.

HALF MOON (HALFE MOONE) Sheepe Streete.

Mentioned in the *Great Fire Court 1675* (27/03/1677). I have found no other references to this establishment and must conclude that it perished in the Great Fire and was never rebuilt.

HALF-WAY HOUSE 48 Kingsthorpe Rd. 1864- Brampton Rd. 1878 -Kingsthorpe Hollow 1884 -Harborough Rd. 1906 & 82 Kingsthorpe Rd.

I thought I would include these alternate addresses on this occasion to illustrate how not only numbers, but also road names change over time, especially out in the countryside.

" Albert Recreation Grounds,"

" HALF-WAY HOUSE,"

KINGSTHORPE ROAD,

NORTHAMPTON.

Aptly called the Half-Way House as it is in Kingsthorpe Hollow, half way to Kingsthorpe and half way up a hill. The earliest date in a directory is 1864, but I am sure this pub goes back further than that although the building doesn't. In the 19th century it would have been standing isolated in the fields between the town and Kingsthorpe village.

R. C. TOOBY, *Proprietor.*

Choice Wines & Spirits,

GOOD COACH HOUSE & STABLING,

ORNAMENTAL LAKE

Running, Bicycle, & Quoit Grounds (Open Daily.)

N.B.--Tents Let on Hire, Good Grass Keep for Cattle.

Northampton Directory 1878-9.

The present site is much smaller than it was, as can be seen from the advertisement from the *Northampton Directory* of 1878-9, referring to the Albert Recreation Grounds. The grass for cattle was probably for farmers taking their beasts to Northampton Market the next day.

It seems to have run something along the same lines as Franklin's Gardens in St. James. In this period running, cycling and quoits were popular. Northamptonshire was famous for its skilled quoits teams – where are they now? The proprietor, R. C. Tooby had his fingers in several pies as can be seen from his advertisement which also boasted *Choice Wines & Spirits.* **Wright** 1884 lists the proprietor, Charles John Smith, as a 'v' proving the business was substantial and another advertisement in **Stevens** 1889 placed by the then proprietor, W. Arnold, said they catered for parties all the year round and that he was a Coal and Coke Merchant-Wharf, Castle Station.

In earlier times it appears to have been smaller, and it was probably Mr. Tooby who enlarged it. The first proprietor in the directories is a John Craddock in 1864, but in the *Northampton Mercury* July 1868 is an announcement of a sale by auction R E Craddock, a Bankrupt and describes the property as: - *containing a front shop, with plate glass window: parlour, tap room, kitchen, two bedrooms, large cellarage, brewhouse and out buildings, now in the possession of Charles Craddock.*

The pub has now been demolished (2010).

HARBOROUGH ARMS 46 St. James' Road.

This pub stood on the corner of St. James' Mill Road, next to the Green Man. In the past both pubs were smaller, *O/S* 1901 shows two houses between them, by *O/S* 1938 the two pubs stood side-by-side. This pub was lost when the road was widened circa 1965. According to the *Northampton Independent* of 30/01/1914 the landlord was a Mr. John Page who had a Yorkshire terrier called Trixie who would beg coppers off customers, carry them in its mouth and drop them into a collecting box for the Crippled Children's' Fund. At the time of writing it Trixie had collected 13s..1$^3/_4$d. (about 65$^1/_2$p).

There are no records of this pub before 1884, even as a beer-shop. *Wright* 1884 has in the main text of his directory *Fdk. Skipp bhs* and in the appendix *John Shaw v* indicating not only a change of landlord in that year, but a change in status.

HARBOUR LIGHTS 1 Gas Street also **Brewer's Arms**.

I don't know why this pub was called the Harbour Lights, we being so far from the sea. It could have been a popular song of the time or simply that the harbour lights are a very welcome sight after a time at sea. It started its life as a Beer-Retailers as  early as 1858, but the name doesn't appear until about 1900. In the 1980s it changed its name to the Brewer's Arms and has since gone through several reincarnations and names. By 2010 it was called the Touch of Heaven and I don't think it could be called a pub anymore.

HARDING STREET TAVERN 44 Upper Harding Street.

This pub stood on the east side of Upper Harding Street, just below the junction with Upper Priory Street, next to the Lord Raglan Inn. In the past the only way a woman could hold a licence was if she was widowed, but this rule was set aside in 1914. William Smith promised the pub to his brother-in-law, Bert Oakenfull, but Bert had been called up into the army. The Magistrates decided that it was a special case and granted the licence to his wife, Ellen Ada on condition she relinquished it to her husband on his return. Ellen ran the pub from September 1914 until April 1919 when it was taken over by an Ethelbert Oakenfull, so it looks like he came back from the Great War. The next entry with a name has John Oakenfull - their son? The last entry is for 1971.

HARE & HOUNDS.

This name is an allusion to the dubious 'sport' of hare coursing. The Hare & Hounds in Duston could have such connections, but the one in Lady's Lane, in the heart of Northampton must been an attempt to give a 'countrified' atmosphere to the pub.

HARE & HOUNDS Harlestone Road, New Duston.

This building is Listed and the description says it is an early 19th century alteration to an 18th century house. The earliest mention in the directories is 1884, it is now a private house, and the last entry was in 1956.

HARE & HOUNDS 1 Lady's Lane and 46-8 Newland.

This pub was quarried away to make way for the Grosvenor Centre. This is one of two pubs that I know of that changed corners. The Criterion did it diagonally, whilst this one simply moved across the end of Lady's Lane. The original pub was on the north corner of Lady's Lane and Newland and is shown as such on both *O/S* 1910 and 1938. The *O/S* 1938 also shows a cleared area on the opposite corner, so the move must have taken place sometime after the 1938 survey. When I was a lad and drank in this establishment the original pub building still stood on the opposite corner and functioned as a guesthouse, it was smaller than the 'new' pub so expansion may have been the motive for the move.

HARP.

The sign of the Harp could be religious, but by the beginning of the 18th century it was the sign of a bird fancier – why I have no idea. It can indicate an Irish connection. We have had at least four Harps in town.

HARP 26 Bailiff Street.

There is only one entry for the pub under its name, in *Wright* 1884, but it also appears as a Beer-Retailers in 1885. The pub seems to have been short lived and was on the east side of the street one door south of the corner with Thomas Street. It is now part of the Vocal Club.

HARP Castle Street.

According to *NN&Q* 1889 the Windmill, Market Square was changed to the Queen's Arms on the accession of Queen Victoria and was at the time kept by a Christopher Gibson, a musician who formerly kept the Harp in Castle Street. In view of his profession the sign is an appropriate one.

HARP Gold Street.

A lease, of 1568 from **NRO** refers to a *Harpe in Golde street.*

HARP Kingswell Street.

There is listed in the *RBN* 1898 a Harp as being mentioned in a deed that I have not seen. There is also one mentioned in the *Assembly Order* of 1585 and another from a will 1493 quoted in *A History of the Church of All Saints, Northampton* by Rev. R. M. Serjeantson. In 1493, November 15th, Simon Rowland of Northampton leaves his body to be buried: - *in the churche yard of the Paryssh chyrche of all Hallowes in Nort: nyghe to the great oke growing there.* The will is witnessed by *Master John Cokks, clerk, and Robert Myddleham, Doctor and Vycar of All Hallowes, and John Marshall, at the signe of the Harpe.*

HART OR HIND Market Square.
According to *NN&Q* 1889 this establishment was called the Hynde before the Great Fire and continued in business, the author believes, until the close of the "last century", i.e. 1799. It is listed in the *Assembly Order* of 1585 as an Ancient Inn and there is a reference to *le hart* in Cornmonger's Row in 1504. This pub was advertised in the *Northampton Mercury To be LETT on July 3rd 1749* and the 24th July announced that James York from the Cross Keys had taken the inn.

It was a large establishment, the Corn Exchange, later the Odeon Cinema and now a 'Rock Café' have occupied the site. The Hart or Hind was one of our more important inns in its time. In the 18th century it functioned as a coaching inn, and swordfights, wrestling matches and plays were all performed here, so some of the rooms must have been quite large. Being on the Market Square also meant that it probably used the larger rooms as market rooms and no doubt catered to the market visitors by providing ordinaries.

HEADLANDS Longland Road.
It has amused me that the sign of this pub shows a headland or promontory above the sea. The district and road after which this pub is named is so called because of the headlands left by the plough turning at the end of a *furrowlong* – it has nothing to do with the sea. The sign was probably ordered and painted by someone who had never been to Northampton, or had no idea where the sign was to end up. The *C&E* 13/02/59 announced the transfer of the licence of the Crown & Anchor, Bridge Street to a site at the junction of Headlands and Longland Road. The pub, it seems, didn't open until 1968.

HELMET see **Sallet.**

HEN & CHICKENS.
We seem to have had two of these in the past so it must have been a fairly common sign as I find references to it elsewhere in the country. In the 17th century it referred to the constellation of the Pleiades and in the 19th century to a children's' game. 'Chickens and

Hens' were also slang terms for small and large pewter pots. The Abington Street pub seems to have been of some antiquity and in Christian art the Hen and Chickens are a symbol of G-D's care, so this may indicate a pre-Reformation date for the pub. The pre-decimal Irish penny used to feature a hen with her chicks. Both humans and chickens have a fondness for the Barleycorn – so, could this be an explanation?

HEN & CHICKENS Abington Street.
This is one of those 16th and 17 century inns from the *RBN* where I have found documents – but not necessarily the same ones! A lease between Edward Lyon *to take possession &c. of that known as the Hen and Chickens situate on the North Side of Abbingdon Street.* A Deed Poll of the same year also mentions the inn. From the Scrutiny of the 1768 Election (only those with property could vote and the Scrutiny was to test claims) we learn that Samuel Shipley had lived there from before Christmas. *His house was lately a publick house.* It seems to have been adjacent, or close to, Albert Place according to the Election Plan.
HEN & CHICKENS Sheep Street.
A single entry, *Burgess'* 1845, the proprietor's name Charles. It was probably a small, short-lived beer-shop.

HENLY ARMS 30 Horsemarket Street.
Probably on the west side, halfway down. A group of buildings of which it was probably one are shown on *O/S* 1901, but not on *O/S* 1938.

HERO OF SCOTLAND see **Welcome Inn.**

HIND Market Square see **Hart.**
HIND 2 Delapre Street.
This establishment was occasionally called the Golden Hind, another case of a name being shortened. The area where it stood is now an industrial estate. The earliest entry is 1884 and the last 1968.

HIT OR MISS 9 Leicester Street.

This pub stood on the north side of the street. The name is probably a wry comment on the uncertainty of success in trade. *O/S* 1901 shows a wider than usual property without a back garden in the centre of the north terrace, this was probably the pub. Entries run from 1845 to 1907.

HOLE IN THE WALL see **George Hotel.**

HOP VINE 39 Marefair also **Vine.**
This pub seems to have been on the south side of Marefair, about opposite the end of Doddridge Street. Its original name almost certainly was the Hop Vine, Vine being a contraction. Perhaps to call an inn the Hop Vine would have implied that the 'new' hopped beer was available rather than the old fashioned un-hopped ale? Dates are 1864 to 1951.

HORSE & GROOM 29 Cow Lane (Swan Lane/Street).
This pub stood on the east side of Swan Street directly opposite the end of Angel Street. Early maps of the area show a number of large houses nearby in Guildhall Road and Albion Place. In the 18th century stables were often located at the back of elegant town houses and it seems that this is when this sign came into use. The earliest entry I have for it is 1845 and it disappeared in 1958, before I started my drinking career.

HORSE & JOCKEY.
This name, no doubt, alludes to the still popular past-time of watching horses race, placing bets on them and losing! There have been four of these signs, two of them quite short-lived – perhaps the proprietors were fond of a flutter as well as their customers?
HORSE & JOCKEY 56 Adelaide Street.
This pub was on the southeast corner of Semilong Road where it joined Adelaide Street. Dates from 1840 to 1966 quoted as a 'bhs' by *Wright* 1884.
HORSE & JOCKEY 153 or 155 Bridge Street.
This sign is recorded twice, both *Taylor's* 1858 and 1864. The proprietor, Normanton Merrill is also recorded as a Beer-Retailer in

Bridge Street in 1861, 1862 and 1867. This could have been the precursor of the Cattle Market Tavern. *Harrod's* 1876 has *Merrill, Norminton, Brass Moulder, Guildhall road*. Did he give up the pub, or was it a sideline?

HORSE & JOCKEY Horsemarket.
A single entry, *Burgess* 1845, proprietor's name Prince – no other details. Probably a small beer-shop and called the Horse & Jockey because of the street name.

HORSE & JOCKEY Lady's Lane and Park Street.
This pub was on the east corner of the two streets; dates are 1858 to 1933.

HORSEMARKET TAVERN 49 & 51 Horsemarket also **Maltster's Arms.**
This pub stood on the north corner of the junction of Castle Street and Horsemarket. It seems to have started life as a Beer-Retailers and the earliest entry under this listing is 1847. It appears to have been run by a James Houghton, Beer-Retailer, Grocer, Landlord and Hop Merchant from as early as 1847 to about 1876 as the Maltster's Arms. In 1884 Issac Garlick was the proprietor and its name had changed to the Horsemarket Tavern. The last entry was in 1907.

HORSESHOE.
I have located three Horseshoes in the area. The two most ancient are in what were villages a few years ago. The horseshoe has long been a symbol for good luck and there are as many explanations for this as there are arguments as to which way up it should be hung. Points up "so the luck won't fall out", points down representing the Moon's north (fortunate) node,

points up to represent the Moon-Goddess, Selene. Iron over the door to ward off witches, avert ill luck or thunderbolts. You take your pick! See Silver Cornet for more on this.

HORSESHOE Kingsthorpe.
Apart from five entries in directories (1830-1854) I have nothing else on this pub. It is not listed as one of the Kingsthorpe pubs of 1874

(see Queen Adelaide) so it had either gone by then or changed its name.

HORSESHOE Weston Favell.

Not a lot on it but it did survive for a long time, I can just remember it and like the above Horseshoe on occasions its proprietor had a second trade, George Dunkley of the Kingsthorpe Horseshoe was a Farmer and Charles Barber of this pub was a Grazier. It is listed from 1850 to 1962.

HORSESHOE Market Square.

There is only one entry for this establishment (1922) so I wonder how long it survived. It described itself as a Commercial Inn.

IRONFOUNDER'S ARMS 179 Bridge Street also **Foundrymens' Arms** (see).

Thomas Halford is listed as a Beer-Retailer at this address from 1847 to 1858. By 1862 Edward Halford had taken over from him and Thomas had moved to 56 Adelaide Street (Horse & Jockey). It seems that this is but an alternative name for the Foundrymen's Arms.

IRONMONGER'S ARMS Location unknown.

NN&Q 1886 refers to two tokens of 1652 and 1668, the 1652 token has: -

OB. THOMAS.COOPER.IN = The Ironmongers' Arms $^1/_4$d.
REV.   NORTHAMPTON.1652 = T. E. C.

Thomas Cooper served in the office of Town Bailiff in 1647.

"JOLLY".

We have four pubs with jolly in their names. The sense here is equivalent to the word 'merry' i.e. slightly drunk. The God Bacchus, the God of wine and merriment has often been called 'The Jolly God'.

JOLLY BRICKLAYERS 69-71 Horsemarket also **Jolly Brickmakers.**

It was reported in a local paper in 1907 that an Owne Young (26) of the Jolly Brickmakers was sent to prison for stealing a money-belt from a man in the Plume & Feathers, Bradshaw Street. It contained 10/6d (52$^1/_2$p.) – Young had 16 previous convictions. Twenty-six is young for a landlord and the directories give H. Ware as the proprietor, so I conclude he was either an employee or a guest. It is recorded from 1877 to 1907.

JOLLY BREWERS Abington Street
See the **Two Brewers** (an alternative name).

JOLLY CRISPIN 134 Great Russell Street also **Russell Arms, Earl Russell, Dick Turpins** and **Jolly Cobbler.**

This establishment is still with us at the corner of Great Russell Street. The street and therefore the pub are named after Earl Russell (1792-1878). This famous politician became Prime Minister in 1865, as the street is named on a map of 1847 it must have been named for his reputation rather than his accession to Prime Minister, or his death.

There is another contender for the name, the Rev. Jack Russell (1795-1883). A foxhunting squire from Devon who came to fame as the breeder of the terrier that bears his name.

The pub changed its name to the Jolly Crispin in 1957. Saint Crispin is the patron saint of Shoemakers. Hereabouts in the past if you called someone "a Crispin" it meant a shoemaker, or at least, a cobbler. As the Cordwainers of old were famous for their drinking it is not surprising to find a Jolly Crispin in the town!

Although it is after the cut-off date of 1993 the 1997 change to the Jolly Cobbler I feel rates a mention. The Dick Turpins was a meaningless name and never popular. The Jolly Cobbler was as the result of a competition to find a new name and this result put the name back almost as it had been from 1957-1994 with the added significance of the name of our local football team which was having some success at the time.

JOLLY SMOKERS (OLD) Mayorhold.
The building was obviously built as a pub and its stucco style is similar to other pubs such as the Green Dragon opposite and the Welcome Inn nearby. The earliest I have it from the directories is 1884.

The Mayorhold is an historic part of the town and marks the North Portgate of the old Saxo-Danish burgh. In later years it was considered a smart part of town and the Town Hall stood here, possibly on the site of the pub. For more, see the Crispin Arms.

Probably the most well known licensee was Mrs. Mary Sherwin who was landlady from 1951 until its closure in 1960. In those days it was unusual for a woman to hold a licence outright. By all accounts she had a good reputation amongst the locals and although it was a rough pub she was well respected and never had to call out the police. "I think they had more respect for a woman," she said in an interview in 1985 during a visit to the town from her home in the USA.

Mrs Sherwin, originally a sceptic, claimed in 1955 that the pub was haunted. The ghost, given the name 'Charlie' seems to have scared the dog, moved objects about and burnt spectral incense. As the whole area is riddled with history and tales of the past, perhaps it isn't surprising that 'Charlie', apparently a monk was around! Alas! The Mayorhold, once so interesting and full of character and characters is now merely a boring road junction and underpass. Does 'Charlie' still haunt the area? I wonder – and if so, in lieu of his 'monks' passages' does he make do with the underpass?

During the demolition of the building in 1966 a well about 40ft. deep was found under the floor of the skittle room. The newspapers description of the "mystery pit" leaves you thinking that it was either an oubliette or an entrance into the fabled system of underground passages beneath old Northampton. However, the description is actually of a typical well and its depth suggested a relatively late date – but we should never allow the facts to interfere with a good story!

JOLLY TANNER(S) Chalk Lane.
This was a small, back street, beer-shop. Its exact location is difficult to ascertain, as Chalk Lane at the time was full of such small properties. Directory records run from 1884 until 1910.

KATHERINE WHEEL see **Catherine Wheel.**

KEEP Kingsthorpe Shopping Centre.
Built as an integral part of the Shopping Centre. I came upon an amusing tale involving a pub with this name in the *Reader's Digest* and although the contributor came from Godalming I suspect it is about our Keep.

It seems this man was working in the pub one night when he got a 'phone call informing him that he was one of the few lucky people to get a free quote for double-glazing. He asked if they knew the pub and was assured that they did and had visited it a few times and liked it. "Well, in that case," he replied, "you'll know that it's in a basement!" (Now demolished 2010).

KING BILLY(S) see **King William the Fourth.**
KING DAVID Newham Road.
The name of this pub could be derived from the Bible, but I feel that it is more likely to have been named after King David I of Scotland, who had connections with this town. A typical smallish estate pub opened in the 1950s and still with us.

KING OF DENMARK 1 Denmark Road.
The building that was once a pub is still at the top of Denmark Road and is now a private house. This pub was the brother to the still extant Princess Alexandra, each deriving their names from the streets. Princess Alexandra was the daughter of the King of Denmark and married Edward VII in 1863. This area was developed between 1864 and 1900.

The King of Denmark was smaller than the Princess Alexandra and probably went out of business because of that pub and the Crown & Anchor nearby. It first appeared in the directories in 1893 and the last entry was in 1933.

It originally had two large windows on the ground floor and these have been removed, partially bricked up and new windows, copies of the ones on the first floor inserted. The lintols above the windows have also been copied. For once someone with taste has converted a pub/shop into a dwelling.

KING'S ARMS.

This became a popular sign at the time of James I (1603-1625). Today we don't have to worry about pub signs becoming politically unpopular and needing to take them down and hide them, but during the Commonwealth many signs disappeared, some resurfacing after the Restoration in 1660. Many of the King's Arms today could be these 'survivors', but in any case it's a safe sign in a monarchy. I've found three in the town.

KING'S ARMS 94 Bridge Street see **Bull and Butcher.**
From *The Local,* Feb. 1982: - *by 1780 it* (the Bull & Butcher) *had become known as the King's Arms and then in 1830 by its present name.* **Mercury** 1796-7 refers to it (2017).

KING'S ARMS 38 Horsemarket **(King's Head?).**
This inn certainly goes back a long way, it has an entry in the earliest directory, the *Universal Directory* of 1791, which seems to have listed for the town only those establishments that a traveller would wish to know about, i.e. large inns with stabling &c. The inn is also shown on *Law's* Map of 1847. On this it is shown as a much larger building than on the *O/S* 1901-1964 and the *O/S* size is as I remember it.

It appears that this inn was also referred to as the King's Head, the author of the *NN&Q* article says that the King's Head stables used to extend down Horsemarket as far as the back of St. Catherine's Terrace, as is shown on *Law's* Map for the King's *Arms.* Various advertisements exist for both signs in the 18th century *Northampton Mercury* and seem to describe the same premises. The King's Head is also mentioned in the *Great Fire Court Book* (05/04/1677) so predates the Fire of 1675. From a deed of 1751: -*In the tenure or occupation of Mary Smalshaw Widow* and *abutting on a certain Street or lane called Kings-Head Street or Kings-Head lane towards the North.*

The pub closed in 1971 and was on part of the Saxon Inn site a little way north from the present Girl Guides' Trefoil House. Trefoil House is now the Northampton Unitarians Meeting House (2017).

KING'S ARMS 22 Market Street.

This beer-shop was on the east side of Market Street about halfway up. This establishment doesn't seem to have lasted long; there is only one entry under the sign *Taylor's* 1864, *Joseph Brooks* and four occasions Joseph appears as a Beer-Retailer between 1861 and 1869.

KING'S HEAD.

What has been said about the King's Arms largely applies to the King's Head. There were, however, King's Heads as early as 1446 and many Pope's Heads were changed to Kings at the time of the Reformation. The head usually depicted was Henry VIII, less common was Charles I or II. Henry VIII's daughter, Elizabeth I, is often the model for the Queen's Head, she being so fond of the inn and tavern. When released from the Tower in 1558 she first went to the Church of All Hallows to pray and then to the King's Head in Fenchurch Street for beef and ale! I understand these two monarchs are also the models for the King and Queen depicted on modern packs of playing cards.

We have had two King's Heads in the town, although one of them seems to have been an Arms at the same time – perhaps in the days of limited literacy these were seen as interchangeable?

KING'S HEAD Horsemarket see King's Arms.

KING'S HEAD 14-15 Mayorhold.

There seems to have been a King's Head on this site for a very long time, directory dates 1824-1971. I got a quick look around this pub just before demolition, (1970s) but didn't have the time or equipment to examine either the roof timbers or the cellar (both good indicators of the age of a building and its origins). When I got back the whole site was rubble – things moved fast in those days! Earliest date I've found in the Mercury is 1751 (2017).

In the past the Mayorhold was an important part of the town and inns and taverns would find a good trade around here and the King's Head stood right at the top of the Mayorhold on the corner of St. Andrew's Street in a prime position. There is more about the Mayorhold's past under; Crispin Arms, Green Dragon and Jolly Smokers.

KINGSLEY PARK HOTEL see **White Elephant.**

KING STREET TAVERN 7 King Street.
The pub stood about where the yard of the Criterion pub was to be. In 1858 Henry Lambert had a Beer-Retailing business here and Samuel Pollard is also recorded as such in 1862 and 1864, in 1889 George Samuel Worley is here and by 1893 is the proprietor of the King Street Tavern. The last record is 1907.

KINGSWELL ARMS 3 Verulam Buildings, 30 Kingswell St.
Verulam Buildings were on the south corner of Kingswell Terrace. I assume this pub was on the ground floor. Many of the references are to a Beer-Retailer; they start in 1884 ("bhs") and continue to 1933.

KING WILLIAM THE FOURTH.
King William IV or "Silly Billy" as he was known because of his mode of speech was a very popular character long before he came to the throne. He was known as the Sailor King because of his eleven years in the Navy, nine of them on active service and some of that time in the company of Nelson who became his friend. When Nelson married the Prince gave away the bride. He was created the Earl of Munster and Duke of Clarence (another pub name) in May 1789. In 1818 he married Adelaide, daughter of Duke George of Saxe-Coburge Meiningen (Queen Adelaide, another pub name). On 26th June 1830 the Duke of Clarence became King William IV and his Coronation was in the following year. His involvement in the Reform Bill and his threat to create Whig peers to combat the Tories could only have

added to his popularity. This is probably why we have had three King William IVs and some of the other names connected with him.

KING WILLIAM IV Commercial and Kingswell Streets also **King Billys** possibly **Grafton Arms** (see) and **Travelling Scotsman** (see).

It seems as far as the directories indicate it was in 1840 the Grafton Arms, becoming the Travelling Scotsman in 1845 and finally changing to the King William between 1864 and 1870, this is more fully explained under those names. This pub is still with us, changing its name a few years ago to the "King Billys". In May 1994, after alterations it reopened under the pointless and silly chain name, "Fitchet & Firkin". It has since changed hands and at the time of writing is once more called the King Billy. This picture is from August 2000 during a 'Hawaiian Week'.

KING WILLIAM IV 2 Green End, Kingsthorpe.
This one, also still extant, shares the village with his wife the Queen Adelaide. The listed as a Beer-Retailer's in 1878 and is named in 1884. (Sold in March 2017 and to become a private house, closed due to falling trade – no car park and no real ales).

KING WILLIAM IV Conduit Lane.
Only listed three times and only once with the name. On all occasions it is entered under "Beer-Sellers" or "Retailers". In all three directories; 1845, and twice in 1847, the name given is Samuel Wright. *Slater's* directory 1850 gives Samuel Wright, Beer-Retailer in Bridge Street, so it looks like he'd moved.

KNIGHTLY ARMS 9 Commercial Street.
The *de Knightleys* used to reside at Fawsley Hall, but what, if any, this extinct noble family has with a back street pub in Northampton I have no idea. Perhaps it was one of their retired retainers who first opened it (William Sabin 1840)?

It was on the south side of Commercial Street a few doors along from Bridge St., a short distance from the King William the Fourth.

I believe in its time trade would have been brisk. It was surrounded by streets of small terraced houses and just across the road from St. John's Street Railway Station, but the station eventually closed and then the Borough began to 'improve' the area – by demolishing the houses and turning the land over to industry. The pub was finally sold in March 1960 for £2,000 - it was the last pub but one that the Abington Brewery Co. had left in the town and one of the few remaining free houses. Although it was bought freehold and fully licensed it was demolished and 'redeveloped'.

LABOUR IN VAIN 55 Upper Mounts see **Black Boy.**
LABOUR IN VAIN 30 Green Street also **Barley Mow** and **Black Man.**
The original sign of this pub is not politically correct by modern standards. The actual name was probably ironic, indicating that no matter how hard the landlord worked he was never going to make a fortune or even get a decent result. The sign used to be very popular in less enlightened days and showed either one or two washerwomen scrubbing a little black boy in a tub of suds, it was often accompanied by a verse such as: -

Washing here can now be seen
She scrubs both left and right
Although she'll get him middling clean
She'll never get him white!

This is supposed to relate to an event that is told of the medieval court. It seems that a traveller brought back from parts foreign a black boy who was presented to the ladies of the court for their amusement. In their ignorance they tried to scrub the black off the lad. They did this so thoroughly and so often that the poor mite caught a chill and died. Dates run from 1884 to 1907.

LAMB & FLAG 40 Bridge Street & Kingswell Street also **Lion & Lamb, Cobblers** and **40s.**
The site of this inn lays four properties below Francis Jitty on the west side of the street. The earliest mention is in 1542 when it was

 mentioned in a document as part of the properties whose rents were given for the upkeep of Northampton Grammar School. The inn was destroyed in the Great Fire, but it seems it was rebuilt as there is a reference to it in a lease of 1766. The properties and probably the inn itself were pulled down in 1828. It is possible that the name changed from the Lamb & Flag to Lion & Lamb at the time of the rebuilding after the Fire. However, Lamb & Flag has Catholic overtones so the change could have happened at the time of the Reformation – about 100 years earlier.

The Lamb & Flag is the *Agnus Dei*, or Lamb of G-D and represents Christ with the flag of His Resurrection. It is found as a crest of the Merchant Tailors and on the coat of arms of the Knights Templar.

Early references to this establishment give the address as Kingswell Street. In Medieval times Bridge Street was very congested and the 'main' road was Kingswell Street. When the King visited to hold Parliament at the Castle the Royal procession would use this street, along Silver Street (now called College Street) and turn left along King Street to enter the Castle by the North Gate.

The other two names are modern and there is no continuity, the Cobblers appeared in the mid 1970s and the 40s about ten years later. In 1986 it was called "40 Bridge Street" – a wine bar.

LAMPLIGHTER Market Square see **Lord Palmerston.**

LAMPLIGHTER Overstone Road see **Overstone Arms.**

LAWRENCE SHERIFF'S ARMS Lawrence St/Wellington Pl.
Only one reference to this beer-house, in the *Northampton Mercury* November 1862. The advertisement describes the premises: - *TO BEERHOUSE KEEPERS, BAKERS and OTHERS. ELIGIBLE FREEHOLD PROPERTY Called THE LAWRENCE SHERIFFS' ARMS. LAWRENCE-STREET, NORTHAMPTON. FOR SALE BY AUCTION, At the ANGEL HOTEL, NORTHAMPTON, on FRIDAY, the 12th day of DECEMBER, 1862, at SIX o'clock in the evening.*

A Substantial brick and slated MESSUAGE, now occupied as a Beer and Refreshment House, and called "The Lawrence Sheriff's Arms" most eligibly situate for business, at the corner of LAWRENCE-STREET, Wellington-place in the town of Northampton, containing Front Shop, Bar-parlour, Sitting-room, Tap-room, Kitchen, four Sleeping Rooms, two good cellars, convient Yard with two entrances into Lawrence-street, containing large BAKEHOUSE, with Meal-room over, Stables, Piggeries, Workshop and Coal House, and two Pumps of excellent Water.

The property, which is new-built is in the occupation of Mr. John Bird, at the yearly rent of £35, and a good business is carried on therein.

LEAMINGTON HOUSE 10 Parade.

Leamington House stood at the top of the Market Square and only seems to have had one proprietor, Edmund Franklin. *Kelly* 1847 records an Edward Franklin as a confectioner and dealer in British wines on the Parade. By *Phillips* 1852 there is an Edmund recorded as a Beer-Retailer here and *Slater* 1862 records Edmund at the Leamington House under the heading *Taverns & Public Houses.* There is one more entry *Taylor's* 1864. This and adjoining properties were demolished to construct the Emporium Arcade, which was built in 1901. Sadly this fascinating arcade full of interesting shops has also been demolished to make way for a dingy, sterile, urine-smelling muggers' paradise.

LEG OF MUTTON 11 Mercers' Row see **Duke of Clarence.**

LEOPARD 15 Wellington Place, Barrack Road.

There is only one mention of this pub by this name (1858) in all others it is a Beer-Retailer. Working from the property numbers on *O/S* 1964 Plan it was located on the south corner of Temple Bar, but numbers could have changed.

Does one of the regiments associated with the Barracks have a leopard as its badge? Perhaps the proprietor played the bass drum and wore a leopard skin? Many of the other pubs in the area seem to have military associations.

LILLY OF THE VALLEY 2 Bell Barn Street.

This pub was at the east end of Bell Barn Street at the junction with St Andrew's Street, it became part of St. Andrew's churchyard, now also gone. The name probably alludes to a popular song.

An advertisement for the letting of the Engineer, Far Cotton in the *Northampton Mercury* February 1868 says; - *Apply to J. Willars, Lily of the Valley, St Andrew's Square.*

LION. Drapery.

One of the Ancient Inns of 1585. In 1607 a complaint was made of the condition of a lane leading from the backside of the Lion (i.e. what is now called College Street) down to the Horsemarket, this meant it ran east-west. It is possible that this lane was not reinstated after the Great Fire of 1675. In a poem about the Fire the author refers to the Swan, the Lion and then the Hind. He was probably listing them in order, if this is so; we know the location of the Swan (Swan Yard) and the Hind (Corn Exchange, Parade). We also know the Lion must have been on the west side of the Drapery (its backside was in College Street), therefore, it must have been between the Swan and the top of the Drapery. It doesn't appear to have been rebuilt after the Fire.

LION & LAMB see Lamb & Flag.

LITTLE BELL 7 or 9 Augustine Street also Prince of Wales.

According to *NN&Q* 1891 the licence of the Catherine Wheel, Abington Street was transferred to this pub in 1841, when a Mr. Pierce Cornfield was tenant. In 1864 the pub changed name to the Prince of Wales. It was located on the east corner of the junction of Augustine Street and Weston Row; the last entry is for 1933.

LITTLE BOAT 78 Brier Lane.

Brier Lane is shown on *Law's* Map and is in effect the start of the Wellingborough Road. The pub has only one entry in *Taylor's* 1864 when a Mr. George Parker was the proprietor. Because the street numbers are not known it is impossible to locate the pub's exact position. However, the New Town Tavern is also listed as being at number 66 Brier Lane. Later directories give the New Town Tavern's address as 80 Wellingborough Road. By counting properties and assuming the plots have not changed I make the present premises of Andrew's Office Equipment (90 or 92) to be its location.

LIVE & LET LIVE 73 Bath Street and 25 Bristol Street.

This establishment stood on the northeast corner of Bristol and Bath Streets. There is only one entry under the name - *Lea* 1900-1 has an A. C. Sanders, there is also an *A. E. Sanders, Beer-Retailer, Bath Street* in *Stevens* 1889. A photograph taken by the Borough Architects Department in 1963 when the area was about to be demolished shows this building boarded up with over the door: - *The LIVE & LET LIVE - Est. 1870 - FREE HOUSE – PHIPPS - ALES & - STOUT.* Directly over the door is: - *R. W. MUDD 6 (GROCER Ltd.)* It obviously still sold beer, but was it on or off sales? In the 1950s it was only listed as a Grocers and did not appear under Beer-Retailers or Public Houses.

The unusual name can be found more to the North of England and comes, I'm told from the 'Hungry Forties' – the period which preceded the repeal of the Corn Laws by Sir Robert Peel in 1846, the high cost of food causing distressing poverty amongst the poor.

LONDON & NORTHWESTERN HOTEL see **North Western Hotel.**

LONDON HOUSE 28 Drapery.

A short-lived establishment, it was located on the east side of the fourth property north from Osborn's Jitty. *Taylor* in 1864 called it the London House and *Kelly* in the same year listed it as a Beer-Retailer - its only other appearance is in *Melville* in 1867 again as the London House.

LONGBOAT
Limehurst Square,
New Duston.
I know little more
than it being a
relatively new pub.
However, here's a photograph taken in 1999.

LORD CAVENDISH see **Marquis of Carabas.**

LORD PALMERSTON 25 Market Square also **Flying Horse** and **Lamplighter.**

The Flying Horse, Market Hill is mentioned in the *Great Fire Court Book* in 1682 so it must have existed before the Great Fire of 1675. I offer two possible explanations for the name, the first is from *NN&Q* 1889 in the form of a rhyme: -

> *If with water you fill up your glasses,*
> *You'll never write anything wise,*
> *For wine is the horse of Parnassus,*
> *Which hurries a Bard to the skies.*

The horse of Parnassus is the flying horse, Pegasus.

The author of the article in *NN&Q* also points out that there was a game where you sat on a kind of swing and took swipes with a wooden sword at a target. However, I understand the term could refer to any swing as a sign I have seen from elsewhere for this name illustrates.

Central to the sign is a pretty young girl dressed in the bonnet, bows and flounces of yesteryear; she is sitting on a swing holding the chains that are entwined with flowers. She is on the upswing, one leg raised, eyes closed and a smile on her face. Behind her ready to give another push is a young man in frock coat, breeches and tricorn hat giving a knowing look to a second young man in similar attire. This second man stands before her, sideways on, hands on knees, peering up her skirts. This behaviour seems ungentlemanly enough, but when you know that in the days of petticoats and hooped skirts ladies did not wear anything resembling knickers you realise the trick these two young gentlemen

FLYING HORSE INN,

MARKET SQUARE,

NORTHAMPTON.

E. WHITE

Returns her grateful acknowledgments to her many Friends and the Public for the very liberal encouragement bestowed on the above House since her residence thereat, and assures them that her best exertions will be used to retain their patronage.

Choice Wines and Spirits, Home-Brewed Ale, London Porter, &c.

WELL-AIRED BEDS.

GOOD STABLING, &c. &c.

N.B.---AN ORDINARY ON MARKET DAYS.

Hickman's Directory 1847.

are playing on this 'innocent maid'. **Or,** she could have been perfectly aware of what was going on.

It seems a Job Bartho kept the inn in 1753 and in 1760 a Surgeon and Apothecary, William Fisher jnr., advertised that he would be at the Flying Horse on Saturdays to ply his trade. An Indenture of the 9th and 10th of August 1834 lists several of the previous tenants but no dates.

The Flying Horse changed its name in 1867. In August 1864 Lady Palmerston cut the first turf of the East & West Junction Railway at Towcester and Lord Palmerston (a Liberal) paid Northampton a visit. The Flying Horse being a Liberal pub changed its name in his honour.

The next big event in the pub's history was on October the sixth 1874, a Parliamentary By-Election involving Charles Bradlaugh had, by nightfall, developed into an unruly mob that gathered in the Market Square. When the result was given out it enraged the mob that promptly tore up the cobblestones and began to hurl them at the windows of the surrounding buildings. The Lord Palmerston didn't escape and the landlord, Josiah Rechab Tonsley defended the entrance of his pub, dressed in a fireman's helmet and armed with an axe. He swore to brain anyone trying to get in. The Mayor, flanked by police, read the Riot Act and Bradlaugh appealed for calm. This had no effect so the army were called out from Weedon. When they arrived they fired a volley over the heads of the rioters, who sensibly dispersed. This was the last serious riot in Northampton; see the George for another good one!

In 1936 the old building was demolished and a new pub rose from the rubble to open early in the following year. The building that stands now, at least from the first floor up, is basically this structure. Around 1974 the "Palmerston" changed its name to the Lamplighter and 'up dated' it's image. However, in 1980 it finally closed – being at that time the only pub left on a Market Square that once had so many.

LORD RAGLAN.

There were two of these in the past; one was probably named because of the street name.

Lord Fitzroy James Henry (1788-1855) 1st Baron Raglan was a soldier of repute. He fought in the Peninsular War and commanded British troops in the Crimean. According to the directory entries the Lord Raglan in Upper Priory Street appears to have opened in 1858, so could have been in honour of the Lord's recent death. Raglan Street was constructed around this time and probably named for the same reason. The second Lord Raglan opened six years later.

LORD RAGLAN 44 Kettering Road and 21 Raglan Street.
The pub stood on the west corner of the junction of the two above streets. A small house, now demolished, was sandwiched between the pub and what was until recently the Unitarian Church. Both the pub and house have gone although the church still stands, but no longer Unitarian – (now they've moved to Horsemarket, see King's Arms, Horsemarket, 2017).

LORD RAGLAN Upper Priory Street and 46 Upper Harding Street.
This pub was on the southeast corner of the junction of two above streets. It was next to the Harding Street Tavern. This pub was almost dead centre of the site of the Priory of St. Andrew. In the early 1970s when I was working as an archaeologist for Northampton Development Corporation we were called out to investigate skeletons that had been unearthed during site clearance in this area. They proved to be the medieval mortal remains of old Northamptonians the skeletons were enclosed in stone 'boxes' called cists (pronounced 'kists') made up of slabs of local sandstone. Some had been disturbed during building operations a century or so before. One had an extra skull between its legs, evidently placed there by a respectful workman from the past. I remember some of the old locals joking about drinking in this pub and not knowing that just beneath their feet lay several medieval skeletons!

LUMBERTUBS Kettering Road North also **The Boothville.**
This pub only just qualifies, being at the very edge of the 1965 Borough boundary and this is probably the reason why there are so few early records of it. *Kelly* 1956 finishes at the Manfield Hospital, the Borough boundary at the time, but *Kelly* 1958 does list this pub even though the boundary wasn't extended until April 1965.

The original name was The Boothville, derived from the district name. Lumbertubs, derived from Lumbertubs Lane was first used in 1960, it is an odd name and there are several explanations as to its meaning. One is that local greengrocers used a field on this lane for the disposal of old wooden vegetable boxes and this led to it being nick-named thus. Another, from Stan Monk, published in the *C&E* March 1994 is that it comes from the Saxon word lumm meaning 'land by a pool' and the suffix, tun is Old English for a wooden vessel.

MAGPIE 154, 156, 173, 173a or 175 Bridge Street.

The above series of numbers illustrates how unreliable property numbers can be in certain areas of town. The first two numbers are even and relate to the west side of the street, it seems the pub moved about 1865. From the unpublished notes of the author of the articles in *NN&Q*:

There is a Publick-House on the East Side of the South Quarter (Bridge Street) now Numbered but still bearing this Name. But this is not the Original site. For less than 20 years ago it was on the West Side of this thoroughfare opposite Navigation Row, & kept by Mr. George Baldwin, also a coal merchant. Where in remote times its Southern Wall was watered by the River Nen & where Barges may have come by and deposited its Cargo in the back part of the premises.

The Magpie's new location is clearly shown on the old brewery plans as being on the east side about halfway between Navigation Row and Cattle Market Road.

The original name of the bird was a Pie, but it acquired the nickname 'maggoty' – hence magpie. Some early versions of the sign have 'Maggoty Pie' – not very appetising! There are many superstitions surrounding this odd bird and it is not at all clear why it should be selected for an inn sign, unless it is because of its reputation for collecting bright things (bright customers and bright conversation or bright coins in the till?) – or it could be because of the type of building.

Half-timbered buildings with black beams and whitewashed infill are called magpie. A 'Magpie' is Cockney slang for a halfpenny and in earlier days a half-pint of ale was known as a 'Magpie', probably because of its price – considering this pub's antiquity that seems a bit steep for a half. There is an old nursery rhyme:-

Round about, round about,
Maggoty Pie,
My father loves good ale
and so do I.

The earliest reference I have found to this pub is an auction notice of April 1763 and it has an entry in the *Universal Directory* of 1791 so it must have been of some importance at the time. *Law's* Map of 1847 shows an enclosed yard at the approximate location of the first Magpie showing it to have been able to accommodate a fair number of travellers and their horses. The second incarnation doesn't seem to have been quite as salubrious as *Wright* 1884 gives it "bhs", not an inn.

MAILCOACH.
This name alludes to the Mailcoaches that carried the King's mail throughout the land. These vehicles were the fastest, had the right of way and didn't pay tolls. A post horn (another pub name) would be blown to clear the way ahead to get the tollgate opened before they reached it. The Mailcoach (and the Post Horn Inn) on the Market Square are named from this service, but the renamed Swan in Derngate is not.

MAILCOACH Derngate see **Swan.**

MAILCOACH Market Square see **Trooper.**

MALT SHOVEL 121 Bridge Street also Maltster's Arms.
Considering this pub's position, close to the town's South Gate it probably goes back a good way. The earliest reference I have to this establishment is a Samuel Wright trading as a Beer-Retailer in 1850 and 1852, he next appears as the proprietor of the Maltster's Arms in 1858. The Malt Shovel appears circa 1870.

It was originally thatched and it also had a protruding first floor. However, after the Great Fire of 1675 no thatched roofs were allowed within the town, but the original Malt Shovel was, like the Bantam Cock just outside a Town Gate. *Wright* gives it the appellation 'bhs' in 1884 but later it styled itself an inn and in 1912 was offering "lodgings". The old building was demolished in 1914 to make way for road widening and the present structure is essentially the replacement built by the Northampton Brewery Company.

In the 1960s when I was working as a self-employed archaeologist I spent the winter working for "Phipps Northampton Brewery Company, Watney Mann (Midland) Limited" and I can remember going into this pub at Christmas. It seemed that this was the custom, at least with the North Brewery. We worked as usual up to lunchtime and then we all clocked out and trooped across the road to the pub, which stood right opposite the main gates. During this session the foremen of the various departments came over with their long boxes of pay packets, which they distributed, to their men (this ritual was usually carried out during the Friday afternoon tea-break in the canteen). Having handed out the pay each foreman was then expected to stand his lads a pint. I had noticed that whilst we were being paid the landlord was pulling scores of pints of "S. P. A." so this must have been a regular custom. I believe the Malt Shovel was the Brewery Tap at the time – I wonder if the foremen got a discount, or even paid for the beer?

The pub was much smaller than it is now as the back has been opened up and the front is no longer two bars, so it was a very crowded, but jovial atmosphere on that day especially after a pint or two. The foremen had a pint with us and left. Suddenly someone called, "It's time!" and we all trooped over the road, queued up to clock-on and, I assumed, prepared to return to work. Instead of going up the steps onto the loading-bay and into the building we all turned about, marched out of the other end of the clock-house and returned to our pints left in the pub.

The Brewery had recently employed a new gate-man, resplendent in his uniform with his medal ribbons from World War II. He was a true 'old soldier' and tried to stop us – all to no avail and although exhorted by many of us to desert his post and join us for a Christmas drink, he steadfastly refused. That is probably why the Brewery gave him the job.

In the afternoon there was a raffle and all the staff were there. Phipps-Walker who I had never seen before, conducted the draw. From the comments about him from the men around me I concluded that he was a very popular and respected man. The prizes varied, from whole hampers, cases of a half-dozen bottles of assorted spirits, turkeys and crates of bottled beer. There were no tatty prizes, and it was fixed – insomuch as by using our clock-numbers it ensured that everyone won something – I won a crate of a dozen pint bottles of Jumbo Stout, most of which my dad drank! The Brewery might have been owned by Watneys then, but the old spirit that must have been around for years still clung on.

Of course, the old Brewery has now gone and Carlsberg now occupies the site. *What's Brewing,* the CAMRA paper described the Malt Shovel in June 1999 thus: - *A Free house which stands at the real ale lovers idea of the Gates of Hell...Carlsberg fizz-factory.*

Since the Watney days the pub has changed a lot, it's better decorated –interestingly decorated, a damn sight cleaner and all the internal walls have gone – but I still think when I'm in there now and then of that Christmas at the Brewery.

In 1983 the pub was acquired by Mick McManus and the name changed to the Tudor House and for a short while later it was called Barney Rubble's, being returned to its old, but not the oldest name of the Malt Shovel by John Harding in 1995.

MALTSTER'S ARMS.

Maltsters make malt, being an essential ingredient of beer, so their skilled trade is very suitable as a sign especially if the landlord is also a Maltster.

MALTSTER'S ARMS 121 Bridge Street see **Malt Shovel.**

MALTSTER'S ARMS 49 & 50 Horsemarket see **Horsemarket Tavern.**

MALTSTER'S ARMS 41 St. James' Road.
This is the Maltster's Arms that didn't change its name. In most entries it is entered under Beer-Retailers, so it was probably a modest affair. The pub was on a bend in St. James' Road, a couple of doors from the Robin Hood. The earliest record is in 1862 when a James Smith had it, a Thomas Smith is in the Robin Hood in 1852, so could they have been related? There is an entry in *Lea* 1906 for an A. Checkley at 41 Main Road I am assuming that this is the same address, as Main Road, Far Cotton doesn't seem long enough to have had a number 41.

MAPLE TREE 12 Lawrence and Maple Streets also **Dulley's Arms.**
Probably first called the Dulley's Arms (1864) because of connections with either Dulley's Brewery of Wellingborough, or Eady & Dulley of Market Harborough. The name change (by 1884) could mark a change in owner or supplier as one would not like to advertise a rival. The second name is derived from the street. It stood on the northeast corner of the junction of the two streets and its last entry was in 1931.

MARQUIS OF CARABAS 59 Bouverie Street also **Rifle** and **Lord Cavendish.**
It stood on the northeast corner of the junction of South Street and Bouverie Street and appears to have been an early example of a pub reverting to an earlier name. It seems that a G. Gibbs changed it from the Marquis to the Lord Cavendish in 1901 and W. C. Lilford changed it back again in 1907. Originally it was called the Rifle (1864), becoming the Marquis about 1884, after Lilford changed it back it retained this name to the end. I understand it closed circa 1957, long before the area was cleared for development.

The name Rifle could be a contraction of a name like the Rifleman, but it could also refer to the 'rifle' – a piece of wood with a strip of emery paper on one side and leather on the other used by clickers to sharpen their knives. The Marquis of Carabas (what a splendid name!) is a title bestowed in gratitude by Christopher Robin in the childrens' story on Puss in Boots.

MARQUIS OF GRANDBY see **Grandby Arms.**

MASONS' ARMS.

There were three pubs with this name. In two cases there is evidence that the proprietors were at some time either Builders or Stonemasons.

MASONS'ARMS St. George's Street.

Only two mentions of this pub, *Burgess* 1845, Masters and *Hickman* 1847, E. Masters. *Kelly,* also 1847 has, *Masters, Edward. Builder and Beer-Retailer.* It looks like he had a brother, Samuel, for he is also listed in *Kelly,* as a builder and shopkeeper in the same street. In *Kelly* 1852 Samuel Masters is at the Fish Inn and a builder. He seems more of a success than his brother for in the street list of *Taylor* 1864 he is residing at number 19 Giles' Street (Black Lion), but not as the licensee.

MASONS' ARMS 29 St. John's Street.

Samuel Howard held the Fountain Inn, Silver Street in 1847 and was listed as at the Masons' Arms in 1858. *Melville* 1861 and 1867 records a *Samuel Howard mason 22 Kingswell Street* and this probably explains the name of his beer-house.

MASONS' ARMS Vernon Street see **Freemasons' Arms.**

MELBOURNE ARMS Melbourne Lane, Duston.

This one is still with us. Like the lane it is named after Lord Melbourne (1779-1848) who was Prime Minister in 1834 and again from 1835-1841. He owned an estate at Duston and probably the pub as well.

The building itself is a Grade II listed building and I have found references in the directories going back as far a 1830 and it was probably a pub long before then.

In the 1970s it was a Watneys pub (few in Northampton were anything else) and in an exchange deal in 1972 it, along with several others, became a Courage pub. It retains some of the original village pub character and possesses a large garden with another across the road.

MELBOURNE GARDENS TAVERN see **Franklin's Gdns. Hotel.**

MIDLAND TAVERN 64 Cow (Swan) La. and 78 St. John's St.
This pub was on the southwest corner of the junction between St. John's Street and Cow Lane. Cow Lane derived its name from the Cow Gate, a small postern in the south wall of the medieval town through which the cows were driven from Cow Meadow into town to the Market Square. In days gone by there was a place about half way up the hill, where the back of the Derngate Centre is now then called "Cowmucke Hille".

Taylor 1858 has a William Robbins as a Beer-Retailer at this address and it also appears as a beer-shop in 1862 and 1864. The first mention of the name is in 1884. The Robbins family kept it for quite a while (1858 to at least 1929). The only other people to keep it were the Hardings (c.1936 to 1954).

MILKMAID see **Gardners' Arms.**

MITRE 8 King Street.
The Mitre used to stand opposite the Criterion and along with this pub and another, the Cross Keys around the corner, shared a rather dubious reputation in the 1960s, if not before. Ron Bayliss, the landlord in those days used to keep scrumpy cider as did the Bell and Tree of Liberty. This was powerful stuff and most landlords would not sell it because of its reputation as 'fighting juice'. Ron had a refinement to this liquor, which I believe he learnt from the black guys that went in there. It was called 'Combo' and came, if I recollect correctly (drinking the stuff affected the memory, I'm sure!) in two forms. The normal one was (I think!) – take a pint glass and add half a pint of scrumpy and a schooner of cheap sherry. The combo-nation was lethal!! The supercharged variety was the same, but you added a double vodka. Blackcurrant juice was an option. Ron always kept an eye on drinkers of these 'cocktails' and threw out anyone who got too excited.

Despite being a rough pub with all the attendant vices I used to like it as no one pretended to be anything other than what they were – so there was a sort of honesty about the place. The pub closed in 1971 and was demolished in 1972; the site is now part of the Moat House car park. Mercury references 1752 & 1767 (2017).

MOAT HOUSE (NORTHAMPTON) Silver Street also **Saxon Inn.**
This is really a hotel, but it does have a public bar. It was built in the 1970s and was first called the Saxon Inn.

I was acting as an Archaeologist for the Northampton Development Corporation during its construction and a large hole was dug to accommodate the heating plant and a cellar bar. This revealed a fascinating section through the medieval town made up of pits full of pottery and burning. The pits seem to have been dug for stone and then filled with rubbish, so the hotel is standing on an ancient rubbish tip.

MOAT TAVERN 53 St. Mary's Street.
This pub stood on the southeast corner of the junction of Doddridge Street and St. Mary's Street. The first mention in a directory of its name is in *Wright* 1884 *Sml. Ths. Betts bhs.* A directory of 1878 lists under Beer-Retailers a *S. T. Betts at 43 Horsemarket* (later the New York Tavern?).

Presumably the name is derived from its proximity to the site of the Castle. I have seen a photograph taken in 1970 showing the pub in a sorry state awaiting demolition. It was lost under Barclaycard House which itself has been flattened. An early photograph shows it was established in 1878.

MOLLY MALONE'S Chapel Place also **Molly's Bar** and **Fagin's.**
Fagin's was opened in 1986 as a bistro by John Maloney. It swiftly became a wine bar and by the end of 1987 it was a pub. It closed for a while a couple of years later, reopening as Molly Malone's in 1990, later still it was extended through to Abington Square and became known as Molly's Bar.

MORNING STAR 23 Great Russell Street.
There are two planets nearer to the Sun than the Earth, Mercury and Venus. Therefore these are always seen from the Earth as close to the Sun i.e. at Sunrise or Sunset. The Morning Star and the Evening Star (Upper Priory Street) are really the same planet, either

Mercury and/or Venus. This is also the name of a locomotive built by George Stephenson for the Great Western Railway. The pub was unusual in that it had two entrances in two streets, the other being through the yard from Earl Street. The earliest directory record is 1858 and it closed in 1974.

MORRIS MAN Witham Way, King's Heath also **Fantasia.**
I have no idea why this pub was called by either of these names. This estate pub was completed in the summer of 1971 and probably was called the Fantasia after Walt Disney's cartoon film. The Morris Man has a nice 'Olde Worlde' feel to it and could have been adopted (in 1979) to indicate a total change of management and style. The pub has long been closed and demolished (2017)

MOTHER CUTHBERT'S HOUSE Location Unknown.
There is a small parchment document written in a small crabbed hand that is almost unreadable in the **NRO**, dated 1588 that refers to this pub.

NAG'S HEAD 79 Kettering Road.
This pub was on the bend of the Kettering Road, a few doors away from the end of Grove Road. It is at present the Kettering Road Off-Licence & General Store. As a pub sign it appears to be a corruption of the Horse's Head. In more modern times it has been the subject of humorous interpretation. Dates go from 1845 to 1933.

NAVIGATION INN Bridge Street.
Only one entry, *Burgess* 1845 under "Innkeepers": - *Fox-Navigation Inn-Bridge street.* Fox does not appear again and I have no number, it is possible that it changed its sign along with the landlord. I would think it was either close to the navigation i.e. the river/canal, or on one of the corners of Navigation Row, the Horse & Jockey was on the north corner 1858-1864.

NELSON Bridge Street.
There are four references to this place in the directories between 1845 and 1852. The proprietor was one, John Burrows who was not only a Beer-Retailer, but according to *Kelly* 1847 was also a Saddler and

Harness Maker and ran an eating-house. I have no number so I cannot locate it, but the Saddler's Arms first appears in the directories in 1864.

NEW INN 150 Kettering Road.
This was on the east side of the road, between Brunswick Place and Market Street, opposite John Clare School. It first appears in 1845 and ends in 1958.

As a lad I went to 'Kett's Kollege for Kool Kats' (John Clare S.M.) in the late 1950s and must confess to having no recollections of this pub whatsoever, but then I was too young to be particularly interested in girls, beer or pubs. I was just a teenager when it must have closed

NEW INN 27 Melbourne Street see **East End Tavern.**

NEWT & CUCUMBER see **Criterion.**

NEW TOWN HOUSE 70 Lower Thrift Street.
This pub, much changed, is still with us. It is at present the R.A.O.B. Club and the exterior has been completely smothered in rendering, making the building strikingly ugly, the product of a committee decision? This now hideous building is at the southwest corner of the junction between South Street and Lower Thrift Street. The photo was taken in 1998.

The name refers to the 'New Town' built out here in the fields (at the time) by Thomas Grundy between 1836 and 1850. The pub is just outside the New Town, which was limited to the north by the Wellingborough Road, West Street to the west, East Street to the east, and – yes you've guessed it, South Street to the south. Its first appearance in a directory was in 1884 and the last in 1951.

NEW TOWN TAVERN 66 Brier La. or 80 Wellingboro' Rd.
At first glance one might think this pub is also connected with
Grundy's New Town (see previous entry), however it is a
considerable distance from it. The building is now the premises of
Benn Security. Directory dates run from 1864 to 1956.

NEW YORK TAVERN 43 Horsemarket.
The first entry for this pub was in 1884; demolished in 1957.

NORTHAMPTON ARMS.
A name you would expect to find here.
There have been two of these, one a
contraction of The Earl of.... We also
have a Town Arms.

NORTHAMPTON ARMS 19 Oak Street.
This was on the northwest corner of the
junction of Oak and Deal Streets and its
earliest appearance in the directories was
in 1864. When the pub was demolished in
the 1960s S. G. Owen, electroplaters and
neighbour acquired the ceramic sign and
installed it in the reception area of their new premises at Ryehill
Close, Lodge Farm. They have since left there, but I have been able
to visit the empty factory and photograph this rather unusual sign.
Thanks are due to Steven Smith of Blacklee & Smith and Scorpion
Security.

NORTHAMPTON ARMS 10 & 12 Silver Street also **Earl of
Northampton Arms.**
This pub must have stood close to the original site of the Criterion on
the east side of Silver Street. The old Criterion was demolished in
1930. This pub survived a little longer, being Compensated for in
1934. There was a drive about this time to reduce the number of
drinking houses in the town and several were closed down and
compensation paid. Another way was for the authorities to request

the surrender of two or three small, unprofitable licences for the grant of a new one on one of the new estates.

NORTHAMPTON CASTLE 4 or 5 Castle Hill/5 Phoenix Street also **The Old Castle.**
The 2500 *O/S* Plan 1901 shows a series of small houses on the north sides of both Phoenix Street and Castle Hill. As the one on the corner of these two streets is larger and both streets feature in addresses it is likely that this is the pub and not where I put it in the *In Living Memory* book. The site became part of the Golden Lion, now flats (2017).

This establishment derived its name either from being close to the site of the actual Castle, or because in the past people have quite wrongly believed Castle Hill to be the site of the castle keep. The mound is far too small to accommodate a medieval castle of any size let alone one of the biggest castles ever built. There may have been a *Motte* here in pre-Norman times. Where is the Castle now? - Quarried away in the 19th century to make space for a railway station.

NORTHAMPTON MOAT HOUSE see **Moat House.**

NORTH STAR Welford Road.
This one was built in 1969 to serve the passing traffic and the adjacent estate. At the time of its construction the town was in the grip of Watneys Brewery and in 1972 there were only six pubs in the town not owned by Watney Mann. They were; the Bear (called the Tavern in the Town at the time), M&B; the Saddlers' Arms, Davenports; the Headlands, Charles Wells; Shipman's, free house; Garibaldi, Bass and this pub – run by Ansells. In 1977 it became the first Ansells pub to serve real ale and in 1986 it had a £200,000 refit and boasted a library. Another £200,000 was spent on a revamp in 1993 when a conservatory was added. When I photographed it in August 1998 it was closed for another change and the sign outside declared, *Another Big Steak Pub Development. Re-Opening LATE SEPT.*

NORTH-WESTERN HOTEL 6-14 Marefare.

Correctly called the London & North-Western Hotel, but it was always called "The North-Western". This railway hotel was on the north side of Marefare right by the junction with Horsemarket. It was demolished in 1970 to clear the area for the building of Barclaycard House. In the 1960s there was a pub opposite called the Shakespeare that my friends and I used. The few forays we made over the road to this pub left an impression of soldiers, teddy-boys (getting a bit dated by then) 'loose' ladies and a 'rough' atmosphere - we tended to avoid the place – so  my recollections are few. Evidence of the directories indicates this hotel started life around 1903.

NOTTINGHAM CASTLE 19 Commercial Street.

This pub was about halfway along on the south side of the street, five doors west of the Knightly Arms. I have no idea why it was called this. The directory dates run from 1845 to 1906, but the licence was surrendered in 1905.

OAK INN 2 Herbert Street and 23 St. Andrew's Street. (21 Sawpit Lane).

This establishment stood on the northwest corner of Herbert and St. Andrew's Streets. St. Andrew's Street was once called Sawpit Lane because of the sawpits and wood yards in the area.

The oak is a symbol of strength, constancy and long life. It is also, like the Royal Oak an emblem of Charles II and it is also our national tree. Entries run from 1858 until 1936.

ODD FELLOWS' ARMS.

This probably refers to the Friendly Society of that name. These 'Friendly Societies' often operated out of pubs and the landlords were often the treasurer as they were in those days considered to be 'pillars of the community'.

ODD FELLOWS' ARMS 2 St. Peter's Street possibly also Boat & Horse.

The premises stood on the north corner of the junction between Freeschool Street and St. Peter's Street.

The first entry under this name is William Negus in 1864; he is to be found as a Beer-Retailer at this address in both 1858 and 1862. The last entry for James Jeffery, proprietor of the Boat & Horse is 1852 so it is possible that they are the same pub. However, there is an advertisement in the *Northampton Herald* in 1862 for the sale of the Odd Fellows' Arms, in the occupation of William Negus at an annual rent of £21, First rate beer trade carried on for 20 years. Does this mean that the pub has had that name all that time? It seems to have been there since about 1844 – a year before the first entry of the Boat & Horse.

ODD FELLOWS' ARMS 39 Mount Street.

Mount Street used to be that part of Lady's Lane that ran from the top of Wood Street to the Mounts. The pub seems to have been on the north side and to have been fairly short-lived, entries from 1845 to 1858.

OLD BAKEHOUSE 19 Bradshaw Street.

There is a strong connection between brewing and baking. This building stands on the southeast corner of the junction of Bradshaw Street and College Street. Although it is much altered this is probably the original structure and almost certainly once was a bakehouse. In directories of 1906 and 1907 (its last entry) it was called Ye Olde Bakeshop no doubt in an attempt to attract the nostalgic drinker. I am surprised that they didn't spell bakeshop Bakeshoppe! From 1845 it was described as a beer-shop, not acquiring its name until 1893.

OLD CASTLE (THE) see Northampton Castle.

OLD GREY HORSE St. John's Terrace and 57 Swan Street (Cow Lane) also **Phoenix.**
There is an entry, under Beer-Retailers in the *Northampton Directory* 1878., *Kilby Geo. St. John's Ter Cow Lane* and this could be the pub. The first entry with a name is *Wright* 1884, who has two, *Frank O. Adams bhs* and *Frank Oliver Adams, baker, shopkeeper and bhs, Old Grey Horse.* Two addresses imply a junction and this one was a tee, according to the Brewery Plans the Phoenix Tavern occupied the southern corner. Arthur William Adams had the Old Grey Horse in 1905 and the Phoenix in 1906, indicating that these are the same pub.

When the Shoulder of Mutton burnt down and was rebuilt it was called the Phoenix and I wonder if this is the reason for this name change? If the bakery and beer-shop shared the same premises it is possible that the bakery caught fire and was rebuilt with this name. Its last entry was in 1941.

OLD HOUSE AT HOME 216 Wellingborough Road.
This name is derived from an old, popular Victorian ballad. To my mind it sums up what the old fashioned local was all about.

According to the directories this pub goes back to 1864 and could have originally been the Crown & Cushion – or its close neighbour (see entry for explanation). The plot on which it stands is empty on *Law's* Map of 1847, but occupied on *Birdsall's* 1878. It is a purpose built establishment and was probably built to serve the thirsty inhabitants of Grundy's New Town. Now the Old House (2017).

OPUS 2 see **Bell.**

OVERSTONE ARMS 66 Overstone Road also **Lamplighter.**
A purpose built street corner pub named after the thoroughfare on which it stands although it changed its name to the

Lamplighter in 1988 and installed real gas lighting. The earliest entry is 1884 about when it was built - it is still with us.

PAPERMAKER'S ARMS Cotton End, Hardingstone.
This only occurs once, in *Kelly* 1847, the proprietor being a William Rutter. The Britannia Inn's address is often given as, *Rush Mills, Hardingstone* and once, in *Bennett's* 1910 as, *Paper Mills*, for the Rush Mills were once a paper mill. From the name of this pub I would guess that it was either nearby or is an alternative name for the Britannia.

PATRIOT & RIVETTERS' ARMS 31 Market Street.
I have grouped these two pubs together, as there is some confusion about them. It is possible that the Patriot became the Rivetters' Arms, but it is also possible that the Patriot moved and/or was resurrected at a later date. The Brewery Plans clearly show the Rivetters' Arms on the west side about halfway between the Wellingborough Road and Brunswick Street.

The pub first appears as a Beer-Retailer in 1862 and is called the Patriot by 1864, all other entries up to and including 1878 give it as a Beer-Retailer, but in 1884 it is called the Rivetters' Arms. Between 1901 and the last entry in 1910 it is called by both names as well as just a Beer-Retailer. From 1901 onwards there are only three directories involved; *Bennett* (1901, 1904, 1906 and 1910), *Kelly* (1903, 1906 and 1910) and *Lea* (1906 and two entries in 1907). Compilers repeating entries from one year to the next without checking them probably caused this confusion. *Lea* in 1907 has both pub names, in Market Street, without numbers, but run by the same person!?

PEACOCK.
We have had two Peacocks and a Peacock & Black Raven, one Peacock is named after the former and the Peacock & Black Raven may be the same inn.

PEACOCK (HOTEL)

28 Market Square. Surprising the Peacock was not listed as an Ancient Inn in 1585, it was of great antiquity but perhaps it wasn't as important then as it became in later years. An early charter of 1456 records: - *The sale of a hospice called Le Pecok by George Longevyle, lord of the manor of Little Billyng to Roger Salesbury, squire of Horton.*

The reference to a hospice is interesting; as these were the early inns (see Introduction). In 1180 All Saints' Church was known as the Church of the Market Place as markets were held in the church and churchyard. Before the Great Fire of 1675 All Saints' Church was about twice the size it is now and could have easily held a market. In 1235 King Henry III ordered that no more fairs or markets were to be held in the church, *but in a void and waste place to the north of the church* – thus was our Market Square created. It is entirely possible that the Peacock began about the same time. In 1456 the Peacock stood on Malt Row as the east side of the Market Square was then called. The two houses next north was called Le Catte and the Green Tree.

The Peacock is the badge of the Dukes of Rutland, but there is no apparent connection. If the Peacock started life as a hospice it would have been attached to a religious house and before the Dissolution it occupied a place in the western boundary wall of the Greyfriars' enclosure. The Greyfriars began in the 13th century - about the time of the formation of the Market Square. The religious meaning of the Peacock is as a symbol of the Resurrection, its flesh supposedly being incorruptible. There is listed in the Great Fire Poem a Phoenix Inn, which by its context must be on the Market Square, as this is its only mention anywhere and in consideration of the similarity of the symbolism of the two birds I feel this is probably the Peacock.

In the 16th century John Mole, the King's Lieutenant and Mayor of Northampton bought the inn for £22 and his will of 1548 lists one of his trustees as Laurence Washington, also a Mayor in his time and great-grandfather of the famous president of the USA.

NN&Q 1889 has a piece on the Inn and the author describes it thus: - *This hotel is situated on the east side of the Market Square. Some idea of its age may be gathered from the fact that it had galleries round its inner court, like the old hostelries of two centuries ago; these galleries have long since been closed, but the remains of them are very plain.*

It appears from this account that the galleries were already filled in, leaving the rails and posts exposed on the outside of the wall. In Elizabethan times entertainments would be performed in the courtyards of inns, many of the spectators watching from the balconies that ran around the yards. These remains were finally removed in 1948 during building work. At the time I was just over three years old and I can remember as a very young child looking into the yard and thinking that it looked like a Wild-West saloon – I'm sure I remember those rails and if that is right it must be one of my earliest memories – certainly of a pub!

The Northampton-Illustrated (circa 1895) has the following description of the interior: - *The accommodation includes spacious commercial and stock rooms for travellers, and a particularly cosy and comfortable smoking room, coffee room, and the usual domestic offices, etc., on the ground floor. There is also a large dining room, where most of the principal civic, Masonic, and other banquets have been periodically held. In the upper portion of the fine old house are well-furnished private sitting rooms, and a number of airy and comfortable bed rooms, affording accommodation for a large number of guests. On market days two ordinaries are served for the convenience of country visitors and commercial gentlemen.*

Bearing in mind that this is a form of advertisement it does give a fairly good impression of what a typical large market inn of the times must have been like. It is true that some of the civic and Masonic banquets were held there, but other inns such as the George, Red Lion and Goat also hosted such functions. An 'ordinary' was a meal provided at a fixed time and price in inns, usually on market days.

There are plenty of advertisements and accounts that refer to this inn, including one account on 1688 of 25s. (125p) for the Mayor and others that was disallowed. The landlord was paid £1..2s..6d. (£1-12½p.) for celebrating the coronation of Queen Ann (1702) – including *two glasses broke*. One popular event was 'Branding Day' when the Freemens' cattle were marked prior to being turned out onto the common. Until the building of a cattle market south of Victoria Promenade (opened 17th July 1873) the cattle were sold in the market. A watercolour by J. A. Perrin painted about 1847 shows these sales and the Peacock Inn was in the right place for such an event.

In 1935 there was some excitement at the Peacock, £14,000 worth of jewellery was stolen from a traveller's handcart left in the yard. It seems people were a lot more trusting in those days.

On May 26th 1957 the inn closed, the licence removed and the 'goods and chattels' auctioned off. There was a refusal of planning permission to turn the site into a shopping mall because of inadequate vehicular access and no proper consideration of façade. There was an appeal in November of that year which didn't get anywhere.

The Peacock is an example of 'Demolition by Neglect' – it goes something like this. A property developer buys up a prime site; he then applies for planning permission to knock down the old building. The Council refuse because the building is of historical or architectural value (in the case of the Peacock the populace wanted to keep the whole building, the Council, just the façade). The developer then delays by appealing &c., during the delay the building is left with no security or maintenance so it becomes vandalised, windows get smashed, pigeons get in and rain damages floors and plaster- eventually the building becomes 'dangerous' and has to be knocked down. It can also, mysteriously catch fire. I am not alone in suspecting this series of events has been deliberately orchestrated several times in our town over the latter half of the 20th century when so many of our important old buildings were lost.

The Northampton Independent January 9ᵗʰ 1959: - *PEACOCK DOOMED. After negotiations lasting more than 2½ years, the Town Planning and Development Committee have decided that the demolition of the Peacock Hotel on the Market Square "should not be resisted". And the council are in agreement. So passes one of Northampton's most beloved hostelries- now too derelict to justify preservation say the experts.*

Thus ended the Peacock Hotel, to be replaced by the hideous Peacock Way – only for this to be demolished in its turn and replaced by Peacock Place, a slight improvement on its predecessor. Now called of all things Market Walk, thus is the name of this venerable inn is lost (2017).

PEACOCK Abington Street, Wood Street.
Opened circa 1981, a subterranean bar in what is left of Wood Street, which has been reduced to little more than the entrance to the Grosvenor Centre. It was named after the Peacock Hotel, but is nothing like it, being a loud, young, bar and very claustrophobic. It changes its name from time to time, I assume in attempts either to change its image or to announce new management.

PEACOCK & BLACK RAVEN No Location.
I suspect that this is another name for the Peacock Inn, but there is a Black Raven in Newland at about the same time. There is only one reference to this inn, from the *Northampton Mercury* June 29ᵗʰ 1732-3 for the sale of trefoil and grass seed at Grendon.

PEDESTRIAN'S TAVERN 69 Woolmonger Street also **The Pedestrian** and **"Isaac's".**
From the Victorian through to Edwardian times there was a great interest in Pedestrianism, or walking as an athletic pursuit, this appears to be the reason for the name. According to a reply by Fred Bailey to an enquiry in the *C&E* 20ᵗʰ April 1996, in the 1920s many pubs fielded football teams such as the Moat Athletic, Hind Rovers and the Pedestrians, as the landlord's name was "Bocca Isaac" (directories give *E. T. Isaac*) it is obvious where the nick-name came from, indicating a long serving and/or popular proprietor.

The pub was on the west corner of the junction of St. James' Place and Woolmonger Street, only four doors from the Harbour

Lights. It appears in the directories in 1864 and the last entry was in 1958.

PHEASANT.

There have been two of these, perhaps they were called this to give an 'Olde Worlde, Sporting', impression, or maybe it was on the menu?

PHEASANT 102-4 Bridge Street.

This was on the north corner of the junction of Weston Street (which disappeared when St. Peter's Way was constructed) and Bridge Street. Directory records go from 1824 to 1922, but it could have been there at a much earlier date. A building corresponding to number 102 in the *O/S* Plan labelled 'Inn'; it had disappeared by *O/S* 1936.

PHEASANT 20 St. Andrew's Square.

One entry, *Taylor's* 1864, Robert Robertson. He occurs as a Beer-Retailer in 1862 at 30 Sawpit Lane and in *Kelly's* 1864 in St. Andrew's Street. St. Andrew's Square is at the junction of Bell Barn Street and what is now St. Andrew's Street. The southern part of St. Andrew's Street, from the Square to the Mayorhold used to be called Sawpit Lane. I have come to the conclusion that this establishment was on the east side of the street, but I cannot be sure of any of the buildings on any of the old plans. As it appears to have been a small beer-shop it could have been any of the properties in the area.

PHOENIX.

Every 100 years this fabled bird is supposed to destroy itself in a fire not made by humans and after a while rise reborn from the ashes to live for another century. It can symbolise rebirth but also a new start, so makes a good sign in certain circumstances. In at least one case in this town the inn was named such because it had burnt down and was rebuilt. The bird is also used in religious, heraldic and alchemical symbolism, with similar meanings. There have been at least three in Northampton.

PHOENIX Market Square?

After the Great Fire of 1675 a poem was written. This poem has references to various inns and the order in which they are written is the one you would have come upon them if walking up the Drapery, into the top of the Market Square and across it to the southeast corner. Only the Phoenix's location is not known, however, the poem does not mention the Peacock; if it did it would occur where the reference to the Phoenix is. Is this an error, a nickname of the time for the Peacock, or poetic licence?

NORTHAMPTON IN FLAMES; OR, A POEM ON THE DREADFUL FIRE THAT HAPPENED THERE ON MONDAY, 20TH SEPTEMBER, 1675.

...The full stretched flames as swift as Jove's fires fly'
Which in an instant lightens all the sky;
Houses of entertainment and of trade
Are together in one ruin laid;
Shops, stables, barns, all buildings fall so fast,
You could not say which was devoured last;
Not even Polyphemus favour's shewn.
THE SWAN INN.
The silver Swan more sweetly sung of late,
Too sad presage of her approaching fate;
In deepest streams she wished to hide her head,
And curs'd the time she left her watr'y bed;
For now amongst the thickest flames she fries'
And there, for want of her own element, dies.
THE LION INN.
The Lion next, when nothing else could fright,
Prepares himself for the unequal fright;
Unknowing how to yield, he scornes the fires,
And, in a generous, sullen rage, expires.
THE HIND INN.
The Hind, she heard, and knew her danger near,
Which came so fast she had no time to fear.
THE TALBOT INN.
The Dog was ne'er afraid of her till now,
Not all so weak an enemy could do;
But now he finds her breath is hotter far,
Than all th' inveterate o' the fiery star.

PHOENIX INN.

Th' Arabian Bird the scattered spices takes,
And of them all a funeral pile she makes;
May she now rise from her flaming nest,
And th' happy emblem prove all the rest.....

This represents about a fifth of a rather long poem. It appears to have been written by, *a clergyman of the diocese, and a spectator of the calamity he here records.*

PHOENIX Market Square also **Shoulder of Mutton.**

This inn only has one mention in a directory, *Pigot* 1824, *Benj. Goodman,* but we have much more information from the *NN&Q.*

When I was compiling my *Place Names of Northampton Town* in 1985 I came across Phoenix Street. Long established inns often gave their name to the thoroughfare on which they stood, such as Black Lion Hill, Swan Yard and Bull Head Lane. The reverse could also happen, Victorian developers giving the street name to their pubs. Phoenix Street, however, is well within the old town and I felt certain that here I had another forgotten pub.

According to the *NN&Q* there used to be a pub on the Market Square called the Shoulder of Mutton from at least 1745. At 1am. on the 17th of February 1792 the inn caught fire and all within perished except the landlord, Mr. H. Marriot who managed to get onto the roof and raise the alarm. His wife, five children and two lodgers all died. A collection was taken up in the town and raised £150. The inn was rebuilt and named the Phoenix. It stood next to the site of what became the Queen's Arms. Sometime in the first two decades of the 19th century it was pulled down and the stone used for building elsewhere.

From the *NN&Q:* - *The figure of a phoenix which was in front of the house is now to be seen at the corner of Phoenix Street, adjoining St. Mary's Place. Phoenix Street was formed about 1828, when the large earthwork, known as Castle Hills, was removed.* So I was right, the street was named after a pub, but one over a quarter of a mile away on the Market Square!

In my youth there was in Abington Park Museum a shelly limestone slab carved in bas-relief depicting a phoenix rising from the flames whilst two cherubic heads blow the flames. In the 18th century flat, carved, stone signs were popular. (After someone was killed by a falling sign Charles II ordered that all signs were to be hung flat upon the wall). On enquiry I located this slab in the Museum Stores in Guildhall Road and Robert Moore of the Museum informed me that he had at least one other bas-relief carving for which there is no provenance or explanation; it appears to be a King's Head. It seems we have here an example of a very old pub sign, if not two. [The stone is now in a sorry condition in the yard of Abington Park Museum.]

PHOENIX Swan Street also **Old Grey Horse**.

PIGEON Near St. Peter's Church.
From a document dated 23rd April 1680, quoted by Brian Giggins in *Hesilrige House, Northampton* 1986, it seems that there was a tenement known by the name of the Pigeon. As far as I can work out it appears to have been in St. Peter's Street at the top of Narrow Toe Lane. A possible candidate for this building is shown on *Nobel & Butlin's Map* of 1747.

PIONEER Haseldene Road.
An estate pub still with us, built in the 1960s, this is one of the pubs that Watneys exchanged with Courage in the big hand over of January 1972.

PLASTERER'S ARMS 19 St. Giles' Street also **Black Lion.**
The main entry for this pub is under Black Lion, according to Bob Brewer, the landlord in the 1960s (who had sight of the deeds) this was its name in 1720. He also told me that it had first been a coffee shop.

PLOUGH.
There have been four of these in the town and as Northampton has been an agricultural market town this is not surprising. It is considered to be a symbol of abundance and fertility, a Plough at Filey has on its sign: -

> *He who by the Plough would thrive,*
> *Himself must either hold or drive.*

PLOUGH HOTEL 87 Bridge Street.

The Plough Hotel was built in 1877 and in 1886 the Plough Hotel Company bought the adjoining Skating Rink, once part of the Victorian Pleasure Gardens. Here they built the Plough Hall later to be known as the Empire Music Hall*. Although it was built primarily to cater for travellers from St. John's Street Railway station it was the nearest large establishment to the new Cattle Market that had opened in July 1873, so it became one of the chief places of refreshment for the Market. On market days it served the traditional  'ordinaries' and hosted the Annual fat Stock luncheons.

In the 1920s it boasted room for 100 cars and used its position on one of the town's main thoroughfares to cater to the motorist. Between 1942 and 1945 all the hotel except the bars were put at the disposal of the American Red Cross. It is said that more than 147,000 members of the US Forces passed through its doors in that time! After the War it was refurbished and modernised and reopened in May 1947.

* I am indebted to Mr. C. Glazebrook for this correction and extra information.

PLOUGH Henley Street, Far Cotton.

One entry, *Taylor's* 1864, Thomas Harris.

PLOUGH Kettering Road.

Three entries under this sign, 1845, 1847 and 1852 - the proprietor seems to have been a William Thomas Jones. To confuse things *Melville* 1861 has a William and Thomas Jones listed. Thomas is at the, Shakespeare Inn & Concert Room, 3 Marefair and William at the, Town Arms, 1 Gt. Russell St. William shows up again in *Taylor's* 1864 at the York Tavern, 1 York Place. I have no number in Kettering Road for this pub, so the location is unknown and the link is broken. I feel the Plough was the enterprise of one man and not very long lived.

PLOUGH (PLOW?) Gold Street.

In the 18th century Gold Street ran from All Saints' Church to St. Peter's Church and an abstract of a title dated 16th November 1756 mentions a Plough, which seems to be on the north side of Marefair near Pike Lane. A *Plow* is also referred to on a document, dated August 1745 as being in Marefair; presumably this is the same pub.

PLUMBER'S ARMS 16 Sheep Street.

The Plumber's Arms goes back quite a while and the building still stands, having until recently been Thursby's Gunsmiths. Bunches of grapes can still be seen over the arches at the front of the building and a wide gateway leads into a yard behind. In the past this yard was known as the Hind Yard and led to the back of that inn.

The Order of Perambulation for the Church of All Saints in 1829 mentions, the Plumbers Arms in Sheep Street. Perambulations were carried out once a year. The boundaries of the parish would be walked thus keeping the exact limits of the parish clear in peoples' minds. The earliest directory mentioning it is of 1824 and it closed in 1959. **Mercury** vol. 70 1789-90 refers to a Plumber's Arms (2017).

PLUME OF FEATHERS.

Heraldically a plume of feathers is always three, as in the badge of the Prince of Wales, which is said to have three ostrich feathers, although no one now knows what they originally were. This pub sign is almost certainly, like the Fleur (Flower) de Luce, a reference to the Prince of Wales. The Fleur de Luce is a badge of France, but in this context it is probably the result of poor painting.

The Plume of Feathers is supposed to go back to the time of the battle of Crecy (1346) when it was acquired by Edward the Black Prince, eldest son of Edward III. It had been the badge of John of Luxembourg, King of Bohemia and carried the motto, *Hou Moet, Ich Dien* that loosely translated means, *Keep courage I am your companion in arms and I serve with you*. It is thought that the Black Prince retained the latter part of the motto, Ich Dien → 'I Serve' as an expression of his loyalty to his father. There is, however, another explanation in the previous century Edward I had been fighting the Welsh and promised them that if they laid down their arms he would give them a prince that spoke no English. Edward II had just been born in Wales so his father presented him to the Welsh saying, *Eich dyn* → 'Here is the man'. Strictly speaking the Plume of Feathers is the badge of the heir apparent and not of the Prince of Wales, although they are usually the same person. There appears to have been two pubs of this name in the town.

PLUME OF FEATHERS 9 Bradshaw Street.

This pub was on the south side of the street near the Sheep Street end. It was open for over 100 years, finally closing in about 1930 when it became R. Hoskins, Tailors.

A will of John Samwell in the **NRO**, dated 1824 has: - *Messuage or Tenement and premises situate standing and being in Bradshaw st. in the said town of Northampton and commonly called by the Name or Sign of The Plume of Feathers.* It is interesting that the first directory entry for this pub is also 1824 and the proprietor's name is Charles Samwell, presumably the son of the above?

PLUME OF FEATHERS Sheep Street.

From the **NRO**, a deed of 1719: - *ALL that Messuage Tenement or Inn commonly called or knowne by the Name or Sign of the Plume of Ffeathers situate standing and being on the* **East** (my emphasis) *side of a certaine Street there commonly called the Sheepe Market or Sheepe Street in the said Towne of Northampton.* At first sight this could be the same pub as above, but it is on the east side of the street and the above pub could only be described as being in Sheep Street in a very loose way if it was referred to as being on the west. I have no more information on the establishment, but I feel that it is very possible that these are, in fact, the same pub, which may have moved sometime between 1719 and 1824.

POMFRET ARMS 10 Cotton End also **Earl of Pomfret.**

This pub is still with us and still a good example of the sort of establishment you would have expected to find on a major road in the last couple of centuries. The earliest entry in a directory is 1830. The passageway to the right now labelled Car Park was intended for carriers' carts and the like. This was never one of your grand

coaching inns; the passageway is too low for carriages and the building too small. Although it is rendered the structure must be of a good date a photograph of 1902 shows a building much like the present one but for the roof-angle, which is much steeper and must have been thatched.

The pub is probably named after Thomas William Fermor, 4th Earl of Pomfret (1770-1833). He served with the Guards in the Peninsula War until his promotion to major-general in June 1813. His eldest son succeeded him and died without issue in 1867.

The most well known landlord was Silvanus Wreford. The directories show him at the pub from 1900 to 1911, but it could have been as long as 1898 to 1914. In 1904 Silvanus – Ben to his friends started up a modest haulage business with one horse and cart. He operated as a general carter around the town and built up his fleet, operating from Euston Road, where his family lived. Today the Wrefords given up the licensed trade, but the 'carting' still goes on!

One curiosity in this pub is the 'smoking head'. This is a sandstone head protruding from the wall of the lounge. If a cigarette is put into its mouth it will slowly be puffed away, no doubt because of a draught coming through a cavity in the wall. Probably it was originally a waterspout and is supposed to have come from St. Thomas' Hospital that stood on the opposite side of the road nearby. The Hospital was demolished 1874. [At this time the pub is closed and boarded up, 2010]. The Felce Brothers have acquired the pub, done it up and re-opened it; it now even has its own brewery! (2017).

PORTLAND ARMS 131 Wellingborough Road.

This pub is named from a street as it stood on the southwest corner of Portland Street and the Wellingborough Road. The earliest mention of this sign is in 1884 with John Smith bhs as the proprietor he is also listed as a Beer-Retailer at this address in 1864, so it would have been a corner beer-shop. The last entry is in 1934.

POST HORN INN 26 Market Square.
In the late 19th century three drinking places stood side-by-side on the Market Square; the Peacock Hotel, the Lord Palmerston (formerly the Flying Horse) and between them this small establishment. In view of the fact that the Peacock was one of the most important coaching and posting inns in the town I'm quite sure that is where this pub gets its name. It first appears in 1889 as a Beer-Retailer; the last entry is in 1910.

POTMAN'S ARMS 1 Green Street and 1 Tanner Street.
No doubt this pub was a small beer-shop and perhaps the proprietor started his career as a potman. Two addresses indicate a corner location. There are only two references under the name, in 1858 and 1864, but a man called Brookes is listed in 1845 as a Beer-Retailer in Narrow Toe Lane, which was opposite Tanner Street. It appears to have been on the southeast corner of the junction between Green and Tanner Streets. The last entry is in 1864.

PRIMROSE (HILL) TAVERN 22 Primrose Hill, Kingsthorpe Road.
The property is still there, three houses south from St. Paul's Road. Most of the entries are as a Beer-Retailer. One, *Melville* 1861 has: - *Wilcox William, Beer-Retailer, plumber, painter & glazier. –* a versatile man! This entry along with a "bhs" in 1884 shows that it was a beer-shop with the landlord carrying on another trade. Entries are 1858 to 1893.

PRINCE ALFRED Barrack Road.
An advertisement in *Northampton Mercury* October 1870 offers *to let a well fitted BEERHOUSE called the Prince Alfred opposite Barracks - Apply Northampton Steam Brewery.*

PRINCE ARTHUR Leicester Road.
The Brewster Sessions in the *Northampton Mercury* September 1878 reported that the licence for the Prince Arthur, Leicester Road has

been transferred to a new pub to be opened in the Artizan Road (later called *the* Artizan). This is the only reference to this pub, a small beer-house, probably close to the Barracks,

PRINCE IN ARMOUR Market Square.

What a strange name for a pub! It is possible that in the 17th century this was an expression in common use that has completely died out like 'The Case is Altered'. It could originally have been The Prince in **Armor** – or Love – perhaps from some play?

The name occurs in a Counterpart of a Settlement of a House dated 1634 "next the Hind": - *Roger Sargent to Wm. Sargent ('s?) Wife....in the parish of all Sts...the Messuage or Inne called the Hynde & being on the West and north part, and the messuage or Inne called the Prince in Armour on the east part....* So we do have an idea of where it was, i.e. the northwest corner of the Market Square, two doors from the famous Hind at the top of the Market Square – it doesn't seem to have survived the Great Fire of 1675.

PRINCE OF WALES.

Royalty has always been a popular subject of inn signs, not only Kings and Queens, but Princes and Princesses as well. Many heirs to the throne have been popular characters before their accession and Northampton has had, and got, four Prince of Wales as well as two Flower de Luce and a couple of Plume of Feathers, badges of the Prince.

PRINCE OF WALES 7 or 9 Augustine Street see **Little Bell.**

PRINCE OF WALES 101 Harborough Road.

This one is now a private house (2017) and commands the junction between the Harborough and Boughton Green Roads. According to the Licensee at the time, Michael Bevington *(C&E 15/3/94),* who had been there for the past eleven years: - *'The Prince' dates back to 1880 and*

was formerly 'Colonel Newham's House' and then a coaching house. "We are only the third set of licensees since then." Said Michael.

This information does not agree with my findings, but I have not had sight of the deeds, whereas Mr. Bevington may have. The earliest entry I have is 1877, a Robert Cross.

PRINCE OF WALES 8 Spring Lane.
This pub stood at the corner of Compton Street and Spring Lane. According to *The Local* Nov-Dec 1980 this pub traded for 80 years (1836-1919), I have dates from directories 1858-1910.

PRINCE OF WALES 7 Union Street, Wellington Street.
This pub was in the centre of the north side of Union Street. According to the same article quoted from above in *The Local* this establishment closed in 1915, I have entries from 1845 to 1910.

PRINCESS ALEXANDRA 1 Alexandra Road.

Princess Alexandra was the daughter of the King of Denmark and the King of Denmark pub used to stand at the top of the next street, Denmark Road. She became the Queen of England having married the future King Edward VII in 1863. Two fields, destined to

become the Alexandra and Denmark Roads were divided up into plots and auctioned off in the same year, hence the street, and pub, names. On his accession the King appointed her a Lady of the Garter – an unusual act the previous one having been, Margaret, Countess of Richmond, the mother of Henry VII in 1488. This typical Victorian street-corner home-from-home pub is still with us and still largely serves the local populace. Refurbished a while ago it now is very 'wooden' with reclaimed wood everywhere, real ale &c. more modern now (2017).

PRINCESS ROYAL 172 Wellingborough Road also **Talareks.**
This pub is still with us, but with a different name to those above. It seems it started out as a Pork Butchers, the first entry (1854) being an Edward Slater & pork butcher. In my youth this was a 'gay' pub, in fact, as far as I know the only gay establishment at the time. This all changed with the name change sometime in the late 1980s – early 90s.

PYTCHLEY ARMS 24 Pytchley Street.
Named after the street. It was located on the northeast corner of the junction of Pytchley and Ecton Streets. All the streets in this area are named after local villages; Harold Street is in fact, Harrold Street. At one time it functioned as the Ukrainian Club. At the time of writing it appears to be converting into a private house (2017). Charles Miles is listed at this address as a Beer-Retailer in 1878 and the last entry is in 1951.

QUART POT INN 52A Marefair and 1 Quart Pot Lane.
When a pub gives its name to a thoroughfare it usually means that the pub has been a long-time landmark. It is listed in the **RBN** 1898 as having documents from the 16-17th centuries, but these have disappeared, like many others. However, the same book says that the passageway alongside the pub was called Quart Pot Lane since the rule of Edward I (1272-1307) making this one of the contenders for the oldest pub.

I never saw this establishment open as a pub, but I clearly remember the quaint yellow sandstone building opposite the PDSA. It closed in the late 1930s, to become a watchmaker's shop and I seem to remember it being a teashop for a while. The only times I entered it was in the 1970s when it sold antiques. The pub has gone, but the lane survives, its name changed about 1900 to Doddridge Street although everyone I knew as a child in the 1950s called it by the old name. **RBN,** *gift of Richard Massingberg 1680.*

QUEEN ADELAIDE 50 Manor Road, Kingsthorpe also **Queen's Head.**

When this establishment first acquired a beer-only licence in 1838 it was the Queen's Head; it had changed to the present one by 1854.

Queen Adelaide was Adelaide Louisa Theresa Caroline Amelia (1792-1849) the daughter of George, Duke of Saxe-Meiningen and the wife of King William the Fourth (1830-1837). The pub was probably named after her death in 1849.

A Cornelius Love bought the pub in 1854 for £165 and he probably changed the name. In 1893 it was sold to Phipps Brewery for £1,500, but the Love family continued to run it well into the late 1930s. The steep hill on which it stands is called Loves Hill – but this could be because the lane used to lead to a well-known courting area. In 1951 it acquired a wine license and a full one in 1961.

Cornelius Love was a good example of a man that in the past often ran pubs alongside other trades; this was especially true in the villages. It seems that in 1937 there still was a room in the pub that had been Cornelius' shoemaking shop. The shoes he made were sent to London in carts drawn by his Shepherd dogs. One story is that one of his dogs got lost in London and made its way home in only two days – I wonder if it was still drawing a cart? He kept Shepherd dogs because he was *also* a Shepherd *and* a butcher – carrying on this business in another part of the premises and slaughtering in the yard at the rear. I imagine that you could have gone to the pub, had a pint of the house-brewed beer, had your shoes mended or brought a new pair, ate a mutton chop while you waited and took a joint home for the week-end.

QUEEN ELEANOR HOTEL London Road.
This pub once stood at the junction of the London and Newport
Pagnell roads, now it sits by the busy dual carriageway that leads to
the M1. The pub looks modern, especially after a considerable
extension and revamp a few years ago, but I am informed that it
actually goes back to the 1880s.

Queen Eleanor was the wife of Edward I (1239-1307). Their
betrothal was political, designed to stop a war between England and
Aquitaine, it took place in 1254 when Edward, then a Prince, was
fifteen and Eleanor was only nine. Unusually their marriage proved
to be a happy one and Eleanor went with him on many of his travels,
in 1270 even accompanying him on the Fifth Crusade. In 1290,
whilst Edward was conducting a campaign against the Scots she fell
ill and died at Harby near Lincoln. Her embalmed body was carried
to London for burial in Westminster Abbey and at each resting-place
the King ordered a cross to be erected. One of these lies on the
London Road only a few hundred yards from the pub – hence the
name. Edward seems to have been a loving husband, but he did have
his bad points, e.g. expelling all the Jews from England in 1290.

QUEEN'S ARMS.
There have been two of these in the town, neither of which survive.
Like the Queen's Head the Queen's Arms is usually thought to refer
to 'Good Queen Bess'. It would have always been a 'safe' name for a
pub.
QUEEN'S ARMS 46 Kettering Road.
This pub was situated on the east side of the bend at the start of the
Kettering Road, at the top of Raglan Street, facing towards Abington
Square. In 1878 W. Knight is listed as a Beer-Retailer, last entry is
1958.
QUEEN'S ARMS 6 Market Sq. also **Royal Oak** & **Windmill.**
According to *NN&Q* this establishment was called the Royal Oak in
the 18th century and from the Plan of 1768 it was run by a Samuel
Easton. As this name celebrates Charles I (see Royal Oak) it is
possible that this was its name directly after the Great Fire of 1675
and it was the rebuild of a pre Fire pub. The author of *NN&Q* 1889
says the name was changed to the Windmill *in living memory* and was

kept by a Thomas Butcher, later to become a Gunmaker. The name was changed to the Queen's Arms on the accession of Queen Victoria to the throne in 1837.

I think the last time I drank here was when the NDC Archaeology Unit was excavating the Green Dragon site. I recall having a session with several of the diggers and some of the men working on the Moat House Hotel. The building still stands largely unaltered externally above the ground floor and is now a bookmaker.

QUEEN'S DRAGOONS see Duke of Clarence (Old).

QUEEN'S HEAD.

We have had two, one, in Kingsthorpe became the Queen Adelaide.

Like the Queen's Arms this is supposed to be a 'safe' sign – often alluding to 'Good Queen Bess'. However, it seems there were pubs with this name long before Elizabeth I and it is thought that it originally alluded to the Queen of Heaven, i.e. the Virgin Mary. At the time of the Reformation such signs would have been swiftly changed into something less controversial and switching from the BVM to the Monarch would be an easy and cheap solution.

By all accounts Elizabeth I was a vain woman and many of the signs showing her were painted by unskilled locals. According to Sir Walter Raleigh's *History of the World* 1614: - *portraits of the Queen's Majestie made by unskilful and common painters were by her own order knocked into pieces and cast into the fire (A Proclamation* of 1563).

QUEEN'S HEAD 14 Gold Street.

This establishment stood on the east corner of College Street and Gold Street; the earliest record from the directories is 1824.

In July 1941 a Stirling Bomber crashed onto the town. It slid along Gold Street ripping into the fronts of several shops on the north side of the street. Parts of the aircraft ended up in the road in front of All Saints' Church and part of an engine on the roof. By all accounts the emergency was dealt with efficiently and the Church was saved.

All the crew bailed out successfully, except for the pilot whose parachute failed to open. He was found on Kingsthorpe Recreation Ground. Only one civilian suffered injury, a firewatcher who was blown off his bike and broke his leg.

Considering it had a wingspan of 99 feet it is surprising that more damage wasn't caused. As it was all of the ground floor of the pub was smashed to pieces and one of the 'plane's bombs ended up in a bedroom.

The Queen's Head survived this onslaught only to be demolished circa 1961 to be replaced by the District Bank, the premises later occupied by Shu-Value.

QUEEN'S HEAD Kingsthorpe see **Queen Adelaide.**

RACEHORSE 15 Abington Square.
Pubs are quite often named after racehorses, but this one seems to have been named after any, or all, racehorses. The name may have some connection with the custom many years ago of racing horses,

bulls and even donkeys (see Bantam Cock) from the Racecourse Crossroad (White Elephant Junction) to Abington Square.

The earliest entry is 1840, but it is probably much older – not, however in its present form. The drawing of circa 1900 shows a three-storey building with a protruding ground floor, as today, but in 1900 the top two floors had three windows instead of four and a covered balcony of wrought iron sat on top of the ground floor extension. The front of the extension was also completely different. A clue to its age can be gained from the fact that it used to

have a bowling green at the back; a visit to the garden today will make this evident.

George Chaloner took this pub in 1852 as an advertisement in the *Northampton Mercury* 17th January of that year states, it goes on to tell that the stables have been repaired and that George is continuing with his plumbing, glazing and painting business.

The drastic changes took place during the Second World War and because of shortages it took many months to complete the work. Interior alterations were decorated in what was then a rather dated mock-Tudor style.   An advertisement from the *Northampton Independent* 18/7/1941 has; - *MR. AND MRS. EVANS wish to Thank all Friends and Customers for their patronage during the last two years of re-building. The BAR and SMOKE-ROOM IS NOW OPEN, and the Large Lounge is temporarily Closed for Refurnishing.*

On his retirement in 1960 the Northampton Borough Licensing Justices congratulated Thomas Evans for 33½ years as licensee of the Racehorse. He took over from his brother-in-law in 1927 in the 1960 passed it over to his son-in-law and daughter, Stan and Mollie Malin. Acquired by Paul and Alyson Hepworth in ---- it is now called the Black Prince.

RAILWAY HOTEL (TAVERN) 16 Cotton End.

This pub is still there and along with its near neighbour, the Pomfret Arms, makes an interesting pair. The Pomfret Arms was evidently a Carriers' pub and the oldest. This one, as the name implies catered to the railway. In the 1890s the present door was a window and the large double doors of the 1890s are now a window.   Unfortunately in the last few years the ground floor wooden sashes have been replaced by plastic frames.

On the upside it does appear to be a straightforward down-to-earth pub. David Keenan, the owner said to the *C&E* 12/6/95, *We run a simple pub here. It's an ordinary pub for working people and it has not changed at all over the past 40 years.* The earliest reference I have for it is 1870.

RAILWAY TAVERN 1 Black Lion Terrace (Hill).
With the arrival of the railway a new sort of pub sprang up. These were often referred to as hotels, and in many cases this is what they were. Unlike the coaching inn they did not need large numbers of stables and could concentrate on accommodating people. They were often very close to stations, convenient for passengers and railway staff.

Black Lion Terrace no longer exists. It only consisted of three houses at right angles to Chalk Lane and faced the Old Black Lion. It ceased to be a pub in the 1950s and I can remember it being a bed-and-breakfast place in the early 1960s when I worked on the Castle Excavations. The earliest record of the pub is 1858 and must have been named for the original small railway halt that was here before the construction of the much larger Castle Station in the 1860s.

The Star & Railway Inn, Weston Terrace, is often confused with this pub, but appears to have started life as the Star in 1845, changing its name to cash in on the new trade.

RAM 19 Sheep Street.
On *Speed's* Map 1610 Sheep Street is called *sheepe market* so it would be reasonable to have an inn of this name here. *RBN* 1898 lists a Ram in Sheep-market, which, no doubt, is the same inn. A document dated 1758 in the NRO has: *And out of all that other Messuage or Inn with*  *the appertances situate standing and being in the Parish of Saint Sepulchre in the said town of Northampton called or known by the*

name or Sign of the Ram now in the Tenure or Occupation of Thomas Gamble Thos: Peach together with the Stable and Garden in Bearward street and little Close of Pasture lying near the Mayorhold belong to the said last mentioned Inn called the Ram....

It goes on to describe the Cross Keys so there can be little doubt as to its location. It is almost certainly pre Great Fire but I not found any references to it in the **Great Fire Court** 1675 Proceedings. However, the pamphlet, *A True & Faithful Relationship of the Late Dreadful Fire at Northampton* 1675 has: - *Burned in Ship* (Sheep) *street as far as the Rose and Crown and somewhat beyond.* The exact location of the Rose & Crown is not known, but it is possible that the fire did not reach the Ram and so it would not have been subject to the Fire Court.

The wool trade was of great importance to the town in the past and the Ram heraldically is the Crest of the Clothworkers' Drapers' and Leatherworkers' Companies – plenty of good reasons to use this sign.

It must have been of some importance in the 18th century, as it got included in the *Universal Directory* of 1791. In the past it hosted Masonic Lodges and during the days when the Racecourse *was* a racecourse, champion jockeys and their mounts.

In my youth I would drink here with my pals on our Saturday night pub-crawl. The bar was equipped with a Shove-Halfpenny board, Dominoes and a unique game to me, which I think was called by the regulars 'Bar-Skittles' and is also called 'Devil Amongst the Tailors'. I understand the game originated in London in the 18th century. There were nine small skittles, about three inches high standing on a platform about fifteen inches square. Fixed to one corner was a post perhaps three feet high and hanging from this, on a chain was a wooden ball, the ball hung clear of the platform by an inch or so. The aim of the game was to swing the ball around the post and across the platform knocking down the skittles. It looked deceptively easy and a rather 'tame' game to us, but I tried it a couple of times and learnt better!

RECRUITING SERJEANT see **Belvedere.**

RED COW.

There have been two, or possibly three of these in the town. Milk vendors in days gone by would announce that the milk they were selling was from a red cow. Red cows were rarer than black ones and so the milk was preferred, it was often recommended in old prescriptions. I imagine the idea was to imply that the 'milk' sold in this pub was preferable to that sold elsewhere.

RED COW 27 or 29 Bailiff Street.

If the street numbers on *O/S* 1964 were the same for the 19th century this pub would have been on the south corner of Elm Street and Bailiff Street. It doesn't seem to have been very long-lived, probably a small beer-shop.

RED COW Horsemarket.

We only have an advertisement from the *Northampton Mercury* of 23rd of September 1734 to tell us of this pub's existence: -*Whereas on JOHN STANLEY (a thin middle-sized Man, full shoulder'd and goes stooping of a red Complexion, full lipp'd, suppos'd to be between 50 and 60 Years of Age, had on a green Shag Frock, and goes under the Denomination of the King's Rat-catcher hir'd a Roan gelding (about 14 hands, full aged, with a whisk Tail if not alter'd, and cuts of all Fours) of JOHN MASON at the Red Cow in Horse-Market, Northampton on Tuesday the 10th of this Instant, proposing to return by the 15th Instant, but has not since been heard of: Whoever therefore will secure the said Man & Horse, and give Notice thereof to John Mason at the Red Cow aforesaid, shall have a good Reward and reasonable Charges allowed.*

RED COW Location Unknown.

Another of those pubs listed in the *RBN 1898* that I have been unable to trace – it is possible that this is the Red Cow, Horsemarket above.

RED EARL Aberdale Road also **Firefly** and **Dallington Brook Inn.**

This pub stood on the corner of Aberdale Road and Camrose Road on the Spencer Estate; the location could be the reason for its name, the Red Earl being John Poynts, 5th Earl Spencer. He was one of the leading Liberal figures during the late 18th and early 19th centuries. His nickname comes not from the colour of his politics, but from his huge red beard.

The pub opened in January 1956 as a purpose-built 'estate pub' catering for children with what was called a large unlicensed garden room – parents, however, could purchase drinks elsewhere and take them in. The pub was furnished in a contemporary style and had a large car park.

During its chequered career it changed name to the Firefly probably after the dinghy designed by Uffa Fox. Its popularity seems to have declined over the years and was demolished in August 1997 after standing derelict for many months.

RED HORSE Bridge Street.
This could have been named after some locally celebrated racehorse – perhaps it won someone enough money to set up a pub. Pedro of Castille, Father-in-law of John of Gaunt had a red, or roan, horse as his badge (see Red Lion).

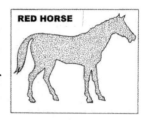

The one record of this pub is a news item from the *Northampton Mercury*, July 22nd 1751: - *On Sunday Morning last one Smith, a Blacksmith, who lodged at the Red-Horse in Bridge-Street in this Town, robb'd his Bedfellows of 18s and his Cloaths, leaving his own in the Room but being persued, was taken at Newport-Pagnell, and committed to Aylesbury Gaol, from whence he will be removed to take his Trial at our approaching Assizes.*

RED HOUSE 157 Weedon Road also **Red Rover.**
Still with us, but since 1996 has been called "Big Hand Mo's". It is at the time of writing (June 1999) undergoing refurbishment.

It may have received the name because it is built of red bricks, there once having been brickworks nearby. It could have changed to the Red Rover after James Fenimore Cooper's novel of that name in June 1967 when the owners, Phipps Brewery redecorated it, and at the time owned a famous stagecoach called the Red Rover.

The earliest reference under this name is in 1900, when the address is given as *Gregory terr.* But there is one reference under Beer-Retailers in 1889 to a *George Starmer of Weedon Road, St.*

James' End – could this be the same premises and a relative of the M. A. Starmer named as the proprietor in 1900?

RED LION.

Reputedly the most common sign today, although if it is, it is run a close second by the Crown. In this town there have been two Red Lions to five Crowns. In reply to a query in a national newspaper recently it was stated that there were 630 Red Lions out of 55,000 pubs in the country.

The origins of this sign probably lie with the badge of John of Gaunt, Duke of Lancaster and fourth son of Edward III. John of Gaunt lived from 1340 to 1399 and the Red Lion began to appear as a pub sign about a century later. When James VI of Scotland became James I of England (1603) he ordered the Red Lion of Scotland to be displayed on all public buildings and this must have added to its popularity.

RED LION *or* RED LYON Bearward Street *or* Sheep Street.

Although there are only two of these they do cause some confusion. It is evident that both establishments were large and popular; there are references throughout the 18th century to the *Red Lion in Northampton* in the ***Northampton Mercury***. By comparison to today the town was relatively small so it was often that street names were not used, so I have no way of knowing which Red Lion is being referred to. However, the Red Lion, Horsemarket was at one time referred to as *one of the three principle inns* – the others being the Peacock and the George, so it is probable that most of the advertisements &c. refer to this inn. This is borne out by the fact that the Red Lion, Bearward Street is only listed in one directory, ***Pigot's*** 1824, *Hy. Bray*. According to the ***C&E*** in 1959 this inn stood *on the present site of the Covered Market*. This indicates that the southern cellar of the double cellars of the Bear could have been the Red Lion's. I visited the Bear's cellars in the 1980s and the landlord thought that the pub had originally been two side-by-side – although this is not the site of the Covered Market it is close enough, however, in the past not only pubs had big cellars.

The **Red Lyon**, Sheep Street, is undoubtedly the same inn as is clearly labelled such on *Nobel & Butlin's* Map of 1747, occupying the site of the east end of the Covered Market (Northampton Municipal Fish and Meat, now Northampton Arts Collective) Market. During the Great Election of 1768 this inn was the headquarters of the Tories, whilst the Whigs were ensconced in the George. Opposing parties at each end of the Drapery – a formula for trouble – see the George for an account of what happened!

At the time of the demolition of the Fish Market I got access not only to the air-raid shelter under the Market; bet a chance to see the inside of the remnant of the Red Lion. It appears that the building was literally sliced in half, the southern part demolished for the Fish Market and the other half left. The frontage of this part still survives and can be seen above part of the 'Select Convience' store attached to the so-called 'Bus Interchange' (2017).

RED LION Horsemarket also **Unicorn.**

That this inn was old is not in dispute, see the previous entry and the bulk of the references in the *Northampton Mercury* are probably to this establishment.

Thanks to Mr. Taylor's research in the 19th century I can reproduce a quote from James Hissey's *A Tour in a Phaeton Through the Eastern Counties* 1889.

Had we according to our wont taken a tour of inspection, I have little doubt but that we should have elected to spend the night beneath the sign of the Red Lion. A most comfortable-looking and charmingly picturesque old half-timbered hostelry this, a picture in itself more pleasing than many a painting, with its curved wood  *front, its projecting upper storey and its grand red tiled roof. Upon the spandrel on one side of the spacious doorway of this delightful old-world hostel is a sculptured representation of St. George with time-honoured lance, on the other the famous dragon is given* (could we have a once named George & Dragon Inn here?). *We were told that this ancient house was built in the year 1412 and a grand old inn it is – you might travel far before coming upon such another, let us hope that it will long be spared to us.*

Further information from James Hissey's book one could conclude that the Red Lion was a Tory stronghold and in view of the knowledge we have from the occurrences during the Great Election of 1768 (see the George) this item could refer to the Red Lion, Bearward Street. In the 'Good Old Days' you had to own property to vote and therefore a reasonable income and what you drank indicated which party you supported. The Tories drank port, whilst the Whigs drank punch, could this be why there was an inn around the corner in Marefair called the Rose & Punchbowl? Entries run from 1824 to 1958

RED ROVER see **Red House.**

RED, WHITE & BLUE Hope's Place (Barrack Road).

Only one entry, *Taylor's* 1864, this could be a transient name for one of the many small beer-shops with patriotic names in the area of the Barracks at the time.

This sign probably does not refer to the Union Flag (Union Jack), but to an old sea song. Another sign, which we have not had here, is the sign of the Three Admirals and here we have a clue. The three active Admirals of the Fleet are called the Red, White and Blue. In a town so far from the sea one would not expect signs with naval connections, but we have a share of them, usually ships such as the Albion. This could just be patriotic fervour or, did the Barracks house Marines at one time?

RIFLE see **Marquis of Carabas.**

RIFLE BUTT(S)
183 Harlestone Road.
This pub is either named after the butts used when shooting game birds or a nearby rifle range. References start in 1884 and the pub is still with us.

RIFLE DRUM Drum (Dury) Lane.
According to the **RBN** 1898 there was in the 16th or 17th centuries an inn called the Drums in Drum Lane and this is probably the same pub. The plans of the Great Election 1768 show a *Wm. Billingham Vict.* occupying this position, he was probably the proprietor.

This pub is still with us and is probably the last of the really small pubs, having only one small bar.

RIFLEMAN'S ARMS.
We have had two of these as well as a Rifle Butt, Rifle Drum and a Rifle, although the latter may have referred to a clicker's sharpening stick.

RIFLEMAN'S ARMS 65 Bailiff Street.
This pub was on the north corner of Lawrence Street and Bailiff Street. On *O/S* Plans 1901 and 1938 the site is shown as two houses, but by *O/S* 1964 it is a double property, so presumably the establishment flourished from a small beer-shop to a street corner pub. Dates from 1864 to 1956.

RIFLEMENS' ARMS 173 Bridge Street.
One entry, *Taylor's* 1864, George Fullard. Perhaps George was a retired soldier, although this pub was in Bridge Street I can find no other references to it. Number 173 is quoted as the address of the Magpie in other directories, but in *Kelly* 1864 the number given is 154 and the proprietor as George Baldwin, so these are not the same premises.

RISING SUN.
A popular sign, there have been three in the town. The Rising Sun is a badge of Edward III, it forms part of the arms of Ireland – but in these cases it was probably used because it is the crest of the Distillers' Company, which is a bit ambitious for pubs with a beer only licenses. It could have been chosen as an optimistic symbol of a new beginning – a new enterprise.

RISING SUN 52 Broad Lane (Street).
This pub stood opposite the Broad Street Tavern, they don't seem to have been open at the same times. Dates 1858 to 1910.

RISING SUN 2 Gas Street also **Sun.**
This pub was on the southern corner of the junction of Court Road and Gas Street, opposite the Harbour Lights. *O/S* Plan 1901 shows the building, but *O/S* 1938 does not. Directory dates run from 1845 to 1907 and from 1884 it is listed as the Sun. In 1861 there was a sale of the pub and brewhouse, *retail trade had been carried on for last 25 years and the business up to the present was in the occupation of Mrs. Sarah Bull.* The two entries up to this date, 1845 and 1858 both give a James Bull as the proprietor, was Sarah his widow? Information supplied by Mr. Starmer.

RISING SUN Gold Street -- Kingswell St./Woolmonger Street.
Part of the Linnell Estate auctioned off in 1847, probably on the corner of Kingswell and Woolmonger Streets. (See Dolphin for details).

RIVETTERS ARMS.
I have located two of these and I could have expected more. The rivetters referred to are of course not shipbuilders, but the boot and shoe workers who worked the new riveting machines in the factories.
RIVETTERS ARMS 13 Market Street also? **Patriot/Rivetters Arms.**

RIVETTERS ARMS 63 or 73 Scarletwell Street.
A typical street corner pub where people would go of an evening for a pint and a gossip. Dates from directories run from 1864 to 1910.

ROAD TO MOROCCO Bridgewater Drive.
An estate pub built in the 1970s with a Moroccan theme; some aspects are still evident. Presumably named after the song.

ROBIN HOOD (& LITTLE JOHN).

Robin Hood crops up with two pubs, one of them originally called Robin Hood & Little John. A popular sign all over the country. I have no knowledge of a sign in the town bearing a rhyme, but many elsewhere do - this is one version: -

> *Kind gentlemen and Yeomen good,*
> *Come in and sup with Robin Hood,*
> *If Robin Hood be a-gone,*
> *Come in and drink with Little John.*

ROBIN HOOD 23 Francis Street.

This pub was about halfway up Francis Street on the east side, it appears to have been an average terraced house. Dates, 1858 to 1952.

ROBIN HOOD also Robin Hood & Little John.

35 St. James' Road (variously; Dallington, Duston and St; James' End).

At one time I thought that there might be three pubs with this name as *Slater* 1850 gives two Robin Hoods and Little Johns, one in St. James' End, run by a Charles Horne; and the other, in Dallington, by Elizabeth Edmonds. However, the two directories of 1847, *Hickman* and *Kelly* both give a Mrs. C. Edmonds as the proprietor, but list the address as St. James and Dallington respectively. You have to be careful with directories! Why *Slater* had two entries in 1850 is probably that that was the year of a change over and the original entry wasn't removed.

This pub stood just before the bend of St. James' Road, after West Bridge, a little nearer town, but on the opposite side to the Green Man. The first entry in a directory is in 1830 when it is called the Robin Hood & Little John. By 1864 just Robin Hood is listed in one- and the last time Little John appears in a directory is in 1876. An old photograph shows a stucco sign with *The Robin Hood Inn-P. Phipps & Co. Ltd.-Noted Ales & Stout.* According to the etched windows and lantern over the door it boasted a Concert Room. It was demolished in 1976.

ROEBUCK.

This sign could be a heraldic crest, it occurred twice in this town, one was still going when I was a child and the other is still with us, but officially known as the White Hart and commonly, Shipman's.

ROEBUCK 25 Grafton Street also **Stag.**

This pub was on the south side of Grafton Street more or less opposite the old Labour Exchange. In my day it was clad on the ground floor with green glazed ceramic tiles similar to the ones on the Old Black Lion today. I never saw this pub open as it closed in 1959.

The earliest map to show this area is *Law's* 1847 when it was an orchard, by *O/S* 1901 a building with a side entrance is shown directly opposite a Court labelled in 1847 '2nd' and in 1901 as Kinburn Place. The general plan of this building does not alter until its demolition in the 1960s; the earliest entry was in 1878. However, an announcement on the *Northampton Mercury* January 1854 has: -

TO BE SOLD BY PRIVATE CONTRACT

ALL that substantial and newly-erected PUBLIC-HOUSE, situate in GRAFTON STREET, NORTHAMPTON, and known by the sign of the STAG, containing three good cellars, bar, tap-room, bar-parlour, pantry, brewhouse, good well of water, with pump: large club-room, 50 feet by 20 feet, and 13 feet high: and five bed-rooms. There is an old-established BUSINESS attached to the House, of 20 years standing which is also TO BE DISPOSED OF, the present proprietor being about to leave the town. The STOCK and FIXTURES to be taken at valuation. – Two-thirds of the Purchase Money may remain on the Property, if required.

For further particulars, apply, to the Proprietor, Mr. W. Manning, at the Stag: or to Mr. E. F. Law Architect, Wood-street

By December of the same year the Stag was being offered for auction, *now and for 20 years used as a Beer-House, known as The*

Stag. As to apply for the particulars is the same as above I conclude that was no result from the first advertisement. Is this, in fact an earlier incarnation of the Roebuck? A sign with a stag on it could easily be called a roebuck, or vice versa.

ROEBUCK Drapery also **Shipman's** and **White Hart &c.**
One of several names that Shipman's seems to have had (see entry).

ROMANY HOTEL Kingsley Road.
Before Northampton was built up, when most of the land outside the old town walls and main roads was just fields and woods, a lane linked Kingsley to the village of Kingsthorpe, now called the Kingsley Road and Kingsthorpe Grove. In the past it has been known as Tinkers' Lane or Gypsy Lane and was a popular site for  Gypsy encampments, especially when there was racing and fairs on the nearby Racecourse.

A stream that issues on the old Northampton Golf Course and joins the north arm of the River Nenn at the top of St. Andrew's Road used to be crossed by a ford at about where the pub now stands. For many years this has been buried in pipes and this is why the Romany is built on a reinforced concrete raft supported by 35ft. concrete piles. The land hereabouts is built up.

The Romany Hotel was opened in November 1938. A purpose built establishment it was provided with a forecourt, for a considerable number of cars. The interior was in Tudor and Jacobean styles, rather better executed than was done in the Racehorse three years later. The three bars, Bar, Smoke Room and Lounge have gone, as have the fine wood veneer. The pub no longer provides accommodation for travelling salesmen &c., but real ale, food, music and other entertainment for University students from the nearby Avenue Campus.

ROSE Gold Street.
One from the **RBN** 1898 16th-17th century list that is untraced. It is possible that it is the same inn as the Rose & Crown in the same street.

The symbol of the rose in early days represented the Virgin Mary, so it could have been pre-Reformation, perhaps converting to the Rose & Crown at that time. A golden rose was the badge of Edward I (1272-1307) and there is the red rose of Lancaster and the white of York as well as the Tudor rose - take your pick!

ROSE & CROWN.
This is a very popular name and I have found five in the town. It is supposed to have come from the Wars of the Roses and symbolised the marriage of Henry VII to Elizabeth, daughter of Edward III.
ROSE & CROWN 1 Alma St. (19th cent.) or 1 Rickard St.
Alma Street changed to Rickard Street to avoid confusion with Alma Street, St. James' End. This pub stood on the east corner of the junction of Rickard Street and Main Road. It is shown on **O/S** 1964 as a substantial corner property with a small yard to the rear. The area was cleared and turned into an industrial estate a few years ago. Entries are from 1864 to1968.
ROSE & CROWN 30 Gold Street.
This establishment was on the north side of Gold Street some idea of its age may be obtained from the earliest document (1750) that mentions it: - *All that Messuage or Tenement with Appertances lately erected and built by the said John Tebbutt now used as an Inn and known by the Sign of the Rose & Crown now in The occupation of the said John Tebbutt....*

There is always going to be some confusion over this sign as there were at least two in existence within the town walls at about this time – if not three. Advertisements and other references often only give Rose & Crown Northampton. The site of this inn is at present the St. John Ambulance charity shop, Wilkinsons, next door is probably where the White Hart stood.

The earliest definite reference to this inn is in 1750 and *Law's* Map of 1847 shows it, it seems to have survived at least to 1911, so perhaps it was a victim of the First World War?

ROSE & CROWN Market Square.

One of the pubs from the *RBN* 1898 list that I have been unable to track down. As the Market Square and Sheep Street are close it is possible that this inn and the one below are the same establishment.

ROSE & CROWN Sheep Street.

According to *A True & Faithful Relationship of the Late Dreadful Fire at Northampton* 1675, *the fire: - burned in Ship* (Sheep) *street as far as the Rose & Crown and some what beyond.*

Was this inn rebuilt? We have the following advertisement from the *Northampton Mercury*, December 1720: - *The Rose & Crown INN in Northampton, a large lately new Shash'd, Wainscotted and hang'd, with stables for 100 horse, large vaults for wine, and other Conviences, and an old accustom'd House To be let with or without part of its furniture at Christmass next. Enquire of Mr. Rogers at Northampton.*

There is no indication of its location, but I assume that as it describes an *old accustom'd house* it refers to one that has been trading for some time, although this could be sales talk. If this is then the Rose & Crown in Sheep Street was rebuilt after the Great Fire of 1675.

ROSE & CROWN Welford Road, Kingsthorpe.

This pub closed sometime before 1956 and became a church. In the 1950s the first 'bus to run on Sundays to Kingsthorpe was after 10am, too late for Mass at the Roman Catholic Cathedral in Barrack Road, a long walk away. The old Rose & Crown was purchased by the Church to act as a Chapel of Ease to the Cathedral, saving the Kingsthorpe Catholics a long walk. Directory dates run from 1830 to 1954. **Mercury** 1782-3 has *Rose & Crown (Old), Kingsthorpe* (2017).

ROSE & PUNCHBOWL 18 Marefair.

There is a photograph of this pub in the Central Library collection and the name on the wall is G. Cosford who had the pub in the 1890s written on the back is the date May 18 1898.

A political sign, the pub was probably first called the Rose. Punch was drunk by Whigs when it became fashionable at the end of the 17th century and many establishments added 'Punchbowl' to their name to indicate their allegiance. The Tories drank sack and claret, reminding them of times past. This indicates a fashionable inn from the 17th or 18th century. Entries are all Widow Cooper 1824 to the last 1898.

ROYAL ENGINEER 21 College Street.
This must have been either on the south corner, or close to the junction between St. Katherine's Street and College Street. Only appears once, *Taylor* 1858, *Marshall, William (Royal Engineer), 21 College Street.*
ROYAL GEORGE Adelaide Street see **Duke of Edinburgh.**
ROYAL HOTEL Gold Street see **Swan & Helmet.**
ROYAL OAK.
I've found four of these, after the Great Fire of Northampton in 1675 King Charles II gave the town 1,000 tunn of timber from the Whittlebury and Salcey Forests and a remission of seven years chimney tax. This is commemorated with a statue of the monarch and inscription above the portico of All Saints' Church. Still today on Oak Apple Day (May 29th) the King's birthday, the statue is wreathed with oak leaves.

In 1651, after the Battle of Worcester, Charles II escaped by shinning up a oak tree at Boscobel – this incident was celebrated during the national rejoicing at the Restoration and an enactment of 1664 fixed Royal Oak Day and it was (and in this town, still is) celebrated for centuries. The King forgave us for our support of Cromwell, and helped after the Fire, so a few Royal Oaks are to be expected.
ROYAL OAK 33 Agustine Street and 31 and 33 Gas Street.
The *Goad Fire Insurance* Plan 1899 shows a double property at the end of Agustine Street on the south side as a public house, *Wright* 1884 gives it a "bhs" so it was a beer-shop. Dates run from 1878 to 1910.
ROYAL OAK 6 Market Square see **Queen's Arms**
ROYAL OAK 133 Harborough Road.

Little about this pub except the entries, from 1884 to 1962.
ROYAL OAK Woolmonger Street.
There are only two entries for this pub, 1845 and 1858 neither with a street number, so it is impossible to locate the establishment. It could be another name for one of the pubs that were on this street at one time.

ROYAL STANDARD.

The Royal Standard is the flag that flies over Buck House when the Queen is in residence and would make a good loyal sign for a pub although I don't think it would imply that Her Majesty was tucked away in the Snug supping a milk stout!
ROYAL STANDARD 13 Nelson Street, Barrack Road.
With a sign like this and its location, this pub was probably opened by a retired soldier to cater for the men in the Barracks opposite. The *O/S* 1901 shows tiny one-up-one-down houses and this pub was probably one of these – a small beer-shop. The dates are 1858 to 1910.

ROYAL STANDARD Woolmonger Street.
Another pub in Woolmonger Street that I have no number for and so cannot locate – like the Royal Oak above. Dates are 1884 to 1906.

RUNNING HORSE St. James' End.
To Be Lett at Michaelmas, or sooner if required. A very good House in St. James's End, near the Town of Northampton, lately the Sign of the Running Horse, containing 3 rooms on a Floor, with good stabling, Brewhouse, Yard and Orchard.
Enquire of Mr. Richard Parr in Northampton.
Northampton Mercury *July 1729.*
The advertisement says lately *the Sign of*, but it may not have been an inn, large private houses often had a brewhouse.

RUSSELL ARMS see **Jolly Crispin.**

SADDLER'S ARMS.
We have had two of these in the town, one of which is still with us and has kept its original name. [No longer]. The name is fairly common and probably indicates a saddler's shop or that the landlord had been, or still was, a saddler.

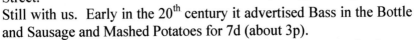

SADDLER'S ARMS 26-30 Bridge Street.
Still with us. Early in the 20th century it advertised Bass in the Bottle and Sausage and Mashed Potatoes for 7d (about 3p).

According to the **Real Ale Guide** 1983 this was one of only two pubs in the town selling real ale. I can remember going in here for that very reason, later it was 'refurbished' i.e. knocked into one and became incredibly noisy with very loud music.

Inflation over the years didn't only affect the price of a pint. "When it's a pound a pint I'm giving up drinking!" How many people said that? An advertisement for this pub in the **C&E** in 1960 said: - *The original sausage and mash shop. Served every lunch-time. 2/- (10p) per person. Orders welcome for parties.*

The first entry is 1850 John Parberry, Beer-Retailer, considering its location; there is no reason why it couldn't have been here much earlier.

SADDLER'S ARMS 25 Marefair.
As far as I can tell it only had two proprietors and the first, Robert Hallam is listed in *Melville* 1867 as *Hallam, Robert, Saddler & Beer-retailer.* It appears to have survived for something over twenty years. By at least 1906 the address was a Pawnbrokers. Pub dates run from 1858 to 1878.

SALLETT or **HELMET** Cow Lane (Swan Street).
Listed in the *Assembly Order* 1585 and probably perished in the Great fire.

SALTERS INN Abington Street.
One of the *RBN* 1898 16th and 17th century inns not found.

SARACEN'S HEAD.
There are two possible explanations for this sign. One, like the Turk's Head it is derived from the Crusades. A fierce depiction of a Turk or Saracen's face was incorporated by many Crusaders into their Arms and this could have filtered through to the inns in the usual way. Two, often these signs depicted a quite respectable Saracen and it thought that these were erected to honour Thomas Becket's mother who was the daughter of a Saracen. Thomas Becket is associated with Northampton, it was in our castle that the barons attempted to try him and it is from St. Andrew's Priory that he fled to the continent.
SARACEN'S HEAD 4 Abington Street.
A pub that had been there a long while, a Deed Poll dated 26th March, 1592, of Agnes Hopkyns, of Northampton, widow, relates to *a messuage or tenement, in the town of Northampton, commonly called Le Saraznes hedd in Abbyngton Streate.* The *Great Fire Court Book* 1675 refers to an Ann Harbert at the Sarazens Head.

The frontage of the south side of Abington Street from Wood Hill to Dychurch Lane was once occupied by two buildings. The Wood Hill half was taken up with the old Guildhall, demolished in 1864 and the other half by this inn.

The inn has been mentioned in poetry, *Poems on Several Occasions* by Nicholas Rowe, London 1747 has the lines entitled "The Lord Griffin to the Earl of Scarfoale"
> *Tho' thy Dear's Father kept an Inn*
> *At grizly Head of Saracen,*
> *For Carriers at Northampton,*
> *Yet she might come of gentler kin*
> *Than e'er that Father dreamt on.*

There is mention of this inn in the minute book of the Court of Aldermen dated December 30th 1702: - *Memorandum Francis Granborow miller at Cliffords Mill in Little Hoton parish Comitat North'ton was convicted before me Benjamin Bullivant Mayor for swearing six oaths sworn at the goate in North'ton on Thurs, last, he comes to the Saracens head Inne every Sat., could not be found.* The *goate* referred to here is probably the Goat Inn in Gold Street.

An advertisement in the **Northampton Mercury** June 1752 for this inn was for a fire-eater, a Mr. Powell from London. The advertisement claims, amongst other things that *He eats red-hot coals out of the fire as natural as bread. and He fills his Mouth with red-hot Charcoal, and broils a Slice of Beef or Mutton upon his Tongue; and any Person may blow the Fire with a Pair of Bellows at the same Time. It also claims that he melts a mixture of various flammable substances such as rosin and wax along with alum and lead and eats them with a spoon (which he calls Dish of Soop)!* Admission, one-shilling (5p.).

The **Great Election Plan** of 1768 shows a William Dorrell in occupation and the churchwardens' accounts of St. Giles' parish for *1802* has: - *Paid at the Saracens Head on Easter Monday as usual..£2..2s..0d.* "As usual" can also be found in the accounts of 1806.

Advertisements in the **Northampton Mercury** of the 18th century gives some idea of the size and importance of this inn at the time. An advertisement in 1765 refers to the inn as the Post-Office, in Northampton and one of 1752 shows that the inn was being used as a place of audit of the Duchy of Lancaster. The advertisement of October 1753 probably gives the best description: - *To be Lett at St. Thomas next, or sooner, if required, The Saracen's-Head Inn in Northampton, being an old and good-accustomed Inn, standing near the Market-Place, and in the Stamford, Peterborough and Cambridge Road; it is a very commodious House, with good Cellars, and Stabling for near 150 Horses. For Further Particulars, enquire of Mr. Richard Moriss, of Northampton.*

The inn had a large assembly room and this was often used for political and social gatherings. In 1859 the licence and sign was transferred to a house in Barrack Road. By 1860 a David Hall had taken possession of the old building and was running it as a Temperance Hotel.

SARACEN'S HEAD 1 Lawrence Street and Barrack Road.

This is the transfer mentioned above, a much smaller establishment. I recall sitting on the top deck of a 'bus and coming level with this sign when the 'bus stopped. If the sign had originally been intended as a compliment to Thomas Becket's mother the one I saw certainly wasn't! Although this pub did not close until 1970 I never visited it, probably because it was so far from our 'beaten track'.

SARACEN'S HEAD Market Square.
This is from the *RBN* 1898 16th and 17th century list and as the Saracen's Head; Abington Street was directly opposite the southern entrance to the Market Square it is possible that this is the same inn.

SAXON INN see **Moat House.**

SECRETS see **Peacock.**

SEWING MACHINE 62 St. Andrew's Street.
This pub was on the east side of the street, between the ends of Cromwell and Regent Streets. The name refers to the machines used in the production of boots and shoes rather than garments. Dates from 1834 to 1936.

SHAKESPEARE 3 Marefair.
Along with my friends I used to visit this pub back in the 1960s, it became our 'local'. Local is perhaps not the right word because we came from all over the county and beyond, such far-flung places as Wellingborough, Towcester, Long Buckby, Newport Pagnell and Aspley Guise. What we had in common was the Campaign for Nuclear Disarmament, girlfriends at the Art School, Jazz and long hair. We 'Beatniks' were not always welcome in the town's pubs. I can remember we were asked to leave one pub because one of us was 'thinking'!!

The landlord of the Shakespeare was different, we were made welcome, he was an artist. "I'd much rather have you lot in here than that lot of squaddies from over the road." He was referring to the North-Western Hotel opposite, renowned for its soldiers from Wootton Barracks and their weekend punch-ups.

The pub was located on the west corner of the junction of Horseshoe Street and Marefair. The reason for the name was because of a theatre that once stood to the east of it. First the theatre went for road widening in 1922 and then the pub fell victim to the Great God Car in 1974, the earliest I have is 1824.

SHAMROCK Grafton Street.
From an auction announcement in the *Northampton Mercury* July 1868: *Lot 6. – All that well-built BEERHOUSE known by the name of "The Shamrock" situate on the south side of Grafton Street, Northampton, comprising a large Bar, Tap-room, Club-room, Three Sleeping rooms, Kitchen, Cellar, with an Entrance Gateway used as a Coal-Store, detached Stable with Loft over, a large Yard, now in the occupation of Mr. Coughlan.*

SHIP.
Although we are about as far from the sea as you can get the Ship occurs three times in the town. It is thought that an inland Ship in pre-Reformation times was a Noah's Ark. The Royal George was a ship and probably the Albion and the portrait of a famous ship on a sign could end up just be called the Ship.

SHIP Drapery.
Taylor refers to this sign in the material for his articles in *NN&Q*. I thought it might be a contraction of Shipman's, but the reference is to the Great Election of 1768 and Shipman's business didn't start until 1790.

SHIP Green Lane.
One of *Burgess'* unique finds, with the bare surname, *England*. I have found in *Melville* 1861, *England, Septimus, Shopkeeper, Abbey lane, West Bridge*. And this is all, except for a Beer-Retailer, Daniel England at 39 Bouverie Street in *Slater* 1862. There is no evidence that these two are connected with the proprietor of the Ship, although Green Lane is quite close to the West Bridge.

SHIP Mercers' Row.
According to a schematic plan based on the 1831 poll, published in *NN&Q* this pub was located on the east corner of Conduit Lane and Mercers' Row, right next to the Duke of Clarence. The proprietor's name is given as *William Butcher Brickmaker* so presumably, like

many landlords of the time, he had two occupations. The *Great Election Plan* of 1768 gives *William Hill, victualler*, but no sign name.

SHIPMAN'S 12 Drapery and 3 Drum Lane also **White Hart, White Hart Tap, Roebuck** and possibly **Crown.**
This pub is licensed under its official name of the White Hart –
however, by the rule of common usage I have put
it under the name that everyone in the town calls
it.
    The *Northampton Mercury* in 1766
mentions the *Crown in Dury Lane kept by
William Peck.* Dury Lane was a "fashionable"
name for Drum Lane in the 18th century. Drum
Lane goes back at least as far as the 16th century
and probably derives from a pub called the Drum,
that's probably the forerunner of the present Rifle
Drum.
    One theory is that the Crown became the
Roebuck which in turn became the White hart,
but there is an advertisement from the
Northampton Mercury 24th January 1767
announcing the letting of the Roebuck and
describing it as: - *That Well-Known and good-
accustomed PUBLICK HOUSE Known by the
sign of the ROE-BUCK.*
    As the Crown was referred to one year before, it is unlikely to
have changed its name and then been described as well-known within
one year. The *publick house* was in the possession of a Mr. John
ROE at the time of letting, and this probably explains the name at the
time.
    The plans of the Great Election 1768, one year later, show a
property facing onto Dury Lane as *Back of the White Hart Rd.
Merrill.* Richard Merrill is listed as a Fellmonger, but could have
owned the pub and let it. To confuse things further in the Drapery
William Peck is shown as occupying the third property up from the
corner with Mercers' Row. There are six in the block up to Osborn's

Jitty. *O/S* 1901 has seven and the third from Mercers' Row is Shipman's!

As the pub has two entrances onto two thoroughfares it is possible that the Crown was the Drapery side and the White Hart Drum Lane. This ignores the fact that the Crown was described in 1766 as being in Dury Lane. It is easy to accept that the Roebuck had become the White Hart for they look similar on a sign.

By 1790 the business of W. & R. Shipman had started, and continued under the same family until 1945. At one time it was run by Dr. J. G. Shipman who was MP for Northampton for ten years. When he died his widow gave their house in Dallington for a convalescent home. During the Doctor's time the pub was known as "The Doctor's" so going to the doctor took on a new meaning!

W. & R. Shipman were originally wine merchants and bottled wine in rooms above the present long bar. Near the stairs can be seen a thick, lead pipe hanging down through the ceiling through which wine was transferred. At two places behind the bar there are groups of six brass taps with brass letters beside them. In days gone by these dispensed spirits &c. from casks above.

In my youth I occasionally went into Shipman's and at the time it was run by Mr. Herbert Pitcher, or 'Pitch' as he was known, a formidable character who ran a 'tight ship', often refusing us because of our long hair or just because he didn't feel like serving us that day. We still went back, even though at the time the pub didn't serve draught beer, and later, when it did start to serve draught, only in halves. It was a place we liked to call in now and then and I think we all respected Pitch. Pitch died at the beginning of 1987 and his wife, Jaquie took over for a while, retiring in July of the same year. The pub at the time of writing is run by Bob and Diane Wise.

The Barrel Bar was opened in 1950 and you could never get draught in there or bring it through from the Long Bar. We were worried about the fate of the interior of this pub when it changed hands after Jaquie's retirement, but the only real alterations was to rearrange the toilets and remove the wall between the Barrel Bar and the Long Bar, making it into a one bar pub. The actual bar in the Barrel Bar was taken out to give more floor space for tables &c.

SHOEMAKER'S ARMS Gold Street.

This establishment is mentioned in *NN&Q* under the Blue Boar, which, according to the author it may have become in the 18th century. See Blue Boar entry for details. Mentioned in Mercury 1766-7 "with Blue boar" (2017.

SHOULDER OF MUTTON Market Square.

This name is thought to have been given to inns where the innkeeper also carried on the trade of the Butcher, or that this is what was put on the table at meal times. See Phoenix for more on this pub.

SILVER CORNET.

Although I doubt either of the two pubs with this name acquired the name for this reason it was probably of religious significance, becoming a musical instrument after the Reformation. The theory is that a silver cornet was originally a halo, probably around the head of a Saint or the Virgin Mary. The paint would weather leaving the halo or cornet (coronet?) and in days gone by when most people couldn't read they called a pub by what they saw on the signboard. This is also one explanation for 'lucky horseshoes' which originally had their ends pointing downwards, the custom of putting it the other way up 'so the luck doesn't fall out' came later.

SILVER CORNET 26 Kerr Street also **Builders' Arms** and **Bricklayers' Arms.**

This pub stood on the end of Kerr Street, on the Mounts. When I was much younger a garage stood on the site, the electricity sub-station at the back of the Courts is approximately the same place. The earlier names obviously refer to a sign depicting bricklayers. The first recorded landlord; William Dunmore 1858 might have been a bricklayer.

SILVER CORNET 21 Welland Way, Kings Heath.

In February 1959 the *C&E* announced that a *Public House for Kings Heath in 1960 Planned.* To get a licence for this new pub entailed the brewery surrendering the licences of the Queen's Head, Gold Street, the Queen's Arms, and the Cleveland Arms, both in the Kettering Road.

For a short while this pub was called the Silvers, but has reverted to the old name. According to an article in the *C&E*

September 1992 one of the landlords was Norman Snow, a star prizefighter in the 1930s and 40s. It seems that in 1940 he was narrowly beaten in the British Welterweight title fight in front of a 7,000 crowd at Franklin's Gardens. Now closed and demolished.

SIX ALE HOUSE Vernon Street.
I assume this pub sold six different ales! It was probably no more than a small beer-shop as the only solid reference I have is from the *Northampton Herald*, March 1878, an advertisement for the sale of brewing plant. For this information I am grateful to Mr. G. Starmer.

In the 1970s my wife and I bought our first house, a small terraced property in Vernon Street. One of my old neighbours told me that at one time my house had been a pub, and when I started on this book I looked forward to discovering something about it. I found nothing for my address, but people do not usually distinguish between beer-shops and outdoor beer houses so I assumed that my house had been one of these. It was unusual as my house had a side entrance when others didn't and the front window had been much larger. Other neighbours told us it had been a shop – I wonder if at one time it *had* been the Six Ale House?

SKULLS AT THE CUPS Bridge Street.
This is a most intriguing name, the origins of which I know not. I know little more than its name – it being listed by Ron Sheffield, the author of *From Tabernae to Fantasia* 1973, there is no number so I cannot locate it.
SLIPPER see **Franklin's Gardens Hotel.**

SPADE & PLOUGH 5 Virgo Street (Terrace), Bedford Road.
When this pub closed it became Watney Mann's sign making department, later a school. In the 1970s I visited here and the bar &c was intact with pumps still on the bar, but stacked behind with lengths of wood.

I can just remember this pub being open when as a child we would go to Midsummer Meadow for a picnic on a Sunday. My mother and I would sit somewhere on the grass near the river, opposite the power station and my father would walk across to the pub and get some drinks. I can remember my father telling me that it was only open in the summer; it seemed strange to have a pub in such an isolated position. Apart from people visiting Becket's Park and Midsummer Meadow there were very few houses in the vicinity, but in the past there had been the Vigo Brickworks and later the United Counties 'Bus Depot and other industry such as Brown Bros. Aircraft. Maybe this is why it managed to keep open until the 1950s. From the directories; 1858 to 1954, it was a Beer-Retailer's until around the turn of the 19th century. All the area is now redeveloped (2010).
SPENCER'S ARMS see **Earl Spencer's Arms.**

SPINNEY HILL HOTEL Kettering Road.
This pub opened its doors in September 1936. It was very much a purpose-built establishment designed to cater not only for the refreshment, but the recreational needs of the  fast growing estates around it. The original plan for the area included a swimming pool, two tennis courts, a large hall for social gatherings, a large garage and a childrens' playground with a shelter. I understand that the proposed site was on the Kettering Road at its junction with Park Avenue. As it turned out it was built about 650 yards further up the Kettering Road and although the tennis courts and childrens' playground were built the swimming pool &c were not.

The first proprietors were Mr. and Mrs. Fred Brightman. They had been stewards of Monks Park W.M.C. for eleven years before moving to the Clarendon (see Two Brewers) for a short period. The N.B.C. surrendered the licence of the Clarendon for this one.

The next landlady was Bertha Wilmott a BBC Radio star who along with her husband, Reg Semour and others would go around during the war entertaining the soldiers.

In 1985 the pub went through a 'British Raj' transformation and two of Osbourne Robinson's paintings that were in the pub and no longer in keeping with the new décor were renovated by Hamden Hosts, the owners, and presented to the Royal Theatre in 1986. The pub has changed again, but not much externally from its 1930s design with the exception of the loss of the elm trees due to disease.

SPORTSMAN'S ARMS 52 Bath Street also **Forget-Me-Not.**

This pub started life as a Beer-Retailers around 1858, by 1884 it was called the Forget Me Not and run by a Mr. Charles Chaplin! By 1900 it was the Sportsman's Arms, it is now (2000) the Shoemaker's Tavern. Now flats (2017).

SPOTTED DOG.

We have had two Spotted Dogs in the town, both of which have now gone. It is thought that the name derives from the Talbot, an extinct breed of hunting dog, now found only in heraldry and pub signs.

SPOTTED DOG 19 Crane Street, or 109 Grafton Street.

The lower end of Grafton Street was once called Crane Street and this pub stood on the east corner of Monks Pond Street. I can never think of this pub without regret, for years I walked past it thinking that it seemed an interesting place and that I should visit one day. I never did get around to it and then in 1971 it was shut. After that I vowed to go into every pub in town that was still open. The earliest entry, as a Beer-Retailer, is 1878.

SPOTTED DOG 48 Kingsthorpe Road.

This pub was in Kingsthorpe Hollow, on the southern corner of Alpha Street and Kingsthorpe Road, the earliest entry is 1878. All this area has been developed and Alpha Street is no more. According to the *C&E* 24/10/97 "50 Years Ago" feature: - *GUEST of honour at the annual dinner of the Northampton Licenced Trade Womens' Auxiliary was Mrs. H. Poulteney, of the Spotted Dog, Kingsthorpe Hollow, who has been a licencee for 56 years.*

The Poulteneys ran this pub for a considerable part of its existence. Charles William Poulteney is shown as having the licence on the earliest Licensing list in 1903 and a Reginald J. Poulteney is recorded in the last directory entry of 1956.

SPREAD EAGLE.

The Spread Eagle is a very common heraldic device; and many monarchs wanted to claim some sort of connections with the Roman Emperors after the fall of the Roman Empire. Both 'Kaiser' and 'Tzar' are variants of 'Caesar'. In the case of inn signs it can indicate the Holy Roman Emperors and therefore the sale of wine. The Black Spread Eagle also has local connections that can be found under that name, these below could be contractions. We have had five in the town; one is still with us.

SPREAD EAGLE 37 Bridge Street.
This pub stood on the east side of the street about halfway between the Angel and St. John's Street. Entries run from 1845 to 1906.

SPREAD EAGLE 47 Hope's Place, Barrack Road.
Probably was one of the shops between the Britannia pub and Louise Road. In view of its proximity to the Barracks it could have had a military significance. Short lived, entries run from 1845 to 1858. An advertisement in the *Northampton Mercury* June 1862 has: -

TO PUBLICANS AND OTHERS
THE "SPREAD EAGLE" opposite the BARRACKS, NORTHAMPTON, TO BE LET, with immediate Possession. Fixtures &c., about £30 – For particulars Apply to Phillips Bros., Northampton Steam Brewery.

SPREAD EAGLE Location unknown.
One untraceable from *RBN* 1898 could have been on the Market Square and a contraction of the Black Spread Eagle.

SPREAD EAGLE Mercers' Row.
There is an advertisement in the *Northampton Mercury;* November 1783 that informs us that *JAMES DURHAM (late Turnkey at the County Gaol)* has taken the Spread Eagle on Mercers' Row.
SPREAD EAGLE 147 Wellingborough Road.
This one is still with us and I've been able to trace it back as a drinking place to 1850 when a William Watts held it as a Beer-Shop- this is probably about the year in which it was built. The pub closed for a time in 1971 being in line for demolition as part of the town improvements. For part of this period it was leased to the Men's Own Ruby Club, but after eleven years it was reopened in 1982.

SQUIRRELS 33 Main Road, Old Duston.
Still with us this building partly dates from the 17th century, still has a thatched roof and is constructed of warm, yellow ironstone. It may have begun life as a private house. It is shown on *O/S* 1886 as "PH", but not as large as now. It first appears in a directory in 1830.

STAG see **Roebuck.**
STAG'S HEAD 7 Abington Street.
The Stag's Head is probably heraldic, but it has been suggested that it could be religious – perhaps from Psalm XLII, v 1: *As the hart panteth after the water brooks, so panteth my soul after thee, O God.* I think I prefer the heraldic explanation!

This inn was on the north side of the street, near the Market Square. At the beginning of Abington Street after a short distance the pavement widens and there is a grey stone block of shops. There is a stag's head carved on the front; this is Stag Buildings, the site of the inn, which was demolished in the 1930s. The bar, I'm told, was the longest in town, running the whole length of Stag Buildings and through to another entrance in the Market Square.

In the 19th century it was one of the best-known hostelries in Northampton and of considerable size, the frontage quoted at auction in 1890 was 88 feet to the street. It was fitted, like all large establishments of the time, with "every convenience for a commercial trade". It had a yard with 10 loose boxes and extra stabling for 20 horses, two covered carriage sheds, lofts, saddlerooms, brewhouse &c. A

STAG'S HEAD

COMMERCIAL INN,

ABINGTON STREET,

NORTHAMPTON.

——

J. WHITWORTH

ACKNOWLEDGES with gratitude the many favors received at the above House; and, stimulated by the past, the Public may rely upon a continuance of his best exertions to add to their comfort and enjoyment for the future, confident that his efforts will not be unrewarded.

———

Choice Wines and Spirits.

WELL-AIRED BEDS.

GOOD STABLING, &c. &c.

Hickman's Directory 1847.

Mr. Manning bought it for £6,000. Is this the Manning of Castle Brewery?

Barley

To be sold by Private Contract, A very fine Crop of Barley, nearly ripe, growing upon two Acres and a Half of Land, opposite to St. Gyles's Church-Yard, in Northampton, adjoining the Road leading from the top of Abington-Street to the General Infirmary, Usual credit will be given upon approved Security; and for further Particulars, apply to Mr. Paine, at the Stag's Head, Northampton. (July 1805). This quote from *NN&Q* 1891 gives an idea of the east side of York Road in 1805.

The inn is listed as a 16th or 17th century inn in **RBN** 1898, but again, I have been unable to trace these documents. The earliest evidence I have is from the Great Election of 1768, although I am sure it was of good antiquity. The last entry in a directory is in 1936. **Mercury** 1766-7 and 1781-2 (200-17).

STAR.

The Star is one of our most ancient signs, if for no other reason that it easy to paint and recognise. The Stella Maria is the emblem of the Virgin; it is also a symbol of prudence and welcome and was often used by monastic inns. In later years to call one's inn the Star implied that *your* establishment shone above all others. The brightest stars are the Morning and Evening ones and these are also represented in our town.

STAR Abington Street.

This inn stood at the end of Ditchers (later Dychurch) Lane on the east corner, right opposite the Stag with the Saracen's Head on the other corner. It pre-dated the Great Fire of 1675 for it is mentioned by the Fire Court Commissioners in 1679. It also crops up in the Churchwarden's Accounts of St. Giles' Church: - *1677, 22nd May. Spent going a processioning att ye Star by ye churchwardens, overseers, and parishioners....0..13..4.*

History of the Church of Saint Giles Serjeantson 1911.

Tanners sold leather here in the 18th century, but in 1723 the sales were moved to the Talbot, the Star being sold. It appears that at this time the Star ceased to be an inn. Reference in the **Mercury** 1765-6 "Dwelling known as the..." (2017).

STAR 25 Castle Street.

There is some confusion as to whether this is also the Globe.

STAR 1 Western Terrace and Elephant Lane also **Star & Railway Inn.**

Although the first appearance of the name of this pub is just the Star, its name changes from year to year and is an example of a name getting shortened by use; however, it seems the Railway part was added when the station was built. First appears in the directories in 1845 and last in 1962, about the time it became a shopfitter's workshop, then a private club, now demolished (2010).

STARS & STRIPES see **Cattle Market Tavern.**

STONE QUARRY New Duston.
This pub is now a Post Office; there is a terrace of sandstone cottages on the west side of Quarry Road, the end one being the Post Office, beyond are the remains of a quarry. The centre cottage bears the date 1862. From the directories I have discovered a John Henry Smith as a Beer-Retailer in Duston in 1864. *Wright* 1884 (earliest entry under Stone Quarry) gives the landlord as John Henry Smith and these two pieces of evidence indicate that the end cottage started off as a beer-shop. This was confirmed by the proprietors of the Post Office on a site visit in 2000. *Wright* 1884 gives the proprietor of the Rifle Butt at the end of the road as a William Smith, a relative? Directories go on to give a last entry for the Stone Quarry of 1911 and in 1903 we have a William Frank Smith at this address described as, *Shopkeeper, Post Office*.

SULTAN see **Criterion.**

SUN see **Bull & Butcher.**
SUN see **Rising Sun.**

SUN & RAVEN see **Bull & Butcher.**

SUNNYSIDE HOTEL Boughton Green Road.
This establishment, which is still with us, was converted to its present use from a large house in the 1950s. I can remember in the 1960s.going to this  pub on Friday nights to a jazz club that was held in a barn behind the main building. At closing time exhausted from 'stomping' all night we would have to trudge the whole length of Eastern Avenue to Kingsthorpe Grove where we would break up and go our various ways.

234

SWAN.

There were three swans in Northampton, one of which remains, but hiding under a different name.

The two most popular birds on signs are the Cock and the Swan. The Swan is supposed to have originated from the Order of the Swan, an Order of Knighthood started by Frederick II of Brandenburg in 1440. It was later adopted by the Cleeves family and was used by Anne of Cleeves, the fourth wife of Henry VIII. It also figured as a badge on the arms of many English Kings and noblemen, e.g. Henry the IV and Edward III. The Swan is usually argent or white, but you do get sable or black swans, often called the 'Mucky Duck'. In medieval times the Swan was considered to be an emblem of innocence. An old rhyme from an Irish pub sign: -

This is the Swan,
That left her pond,
To dip her bill in porter,
Why not we,
As well as she,
Become regular Topers?

SWAN also **Mailcoach** 6-8 Derngate. The *RBN* 1898 lists this establishment as one of the 16th or 17th century inns. The earliest record I have is 1830 and it changed its name in the 1970s to the Mailcoach as a result of a competition, the new name alluding to the Postal Sorting Office that was opposite at the time.

TO INNKEEPERS, FARMERS, AND OTHERS.

20 QUARTERS OF MALT.

TO BE SOLD BY AUCTION,
By W. J. PEIRCE,

On Wednesday, 16th February, 1859, at the Swan Inn, Derngate, NORTHAMPTON, at Three o'clock in the afternoon,

20 QUARTERS of MALT, of first-rate quality. May be seen on the Morning of Sale.

I used this pub at the time and the bar would fill up with uniforms, Postmen and 'Bus Drivers from the United Counties 'Bus

Northampton Mercury 1859.

Station just down the road. The lounge would fill in the evenings with theatregoers from the Rep. just around the corner, and sometimes quite famous people, including Errol Flynn in times gone by, could be seen in here.

SWAN Drapery.

The Swan in Derngate gave its name to Swan Lane when it was changed from Cow Lane, so this Swan gave its name to the jitty half way up on the west side of the Drapery, Swan Yard.

This is one of the thirteen ancient inns listed in the *Assembly Order* of 1585 and from the records of All Saints' Church we learn that in July 1645 they buried a soldier from the Swan, one of the wounded from the Battle of Naseby a month before.

The Swan is the first inn to be mentioned in the poem *Northampton in Flames*. It was rebuilt and the *Northampton Mercury* is full of advertisements concerning the inn in the 18th century. I have no definite closure date, but *Law's* Map of 1847 has Swan Yard marked and I'm sure if the inn was still running it would have been included. The **Mercury** 1836-7 has "Joseph Yates" and 1838-9 "Charles Sanders" (2017).

SWAN Sheep Street.

To be LETT and Entered upon immediately THE SWAN INN in Sheep Street, Northampton. For particulars enquire of Mr. Richard Jeffcutt, in Northampton.

Mercury February 4th 1754

Also, as above, but with: -

NB. One great advantage that a Publican in Northampton will have in time, is, that the Magistrates of the Corporations will grant no Licences to any new Publick Houses in the said Town.

Mercury September 9th and 23rd 1751

SWAN Woolmonger Street.

Only one reference, an Indenture of 1837: - *In a certain street there called Woolmonger Street herefore known by the name or Sign of the Swan but now used as a private house....*

A sign in the past didn't guarantee that a property was an inn as houses, shops and other premises would also carry them, but in this case as it says, *now used as a private house*, I think I am on safe ground.

SWAN & HELMET.

We have had two, one of which is still with us. The sign is heraldic, the badge of Buckingham.

SWAN & HELMET 23, 23a &/or 25 Gold Street.

This is a confusing address that is explained (?) under the Foresters' Arms, this entry deals only with the Swan & Helmet.

There is a reference to a Swan & Helmet in Gold Street as early as 1723. As it also appears in the *Universal Directory* of 1791 it must have been of some importance.

Taylor wrote of it thus: - *There was a Inn or publick-House situate on the South side of Gold street, bearing the above Name, and continued to exist up to the Year * *. When the premises were taken down and rebuilt. And the new House assumed the name of 'ROYAL HOTEL', under which it is now carried on by Mr. C. Cain. But at what period the Old Inn was opened we cannot now say. But by its venerable appearance it seems like a House or...large Tenement run up immediately after the great Fire of 1666* (sic).

*Unfortunately he didn't get around to filling in the year.

An advertisement in the *Northampton Mercury* 1742 to let the inn, *now in occupation of John Tebbutt* describes amongst other things a brewhouse and stabling for 50 horses. Other advertisements for auctions indicate that it must have had at least one large room. The **Mercury** has three references to this pub; 1763-4, 1772-3 & 1813-4.

SWAN & HELMET 65 Grove Road. This pub is still with us, another purpose-built street corner pub constructed

SWAN & HELMET INN,
GROVE ROAD, KETTERING ROAD,
NORTHAMPTON.
W. BARKER,
Dealer in Wines and Spirits,
ALSO
PHIPP'S CELEBRATED ALES & STOUT.

at the same time as the surrounding terraced houses, shops and small factories. The ground floor still bears externally the vitreous green tiles that were so popular for pub exteriors in the 1930s. The Old Black Lion is another one, but they are a marmalade colour. The earliest I could trace this pub back was 1877; probably about the time it was built. William Barker, the first landlord was also a Coal Merchant and Dealer.

TABARD.

A Tabard was a jacket with short, pointed sleeves worn by knights over their armour. It would have been emblazoned with their field of arms. Their servants often wore such garments as an indication of their fealty and authority, as it was a noble garment only worn by the upper classes. Tabards are still worn by the Heralds of the College of Arms on State occasions. It is a sign of some age as Chaucer had his pilgrims start from a Southwark pub of the name in 1383. I've found three of these in the town, all of them of good age.

TABARD Cotton End and **TABARD** Woolmonger Street.

I've grouped these two together because in both cases they are in the *RBN* 1898 16th or 17th century lists and that is all I know about them.

TABARD Swinel-strete (Derngate).

Victoria County History Vol. III p.19 quotes a Rental of 1504 that mentions several inns in the town including *le Tabard*.

TAILOR'S ARMS Wellingborough Road.

Only one reference and no street number, from an advertisement in the *Northampton Mercury* April 1868: - *TO BE LET With Immediate Possession. AN old-established BEERHOUSE, THE TAILOR'S ARMS, WELLINGBOROUGH ROAD, Northampton.*

When an advertisement says "immediate possession" it indicates to me that the premises are unoccupied and therefore not conducting business. This may explain why many beer-houses only appear once and that's in such advertisements as above. They either did not continue as beer-houses, or the premises changed name or use.

TALBOT.

A Talbot is an extinct form of hunting dog. It was white, rather like an old-fashioned hound, but with black or blue spots all over, somewhat like a Dalmatian. Talbot inns often ended up being called the Spotted Dog. Talbot is the family name of the Earls of Shrewsbury and

the dog features in their arms. Talbot inns often indicate a connection with this family.

TALBOT Market Square, near Newland?

It was to this inn that the leather market moved when the Star closed down, it must have been pre-Fire as the *Great Fire Court Records* have a petition from a Raphael Coldwell, September 25th 1676 that refers to the *Talbutt* having been destroyed in the Great Fire. This *Talbutt* was probably the Ancient Inn in the *Assembly Order* of 1585. An order was made for its rebuilding with four tenements in Newland adjoining or lying near to, the backside of the inn. In the 1720s the inn was run by Thomas Miller according to advertisements of the time. I do not know when it finally closed. However, from the advertisement below it must have been flourishing in the 18th century:-

To Be LETT.
And Enter'd upon at St. Thomas next, THE TALBOT INN, situate in the Market-place, in Northampton, with The Utensils for Brewing, and Stabling for a great Number of Horses.
Enquire of Mr. Snowden, Shop-keeper in Northampton.

The historical panels painted by Osbourne Robinson, the late scenic designer at the Repertory Theatre that were in the Grosvenor Centre (where are they now?) show the sign of this inn on a panel illustrating the times of Henry VIII (1529).

This is probably the inn referred to in the poem *Northampton in Flames* the writer seems to be travelling up the Drapery, calling at the Swan, then the Lion (probably the Red Lyon), the Hind on the top corner of the Market and then the Talbot and finally, the Phoenix (probably the Peacock).

TALBOT Sheep Street.

According to *NN&Q* there were two Talbots, one in the Market Square and one in Sheep Street. Taylor thought that they could have been the same inn, but the Fire Court Records puts one of them close to Newland, well away from Sheep Street. Taylor quotes an advertisement dated 1749 for the letting of: - *A Good-Accustomed Inn, in the Sheep-Street, Northampton, known by the Name of the Talbot.*

TALBOT 35 & 37 Wellington Street.
This pub stood on the west side of the street, near the top, on the corner of Union Street. It was lost in the 1970s during redevelopment. I have traced it as a Beer-Retailer back to 1858.

TALEREK'S see **Princess Royal.**

TAVERN IN THE TOWN see **Bear.**

TELEGRAPH 103 Bridge Street.
I have discovered that this is the name of a coach and the pub was probably named after it rather than the electric telegraph. As it stood on Bridge Street this seems most likely. There is only one reference to it, *Taylor's* 1858, *Morley William (Telegraph), 103 Bridge Street.*
    It was on the river side of the Tom Thumb, it is possible that it didn't survive because of the proximity of this pub.

THESE GATES HANG WELL see **Gate Inn.**
THOMAS BECKET see **Green Man.**

THREE.
There is no pub that I know of just called 'Three', but I have discovered nine in the town with three in their names.
    The number three is a special, lucky number; not only because of the Trinity, but earlier, such as the triple aspect of the Moon Goddess and the innumerable trinities of Pagan Gods such as Osiris, Isis and Horus. As well, there is the fact that once is just once, because it happened; two and it's a coincidence – but three and there has to be *something* in it. The Kelts were fond of three, they liked three severed heads in their sanctuaries – it goes back a long way.

THREE COFFINS Bridge Street.
Taylor made a note of this sign under Bridge Street, but never published it, probably because he doesn't seem to have found anything more on it. It could have been a nickname – perhaps for one of these below?

THREE CROWNS Bridge Street.

This name either represents the Three Wise Men, the Papal Crown, the Three Crowns of England, Scotland and Ireland, or the Arms of the Drapers' Company. The pub is more fully discussed under "Crown(s)".

THREE CUPS Bridge Street.

Three cups appear in the arms of the Salters' Company, but I think this could be the "Three Pots for a Penny" – see below. Only one reference in a directory, *Pigot*, 1824 *Ths. Lake* and an item in the *Northampton Mercury* 9th September 1820: - *At the house in Bridge street in this town known by the name of the Three Cups, which this week has been part taken down, for the purpose of being rebuilt, while the workmen were excavating a portion of the old site to make a cellar, they dug up in the course of Tuesday and Wednesday last, upwards of 400 skulls and other human bones.... The premises form part of St. John's hospital.* The author of this article said that the bones appeared to be male (how could they tell?) and therefore they were probably the result of some great battle. However, it is more likely that they had disturbed a burial ground associated with St. John's Hospital.

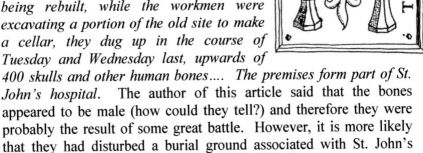

THREE POTS FOR TWO-PENCE or **THREE POTS FOR A PENNY** Bridge Street.

Three Pots was on the corner of Three Potts Lane, now called St. John's Street, the sign is self-explanatory. In April 1751 the *Northampton Mercury* advertised an auction of six tenements in St. John's Street, *At the house of James York the Younger, known by the Sign of the Three Pots-Twopence in the Town of Northampton.* We have a copy of a will dated 1758 that refers to the sign of the Three Potts on the east side of Bridge Street. It is also mentioned in *A True and Faithful Relation of the Late Dreadful Fire at Northampton: - Burned in Bridge-Street as far as James Bailes at the Sign of the three*

Pots for twopence. Did this inn change its name because of inflation, I wonder?

As all the above and the next entry are all in Bridge Street or St. John's Lane I wonder whether they are, in fact, all the same premises?

THREE PIGEONS St. John's Lane.

This pub is one of those in the 16th and 17th century list from **RBN** 1898, the name also occurs in a document of 1704.

Not only has its location led me to believe that this is the same establishment as the Three Potts, but the name itself. The Saxon word for a pail was a 'piggen' and it is claimed by some that this became corrupted into 'pig' as in Pig & Whistle – it is entirely likely, in my opinion, to have also been corrupted into 'pig-eon'.

THREE TUNS.

These last four present no real problems, they are all at different addresses and the meaning of the sign is known.

A tun or tunn is a brewer's fermenting vessel, or it's a cask, 252 gallons capacity if its wine and 216 if its beer. The arms of the Vintners' Company, incorporated in 1437 display three tuns, it is therefore an indication that the establishment served wine as well as ale and beer. The Brewers' Company also features three tuns or casks, in this case three  barrels (36 gallons) although I am not sure how you judge the capacity of a cask illustrated on a field of arms.

THREE TUNS Drapery & Market Square.

To quote *NN&Q* 1881: - *A public-house on the east side of the square still bears this name. It is probable, however, that this forms but a portion of the original site of the Chequer. The Three Tuns was, up to 1750, the sign of a 'good-accustomed publick-house' in the Drapery.* So this represents *two* pubs.

It was advertised for let in April 1749 and was described as an old public house, so it must have been around for a while. As we don't have a definite location we do not know if it changed its name when it was let, presumably by 1750, and the sign transferred to the Market Square, or ceased to trade.

THREE TUNS Gold Street.

From an Abstract of Mr. Morgan's title to the Rose & Crown Inn, Wheatsheaf Inn and several houses in Gold Street in the town: - *21 April 1634...called or known by the Name or Sign of the 3 Tuns....* I think this must have been close to the Rose & Crown.

THREE TUNS Horsemarket.

From the Great Fire Court Book 1675: -...Toft with the backside or Garden and the app-tenances scituate & being on the West side of the horse Markett...on which Toft stood formerly a Messuage or Tenement...lying on the North called formerly the Three Tuns. April 26th 1684. It appears that it perished in the Great Fire, never to be rebuilt.

THREE TUNS 23 Market Square.

This is another from the **RBN** 1898 list for which we haven't the documents, but it did survive up to 1910. **Taylor** was right (see above) it was part of the old Chequer and would have been one property closer to Abington Street than the Lord Palmerston. When I surveyed the old cellars under the Market in the 1960s a sign in one of the passages near this part of the Square said "To the Three Tuns Shelter" - one of the Air-Raid Shelters from World War Two.

TOLL HOUSE INN St James' End.

The late Lou Warwick quoted this inn in an article in the *Northampton Independent*, September 1978. He referred to an advertisement for a sale that was conducted at this inn in 1737: - *William Roe and James Williamson at the Toll-House, St. James selling all sorts of Silk, Mercery and Linen-Drapery Goods – Our Stay here will be but Short.*

Northampton Mercury 6th June 1737.

Another advertisement I have found in the **Northampton Mercury** dated 25th April 1763: - *Publick NOTICE is hereby given. THAT the INN in St. James'-End, near Northampton, in very good Repair, is taken and entered upon by Nicholas Blackwell of Kislingbury: Where all Gentlemen, Ladies, and Others may depend on good Entertainment and Civil usage, and their Favours will be gratefully acknowledged by Their Humble Servant NICHOLAS BLACKWELL.*

Beeby Thompson wrote that the old Tollgate was at the junction of the Weedon and Harlestone Roads and that there were two gates side-by-side. He did not make it clear whether these were across one road or one each across each road. If the latter is so the tollhouse would probably have been between the two roads where they diverge, where the cake shop and bank are at present. This would also have been the inn or it was close by.

TOM THUMB see **General Tom Thumb.**

TOWN ARMS 59 Upper Mounts and 1 Great Russell Street.
This pub was on the site of the Chronicle & Echo building on the Mounts. It stood on the corner and as I remember it, it had a rather peculiar sign. It was a sort of lop-sided arms of the town, there was the 'castle' with its three turrets, but supported by only one lion. I understand this was because the council, in their wisdom, had

refused permission for the pub to display the town's arms. Heraldic devices are the property of to whom or what they are awarded to and as such are copyright. I would imagine if a pub displayed the town arms today without permission nothing would be said. However, if some jobsworth did object one would have the perfect defence in the fact that the town council have recently murdered the town arms producing a hideous 'trendy' abomination that breaks all the rules of heraldry and good taste! The earliest date I have for this pub is 1862 and the latest 1973.

TOWN ARMS St. Andrew's Square.
Burgess 1845, *Williams", Phipps 1852, "Samuel Williams.* This is all we have. It probably stood opposite the Welcome Inn. In *Taylor* 1864 there is a Samuel Williams at the Lord Raglan, Upper Harding Street, so it looks like he moved around the corner.

TOWN CRIER College street.
One entry, *Burgess* 1845, Ward. There have been several pubs along this relatively short street in the past and without a number there is no way to tell where it was, or if it's another pub with a name change.

TRADESMAN'S ARMS 47 Brunswick Street.
This pub stood on the south side, facing up Dover Street, opposite the Dover Castle. The first mention is in 1884, but there was a beer-shop next door at 45 from 1858 to 1864, so did it move into the larger number 47 and give itself a name?

TRAMCAR.
The tram was a popular form of public transport in days gone by and two pubs are named after them. One, in St. James' Road was at a terminus and the other one, halfway up the Kettering Road was on the route of the first section, opened in June 1881.
TRAMCAR 110 & 112 Kettering Road also **Tramway Inn.**
This pub stood on the northeast corner of Kettering Road and Portland Street. The earliest reference is in 1881. I visited this pub on a few occasions and remember that it had hard, plywood benches along the walls with designs of hundreds of holes drilled through them. These benches were either from tramcars or had been made to imitate them.

The pub finally closed its doors in 1974 and the site is now part of the patch of grass by the Kettering Road.

TRAMCAR TAVERN 126 St. James' Road (Café Square) also **West End Tramcar.**
I can remember this pub, but I never went in it. It used to stand on the southwest corner of St. James' Road and Devonshire Street, opposite the bank. The whole area has now been redeveloped.

The first trams (horse) ran in Northampton in 1881, the Company having been formed the year before. The first section, West Bridge-Racecourse was opened in June of that year and extended to Café Square (often wrongly called St. James' Square) by the end of July. The pub was built shortly afterwards, the last entry from the directories is 1970.

TRAVELLER'S HOUSE 10 Castle Street.
This pub must have been on the north side of the street, near the Horsemarket end. Both *O/S* 1901 and 1938 show a group of assorted buildings at this end of the street, the pub is probably one of these. By 1938 both St. Peter's and Doddridge Houses are shown in the process of construction, so the pub probably closed about then. It only appeared in five directories, from 1911 to 1933.

TRAVELLING SCOTSMAN 64 Kingswell and Commercial Streets.
The name of this pub was a mystery. At first I thought that as was a famous train called the Flying Scotsman, which I understand was a T. P. O. (Travelling Post Office) that sorted the mail as it travelled over-night to the North; that this could have been (in jest?) a name of a slower version. The National Railway Museum, York knows nothing of it.

Since the publication of the first edition I believe I have found the origin of this name and it has nothing to do with Scotsmen. On the north end of Foundry Street opposite the Albion Brewery are still some stables which I was told when I worked at the brewery in the 1960s were for extra dray horses. A fully laden dray would have had difficulty in getting up Bridge Street and extra horses were hitched up to assist the dray up the hill. In the past a wooden roller or wedge would be used to stop carts from rolling backwards on hillsides, this was called a 'scotch' it seems that on the steep Bridge Street a man with a scotch would walk alongside the rear of the dray to make sure that it didn't roll backwards he was known as a 'scotch man' – hence the name?

Only one entry 1864 gives a number and this is not a great help. Using *O/S* 1964 it seems to coincide with the present pub on the corner of the two streets. I am left with the same problem as I had with the Grafton Arms (see entry) but in this case the dates do marry up better, the last entry for the Scotsman is 1864 and the first for the King William IV, 1870; whereas the Grafton Arms only has two, the last being 1845. This year coincides with the Scotsman's first date, both in **Burgess**, but the Grafton is listed under "Innkeepers" and the Scotsman "Beer-Sellers". In 1884 the King William is given a 'v' so has the same type of licence as the Grafton. A past landlord, who has had sight of the King William deeds tells me that the Grafton is mentioned in them, so the Scotsman must be an adjacent beer-shop. The dates for the Scotsman are 1845 to 1864 and the Albion Brewery was established next to the King William in 1864, so the pub could have disappeared then.

TREE OF LIBERTY 24 Albert Street.
Thomas Jefferson, *"The tree of liberty must be refreshed from time to time with the blood of patriots and tyrants"*. The original Tree of Liberty was an elm that stood in Boston and was a rallying point for disaffected colonists prior to the American Revolution, no doubt here connected with the Radical shoemaker of this Town. This establishment was about three-quarters of the way along the street on the east side. It was tucked away in a back street, one of those pubs you discovered when you were on a pub-crawl and returned to later.

This was one of the three pubs in the town in the 1960s that sold 'scrumpy', but Bob Lay's was best. When you walked in he was often out of sight around the back somewhere. People would politely stand by the bar and wait for him to appear; you could often hear him shifting things about 'off-stage'. Bob kept a talking mynah bird and its cage was half out of sight behind and along the side of the bar. After a minute or two people would make a slight noise, cough or shuffle their feet, but never tap a coin on the bar, people had manners then. The bird, on hearing this sound would, in a loud and raucous voice call out. "Waddya want!" Invariably the potential customer would jump, much to our amusement, and look around in vain for the owner of the voice - ordering a drink as they did so. This response would trigger the bird to repeat its phrase, resulting in the customer repeating their order whereupon the bird would repeat... you get the idea. Like everyone else I too was caught on my first visit – in fact, I must confess I was caught more than once and even when I knew what was coming that bird always made me jump.

The earliest entry is for 1852 and the pub went when the area was cleared to build the Grosvenor Centre, around 1970. Bob had the pub to the end and died shortly after he retired; said by some to have been killed by the demolition of what had been his home and livelihood since 1932.

TROOPER 2 Market Square also **White Hart** & **Mail Coach.** Victoria House still stands at the northwest corner of the Square and this establishment stood immediately to the south of it.

The author (**Taylor**) of *Glimpses of Old Northamptonshire Signs, NN&Q* 1889 says: - *Was occupied up to 1823 by Mr. Rawlins of the firm of Rawlins Bros., distillers, Bedford, when the late Mr. Thomas Walker succeeded; he was previously the Bedford carrier. Mrs. Walker remained at the Trooper until 1860, and was followed by Mr. William Swallow, When Mr. Rawlins purchased the property it fetched £700 who was succeeded in February, 1875 by MR. Charles Cooke He left at Lady-day (25th March), 1883. The property now occupied by Mr. William Warwick was sold to Mr. Dulley of Wellingborough, at the Angel, by Messrs. Pierce and Thorpe, on April 18th 1881, for £1840.*

Additional information in the Addenda tells us that it was known only as a Messuage or Tenement, i.e. a dwelling until 1750 when it was known as the White Hart and occupied by a John Roe. (There was a John Roe at the White Hart or Roebuck, Drum Lane in 1767, see Shipmans). In 1781 it was occupied by Thomas Hill, and by 1794 it was known as the Mail Coach, sold for £330 and occupied by Henry Spurr. In 1808 Thomas Campion bought it for £350. By 1821 it was the Trooper and bought by John Rawlins, of Bedford, wine merchant, for £640.

The discrepancy between the purchase price in the latter paragraph and Rawlins apparent payment of £700 in the previous is probably accounted for that in the former it says the inn fetched £700, whilst the latter says John Rawlins purchased it for £640. It would seem that John paid another £60 for fixtures, stock &c. Dates run from 1824 to 1904.

TRUE BLUE.
We have had two of these in town, and they both seem to be connected. The sign, like the next one, the True Briton appear to be references to the names Tories used as signatures to political letters

they were fond of writing to newspapers at the time. Other examples are Ancient Briton, North Briton and Generous Briton, none of which were used as pub names in Northampton.

TRUE BLUE (OLD) 29 Grafton Street.
There are only two records of this pub, 1858, Henry Stringer and 1864, James Walker. This pub stood on the south side of the street; two doors west of what became the Roebuck. The Roebuck is recorded as being here in 1878, so it could have been here at the same time. It is also recorded in *Slater* 1862 that a Beer-Retailer called Septimus Jones was at number 27. This meant that three properties in a row could have all been selling beer at the same time, and this could have been the reason for Henry Stringer, moving away to the new location listed below and leaving the pub to James Walker.

TRUE BLUE (OLD) 51 Bearward Street.
By 1864 Henry Stringer had opened another True Blue at this address and this accounts for James Walker at the previous address adding the word 'Old'. It does not seem to have done James much good as the pub disappears from the directories after 1864. It may have continued for a while for in 1900 this pub added 'Old' to its name, perhaps in rivalry?

This establishment was on the south side of the street at the bottom of the road near the Mayorhold. I can remember when working with the Northampton Development Corporation Archaeological Unit in the 1970s on the Green Dragon site taking my level over the road to establish a temporary benchmark. I sited up Bearward Street and saw in faint letters on the first floor of the paper shop the legend, "Old True Blue" regretfully I didn't take a photograph. Entries are 1864-1907.

TRUE BRITON.
This, like the previous entry is clearly political, again we have two of them, but this time unconnected.

TRUE BRITON 17 Cyril Street.
The location of this pub has caused some difficulty, but was finally resolved in 2002 through other research concerning Victorian Domestic Terraced Street Architecture. I am now certain that it stood

on the north corner of the tee junction between Cyril Street and Woodford Street. Dates run from 1878 (about the time this area was being built) to 1958.

TRUE BRITON 28 Maple Street.

This pub stood on the south corner of the junction of Maple Street and Temple Bar, a grand name for a jitty! Dates run from 1878 to 1956. A True Briton is referred to in the Mercury 1800-1, could this be the one above? (2027).

TRUMPET.

This could have a religious or military meaning. In Numbers X. I. the Almighty commands Moses to make silver trumpets to call an assembly and an assembly is what any landlord would want in his pub! But it probably refers to mail coaches and their post horns.

TRUMPET Horsemarket.

An untraced inn of the 16th and 17th cents. from the *RBN* 1898.

TRUMPET 29 Silver Street.

Considering the street name this *could* have been a silver trumpet. The pub stood halfway along the street on the south side, by *O/S* 1938 the area had become a school and now is lost under the development of the area in the 1970s. First as a Beer-Retailer 1845 and the last entry 1910.

TRUMPET 2 Wellingborough Road, Weston Favell.

This pub was rebuilt in 1935 behind the original, which was then demolished. The earliest reference to it is 1820, but considering its location it could go back a long way and the trumpet referred to  here could be a post horn. *WESTON FAVELL STATUTE For Hiring Servants WILL be held at the TRUMPET INN, on Tuesday, the 26th Day of SEPTEMBER. 1820. Dinner at One o'Clock.*

Northampton Mercury 9th September 1820.

TUDOR HOUSE see **Malt Shovel.**

TURK'S HEAD 10 St. Edmund's Street.

The probable explanation for this sign is the same as for the Saracen's Head, although this pub definitely did not date back to the time of the Crusades. The Turk's Head is also a species of thistle, a cake tin, a type of broom and a complex rope-work knot on a narrow boat.

I think this is probably had the smallest bar I've ever been in. It was a few yards down the street from the Wellingborough Road on the left. As a young man I lived a little further up the road, nearer Abington Park. Sometimes we would 'do the Welly Road'. The first stop would be the Crown & Cushion and the Turk's Head would come sixth. I don't recall the landlord's name, but a friend of mine, Alan Richards tells me it was Bill White whose parents held the licence before him. Bill was a very pleasant chap and if I remember accurately he was an ex-serviceman and completely bald. This alone was a novelty, the only bald man most people knew of in those days was Yul Brinner from the film The King and I; whereas most of us had hair well past our shoulders – nevertheless we were always made welcome.

At the time I thought the pub was two houses knocked together but it proved to be to have been a purpose-built double house. The bar was the size of a normal terraced house front room with the serving area taking up most of the space. There was a bench seat along the front wall and room for a couple of chairs towards the rear. The back room was served through a hatch at the back of the bar. The whole of the other house front and back rooms were one room given over to skittles, darts and a couple of tables.

We always went into the bar and in doing so (there were never more than four of us) completely filled it! We never stopped for long, it was a local and it wasn't ours. The inhabitants were friendly, but we were young and always on the way to somewhere else. So having had a pint or two would say goodbye - for even two extra customers in a pub so small constituted a crush at the bar, the whole room accommodating no more than six to eight persons.

Dates run from 1857 to 1936, but the pub closed much later than this, I think about the time the Clearance Orders went out in the 1970s.

TURNER'S ARMS 74 Newland.
This pub was at the top of Newland, on the east side, close to the Lotus shoe factory. *Goad's Insurance* Plan 1899 show this pub as being next door to a factory titled, *Turner Bros, Hyde & Co. Boot & Shoe Factory.* I think this explains the name and is the first case I've found of a factory having its own tap. Before it was made illegal to pay off workers in a pub this was one way the bosses could claw back some of the wages, so this may explain its existence. Dates run from 1889 to 1932.

TWENTY FIVES 55 Lower Harding Street also **British Banner.**

Twenty Fives is a card game and the British Banner may have been influenced by the American Banner just up the road. The pub stood on Grafton Square directly opposite the Welcome Inn; all this area was redeveloped in the 1970s. There is a Beer-Retailer called Moore or Moon in Lower Harding Street from 1845 to 1852, but as we have no street numbers we cannot be sure this is the same establishment. In 1858 Joseph Webb is a Beer-Retailer at the address and in 1884 the pub's name is recorded, the last entry is in 1956.

TWO BREWERS 25 Abington Street also **The Clarendon.**
This is a very ancient sign, often called the Jolly Brewers, it usually depicts two, rotund men in aprons carrying a cask between them on their shoulders, suspended on a pole. In Roman times this was the sign of a vintner and the cask was an amphora.

The Two Brewers is traceable back to 1824. It stood on the north side of Abington Street a few doors west of what is now the entrance of the Grosvenor Centre. It was an establishment of note and probably its most renowned proprietor was Alfred Leoni Clarke who acquired the premises about 1896. Before this he had had a music hall act as the 'Cat King'. I'm not sure if this meant that at one time he worked with big cats but he did have a boxing kangaroo and travelled around the world twice with this act. When the kangaroo died he had it stuffed, bought the pub and displayed it in the bar!

In 1929 the pub was acquired by William John Watson who changed the name to the Clarendon, probably in an attempt to change the clientele (nothing's new!) I don't know if he succeeded, but the pub closed in 1936. The licence was surrendered to obtain one for the new Spinney Hill pub in the Kettering Road. The last proprietors, the Brightmans, moved with the licence to the Spinney Hill. A reference in the **Mercury** 1839-40 (2017).

TWO WRESTLERS "The Parrish of St. Sepulchre". From an Indenture dated 21St December 1724: - *Called or known by the name or sign of the two wrestlers, now in the occupation of James Walter, situate and being in the Parrish of St. Sepulchre.* This is all that is known of this establishment and at the time the whole of the town was divided into four parishes, St. Sepulchre's, St. Peter's, St. Giles' and All Saints' – St Sepulchre's occupied most of the northern part of the town.

UNICORN.
There have been two and possibly three of these in the town. The Unicorn is a sign of Goldsmiths, Apothecaries and Waxchandlers. For some reason it was also used by early printers. The Red Lion was made even more popular than it had been by the order of James I of England that the Red Lion of Scotland should be displayed on all public buildings and if publicans took this

up why not the other supporter of the Royal arms? In any case, it is a good sign for an inn as the Unicorn symbolises purity. Albertus Magnus wrote: - *It is reported that the Unicorn's horn sweats when in the presence of poison, and for that reason it is laid on the tables of the great, and made into knife handles, which, when placed on the tables, show the presence of poison. But this is not sufficiently proved.* A unicorn horn is actually the tusk or tooth of the narwhal.
UNICORN Horsemarket also **Red Lion.**
In Taylor's notes for the *NN&Q* he has, *beside the Red Lion formerly called the Unicorn* and the **NRO** have a document dated 1618

referring to this inn. **RBN** 1898 have a Unicorn, location Unknown on their 16th and 17th century list and I think this could be it. It is interesting that here we have the Unicorn of England becoming the Red Lion of Scotland and there is a possibility that it was once a George & Dragon (see Red Lion).

UNICORN Bridge Street.

In the *Northampton Mercury* there were a whole series of notices and advertisements from 1726 to 1765 and possibly longer which refer to the Unicorn. Most of these mention Bridge Street and none Horsemarket. As advertisements are appearing at the same time for the Red Lion, Horsemarket I conclude that they all refer to the Unicorn, Bridge Street. I have been unable to fix its location.

VALIANT DRAGON (Dragoon?) Newland.

The Book of Election Minutes 1768 mentions: -   the Valiant Dragon Alehouse and later refers to it as being in Newland.

VICTORIA.

I don't feel there is any need to explain the origins of this popular sign; the town has had four of them – one of which survives.

VICTORIA (HOTEL) 1 Market Square.

This is Victoria House, which still stands at the northwest corner of the Market, facing the Corn Exchange. Only two entries, 1864 and 1869.

VICTORIA TAVERN 65 Kingsthorpe Hollow.

This pub stood at the road junction at the top of Semilong Road. It was lost during redevelopment in the 1970s. Entries run from 1864 to 1973.

VICTORIA 2 Poole Street.

A purpose-built Victorian pub that's still with us, although it was for a time the Social Club of the Northampton Nene Angling Club. The earliest date I have for it is 1878 although the present sign over door declares that it was established in 1897. This photograph was taken when the Angling Club still had it. It is now flats (2017).

VICTORIA Victoria Street see **Britannia.**

VINE 38 Abington Street.
We have had two Vines in the town, but one was an abbreviation for the Hopvine, a different thing entirely. This sign wasn't because the proprietor wanted to indicate that wine was available, but because of a large vine that grew outside the door. This was cut down in the 1880s and the inn itself was demolished in 1958. The pub stood one door east from the corner of Fish Street.

An indication of its age can be got from a reference of 1891 to a landlord of 60 years before (circa 1831) and no indication that he was anything like the first. As I understand it the inn was originally on one site and the house next door was a pub *with no name.* This nameless pub was opened by Mr. James Durham in about 1830 who left some time later. On his departure the landlord of the Vine, a Mr. James Ager, moved to these premises and took the sign with him.

The freehold of the property appears to belong to a 16th century St. Giles' Estate Charity and in the 1950s still had 800 years to run.

VINE see **Hopvine.**

VOLUNTEER 32 Wellingborough Road also **Forget Me Not.**
Still with us, but with a pointless name. At first it was called the Forget Me Not, one of those whimsical names like the Welcome Inn. The name by which most Northamptonians know it by is the Volunteer, an old popular name recalling the Militia of the old days I wonder if George Garrett, the landlord at the time of the change might have been one of these men?

In 1994 the pub had a facelift and the landlord appealed for ideas for names of the bars that were being created. The result was the Mobbs Room after Colonel Edgar Mobbs whose memorial stands facing the names on the War Memorial opposite the pub and the Whistling Walter. Walter "The Whistler" Flint used to wander around the town in days gone by happily whistling to himself no particular tune I could ever discern – a loveable eccentric who has long gone.

WAGGON & HORSES 34 Bridge Street.

From the 17th century carriers were a vital part of the nation's trade. They would travel the land with their wagons stopping on the way to collect and deliver goods. Bridge Street with its national traffic would be an obvious site for this sign.

Wright 1884 has a 'v' after the proprietor's name so this confirms it as an establishment that provided victuals and accommodation. It no doubt goes back a lot further than its earliest appearance in a directory of 1824 and was probably in business at the time of the *Universal British Directory* of 1791, but, no doubt, was not 'posh' enough to rate a mention in it. The last entry was in 1906. It stood on the south side of the jitty in Bridge Street known as Francis Jitty, more or less opposite Angel Street.

WALLACE see **Welcome Inn.**

WARDS ARMS.

There is a family called Ward with local connections. Sir Edward (1638-1714) was chief Baron of the Exchequer and second son of William Ward of Preston, Rutland. He had Whig connections, so it could be a political sign.

The other possibility is that 'ward' is an occupation, as in 'warden' this sounds rather archaic and I don't believe that either of these two pubs is of any age. Both appear around 1900 neither lasted very long. Did the name have some short-lived significance that we are no longer aware of?

WARDS ARMS 55 Bridge Street also possibly **Crown(s)** and **Warwick Arms.**

Only two entries (1901 and 1905) neither give landlords' names, one gives a number and the number could indicate that this was the Crown(s).

WARDS ARMS 50 Lawrence Street.

This pub stood on the west corner of Oak Street and Lawrence Street. Beer-Retailers, 1878, the name, 1900, last entry 1910.

WARWICK ARMS 55 Bridge Street also possibly **Crown(s)** and **Wards Arms.**
The licence of this pub was given up and the proprietors, Mr. and Mrs. Bailey moved with the licence to the new Romany Hotel in 1938. Entries for this pub date from 1840 until 1938, but *Aubrey* 1940 and 1941 still have it in them.

WATERLOO ARMS 58 Gold Street.
The Battle of Waterloo on the 18th of June 1815 was one of the hardest fought in English history and the victory resulted in the creation of many place-names involving 'Waterloo' and 'Wellington'. This pub could have been one of them, although it is untraceable before 1893.

It stood on the north side of Gold Street a few doors from the junction with Horsemarket. *O/S* 1964 shows a small property at this number, so it was probably a beer-shop, although it doesn't appear in any of the Beer-Retailer lists I have consulted. It ran from 1893 to 1910 according to the directories.

WEDGEWOOD 79-81 Abington Street.
Originally, in the 1960s this was a restaurant, but Berni Inns purchased it and turned it into a pub-restaurant. It has been called the Mumu, later the Rhubarb Barrel and is at the time of writing boarded up (2017).

WELCOME INN 1 Upper Harding Street also **Hero of Scotland** and **Wallace.**
This is one of those pub names that use the word 'Inn' as an invitation; the other popular one (we haven't got one) is the 'Dew Drop Inn'. The earliest reference to this pub is 1845 when it was called the Hero of Scotland. Presumably the proprietor, Mr. George Roberts, was a patriotic Scot, for by 1864 it was being called

the Wallace and since the film Braveheart we all know who William Wallace was – or do we? Somewhere between 1878 and 1893 it changed to the Welcome and has stayed as such to this day. Became the 'Motown' around 2010 and by 2017 has ceased to be a pub and is now 'The Grafton Rooms'.

WELLINGTON 38 Albert Street also **Black's Head.**
This pub stood on the northeast corner of Albert Street and Lady's Lane. There is one appearance of a pub at this address in 1864 when it is called the Black's Head, it does not appear again until twenty years later when it is called the Wellington. It is possible that these are two separate pubs. The name Wellington runs from 1884 to 1911.

WELLINGTON ARMS 19 Wellington Pl. & 19 Barrack Rd.
Law 1847 shows Wellington Place as on the east side of Barrack Road from Bull Lane (Campbell Street) to Lawrence Street. According to *O/S* 1964 number 19 is a small shop opposite Regent House, part of a terrace, but distinguished from its fellows by a side entrance. It is now a patch of grass having been redeveloped. The name is a good one for a pub so close to the Barracks, for many years it was listed under Beer-Retailers (1845-1878), was first named in 1884, the last entry is in 1948.

WEST END TRAMCAR 126 St. James' Road see **Tram Car Tavern.**

WHARFINGER'S ARMS 7 Weston Street.
A Warfinger is a wharf owner. This pub stood on the east corner of the junction of Weston Wharf and Weston Street. The area went as part of the construction of St. Peter's Way. Entries run from 1845 until 1956.

WHEATSHEAF.
A popular sign, both locally and nationally, not only for pubs, but bakers. The arms of the Livery Companies of Innkeepers, Publicans, Bakers and Brewers all carry a wheatsheaf as a charge.

WHEATSHEAF Bridge Street.

Untraced from the *RBN* 1898 list of 16th and 17th century inns.

WHEATSHEAF 126 Dallington Road.

Dallington was a village outside the Borough so there is little information on its early days. It first appears in the directories in 1830 and I see no reason why it shouldn't be much older. The building is a Grade II Listed Building and is described as being 18th century. It is still a working pub.

WHEATSHEAF Gold Street also **White Hart.**

There is mention in a document of a White Hart on the north side of Gold Street in 1636 and I have also learnt that it was next door to the Three Tuns. By 1739, after the Great Fire of 1675, we have *White Hart now commonly called Wheatsheaf* although a deed of 1750 is still calling it the White Hart. The earlier date of 1636 is from an Abstract of Title of the Rose & Crown Inn dated 1767 from this document it is possible to work out that the inn occupied at least some of the site of the present Wilkinson's store. Directory dates run from 1824 to 1854.

It must have been of some substance as it had a cock-pit in the 18th century: - *AT THE WHEATSHEAF in Northampton, on Whitsun-Monday and Whitsun-Tuesday the 14th & 15th of May, will be a Match at Cock-fighting, between the Gentlemen of Daventry and Northampton, for 2 Guineas a Battel, and 10 Guineas the odd Battel. Each side to show 21 Cocks and Stags.*

Northampton Mercury, April 9, 1722

WHEATSHEAF 18 Regent Square.

The site of this pub, just inside the North Gate of the Medieval Town implies, along with the name, a possible early origin, however, the building must have been a replacement. The earliest directory entry is 1864 and the building could have dated from this period. The superb stucco-work shows that this could have only been a pub called the Wheatsheaf with the frontage surmounted by a stook of wheatsheaves. It closed as a pub in about 1957, but continued as a club for a time, it is now lost to road widening.

WHITE BEAR No Location.

The word 'bear' has been used as a pun on 'beer', a trade token, not local, of 1670 for an inn called the Bear has on it "Beware of ye Beare" – alluding to the beers strength. Anne, Richard III's Queen, daughter of the Earl of Warwick had a White Bear as her badge as a difference from her father's Bear & Ragged Staff and I think this is the most probabe explanation for the sign.

This inn is one from the **RBN** 1898 16th and 17th century list, but in this case I have found a reference from the Vernalls Inquest (property rights and disputes) of 1681 where there is mentioned a, *White Beare – widow Drables house.* Sadly, I do not know where Widow Drable lived.

WHITE ELEPHANT 2 Kingsley Park Road also **Kingsley Park Hotel** This is still with us and stands in a prominent position on the Kettering Road at the northern end of the Racecourse.

Throughout most of its existence this pub was known as the Kingsley Park Hotel and it was only in 1955 – 72 years after it was built that an application was made by the owners, Northampton Brewery Company to the magistrates to change the name to the White Elephant. I was ten at the time of the change, but I had always known it as the Elephant, even though it had "Kingsley Park Hotel" outside – one of childhood's mysteries!

The Racecourse was at one time an actual

racecourse. When racing began in 1727 this was a piece of Common Land well outside the town. The races proved to be very popular, even King Edward VII (1901-1910) attended on occasions. The pavilion still stands, set back from the Kettering Road and now a restaurant. As the land is Common Land it cannot be permanently fenced or paths diverted and this caused problems leading to some dangerous and fatal accidents during races. In 1901 a man ran out to rescue his son and both he and the rider were injured, the man dying from his injuries two years later. In March 1904 a horse swerved on a bend, struck a post and threw its rider. The horse then somersaulted over the fence, landing on a spectator and ran off into the crowd. This was the last straw and no more racing took place here.

This was not good news for the Kingsley Park Hotel; it had been built by a syndicate of 'Sporting Gentlemen' in 1883 as a residential club for owners, trainers and jockeys. Now only 21 years later it became redundant, standing as it did in splendid isolation outside the Borough at the top of a hill by a crossroads.

The other two roads at this crossroads ran to the villages of Kingsthorpe and Abington and in time gone by this junction was the place of public execution. Recently a concrete information ball has been sited on this corner of the Racecourse that declares that the gibbet was on the site of the White Elephant pub – this is incorrect; it was on the diagonally opposite corner to the tram shelter. Later it moved to public land i.e. the Racecourse proper. The condemned would leave the town by the East Gate and if legend be true gain their last drink at the Bantam Cock on Abington Square. They would then be conveyed along the Kettering Road to be hung here. In the early 1970s during the construction of an extension to a doctor's surgery in Abington Grove human remains were found that could have been the victims of the gibbet.

Thus the Kingsley Park Hotel stood near this unhallowed spot, a landmark, empty and isolated for 18 years and acquiring the apt epithet of 'The White Elephant'. But things move on and towns grow and in 1922 the Northampton Brewery Company purchased it and commenced trading, but it wasn't until 1955 that they applied to change the name. Dr. Eric Shaw, Chairman of the Magistrates said in granting the change, *"We hope that in its new official name the White*

Elephant will prosper over the years." If in the past one had to apply to the Magistrates to change a pub's name – **why not now?** They are part of our heritage and merely buying the property should no more give one the right to change its name as one the right to knock it down or paint it a silly colour!

WHITE HART.

We have had four of these, but it seems this is a sign that often changes to something else – only one of ours retained its original name throughout its career. The consensus of opinion is that it is the badge of Richard II. It seems that he declared in 1393 that all pubs must have signs and the theory is that many chose his badge.

WHITE HART (OLD) Cotton End.

This is still with us, its sign still in view as it is in mosaic set into the front of the building. The present building was constructed about 1900 and there is an inscription on the staircase newel "P. Phipps 1899". An old photograph shows a steep roofed (thatched?) building at right angles to the present one. The earliest reference I have to it is an advertisement for

patent medicine from the *Northampton Mercury* 1724, the last is 1966. The pub has been reopened by the Richardsons Group once more as a pub with the original name.

WHITE HART Drum Lane see **Shipman's.**
WHITE HART Gold Street see **Wheatsheaf.**
WHITE HART Market Square see **Trooper.**

"THE WHIT HIND"

In the 17th century there was a shortage of small change and many tradesmen issued their own tokens. An undated one from Northampton for a ¼ d. has: -

O: AT . THE . WHIT . HIND = a hind statent.
R: IN . NORTHAMPTON = G . E . E.

It was probably issued by one of the pubs listed above.

WHITE HILLS HOTEL Whitehills Way, Kingsthorpe.

This was, and still is, right on the Borough boundary. The pub was built in 1937-8 to serve the new Whitehills Estate. According to the *Real Ale Guide 1983* it is claimed to be the largest pub in town.

The name of the estate and pub derive from a pit of white sand that was here. It was purpose-built by the Northampton Brewery Company who surrendered the licence of the New Inn at Hackelton for it.

It seems a green spectre was seen in the cellars of this pub in 1978 passing through the walls and several barrels. I wonder if it affected the beer? Perhaps with a sand pit nearby there could have been plague burials in the past – it would explain the green colour.

WHITE HORSE.

I have found five White Horses in Northampton. The symbol of a horse has always been popular, whatever its colour if for no other reason it is easily recognisable. Often this sign can celebrate some local or national horse of renown. The White Horse was a standard of the Saxons and one of the chalk horses has become the badge of Kent. A galloping White

Horse was the device of the House of Hanover and it also occurs on the arms of Carmen, Coachmakers, Farriers, Saddlers, Wheelwrights and Innholders – so there has always been a good excuse to use it.

WHITE HORSE (OLD) 1 St. Andrew's Terr. and Grafton St.
St. Andrew's Terrace only is shown on *Law's* Map of 1847 at the acute corner made by Grafton Street and St. George's Street. *O/S* 1901 shows a short terrace of four dwellings and number one is probably at the Grafton Street end as the building shown has quite a large yard with an entrance through a gatehouse in Grafton Street.

There is only one reference to this establishment, in *Lea's* 1900-1. Oddly, this pub is not listed, but is in the form of a strip advertisement across the tops of pages 35-38: - *1 St. Andrew's Terrace & Grafton st. - OLD WHITE HORSE - (G. Britten, Proprietor).* It was probably short-lived and by *O/S* 1938 the area is shown as void house shapes that could be the present houses under construction.

WHITE HORSE Kingsthorpe.
In 2009 Tony Horner produced a map of Kingsthorpe based on the Inclosures Map of 1767; this shows the White Horse and its bowling  green across the road to the east.

The present White Horse is not the original building. In the past it had a reputation for its bowling green and cheesecakes. It is said that during Charles I's captivity at Holdenby he visited here to play on its famous green. During the War the house was used by Canadian and American troops as well as the Home Guard and as a result of its condition after the War it was decided to demolish it. The earliest date I have found in the directories is 1830, however from the *Mercury* we have: -

By Order of the Gentlemen.

THE BOWLING-GREEN AT THE White-Horse at Kingsthorpe. Near Northampton will be opened on Thursday the 9ᵗʰ of May 1751, and the Ordinary will be at Twelve o'Clock and continue every Thursday Fortnight following during the Bowling Season by Their obedient humble Servant. WILLIAM BARNARD.

Northampton Mercury, 6ᵗʰ May 1751.

Before the advent of the lawn mower in 1830 bowling-greens were cut by hand with shears and represented a considerable investment in time and effort, so this inn would have been of some local importance hence the King's visits in the previous century. The "Ordinary" referred to in the advertisement is a set meal at a set price and at a set time. The pub was closed in February 2009 and boarded up and planning permission sought for housing, its fate is still unknown (2017).

WHITE HORSE Marehold.
Untraced inn from the *RBN 1898* 16ᵗʰ and 17ᵗʰ century list.

WHITE HORSE 64 Sheep Street.
Although this pub features in many directories, I have no more on it. It was three doors along north of Church Lane, just south of St Sepulchre's churchyard. It had a victualler's licence in 1884; perhaps it never harboured a felon or drew the attention of the press in other ways, or felt the need to advertise? Dates run from 1824 to 1907.

DRUMMERS

WANTED immediately, SEVERAL experienced DRUMMERS – They will have good Wages, which will be paid them Weekly.

Apply to Sergeant Cole at the White-Horse, in Sheep Street, Northampton.

WHITE HORSE Horsemarket.
A good name for a pub in this street, two references. Document in the **NRO** 1640 describing a property in Horsemarket and mentions: - *signe of the White Horse on the South*, and an advertisement for letting the pub dated 1716.

WHITE LION

WHITE LION.

Although a fairly common sign the only explanation I've found is that it was the badge of Edward III. Northampton has had three White Lions.

WHITE LION Abington Street.

This inn was on the south side of Abington Street, about halfway between Fish Street and the end of Dychurch Lane. It definitely existed before the Great Fire of 1675 as it is mentioned in the Fire Court books in 1678. We also have references in St. Giles Parish records: -

1663 Imprimis. spent at our choice at the White Lyon 00-05-00
1666 April 26 Spent at the White Lyon at making the poor rolls
00-00-08
"   "   29 Spent at the White Lyon At the Visitatio 00-06-08

It had ceased to be an inn at the time of the writing of *NN&Q* (1890).

WHITE LION 7 Arthur Terrace, Kingsthorpe Road.

The site is now a block of flats *O/S* 1938 shows a property labelled "Inn" on the south corner of Arthur Street and Kingsthorpe Road.

WHITE SWAN 28 St. James' Street.

I have very little information about this pub. It appears to have stood on the west corner of St. James' Place and St James' Street, which were not in St James' End, but amongst the streets, now demolished to make St. Peter's Way car park, south of Marefair. Dates run 1864-1941.

WILLIAM IV 2 Commercial Street see **King William the Fourth.**

WINDMILL Market Square see **Queen's Arms.**

WINDMILL

Welford   Road,
Kingsthorpe.
This is a fine, early
19th   century
Northampton
sandstone   house
standing   beside   the

main road; it is a Grade II Listed Building. The first entry is in 1884 and it is still open. **Mercury** 1795-6 refers to this pub.

WOODBINE TAVERN 49 Upper Mounts.
The Woodbine or Honeysuckle was a popular image in days gone by. According to a 1920s book of household knowledge in my possession the woodbine flower symbolises devotion – a feeling the landlord may have wished to engender in his customers!

From the *O/S* Plans I calculate this pub must have been on the south side of the upper Mounts about halfway between the ends of Earl Street and Great Russell Street opposite. Dates run from 1893 to 1910.

WOOLPACK 25 Bridge Street.
A Woolpack is a pack of wool weighing 240lbs. This sign is common in wool producing areas such as here, once being an important wool market.

This inn stood on the west side of the street not far from the top and must have been of some importance as it is listed in the *Universal Directory* of 1791, there are directory dates until 1958. Earlier is, Mercury 1762-3 *with Bell (2017)*.

WOOLSTAPLERS' ARMS 8 Commercial Street.
According to **O/S** 1964 number 8 is two doors west of the King William the Fourth (King Billy) and if this numbering holds for the last century or so it must have been where the pub garden is now. The reason for the sign is probably the same as above, a woolstapler being a wool dealer. There are only two references to this pub, 1845 and 1864.

'X'.
There are no pubs starting with this letter, no Xebec, Xerxes, X-Rays or Xylophones, but 'X' can stand for the unknown and I have an alehouse with no known name. The illustration is of a possible

sign for a pub called The Xebec, a sailing vessel. So 'X' will stand for the Pub With No Name.

AN UNAMED ALEHOUSE 176? Bridge Street.

This establishment was to the north of the Crown & Anchor and adjoining it. Deeds often define a property by the properties around them. According to a deed of 1772 there was *to the north of the Guy of Warwick, later the Crown & Anchor, a property, now alehouse occupied by Amy Dray* – this is all we know of it, but at least we know the name of its proprietor. It seems to have been a humble alehouse and may never have had a sign.

YORK TAVERN.

We have had two of these, one in York Place and the other in York Road, so there is a simple explanation for their names. However, it is said that this sign was often given to a pub run by ex-soldiers and can be an abbreviation of the Duke of York.

YORK TAVERN 1 York Place and 7 Weston Street.

This pub stood on the southwest corner of York Place and Weston Street; that both disappeared under St. Peter's Way. The known proprietors are; William Jones 1864-1879 and Charles Henshaw 1884-1906, there are entries with no names from 1910 to 1933.

YORK TAVERN 35 York Road.

One entry for this pub, probably short-lived, G. M. Lewis 1936, it was at the north corner of the junction on York Road and St. Edmund's Road, now a shop.

'Z'.

Like 'X' - 'Z' has no pub name to represent it. A Zebra would make a good sign, as would a Zulu, Zeppelin, Zenith and Zodiac – even a Zero! We have had X – the pub with no name, so for Z I've chosen the last entry in. my book. The tribute to all the pubs that have been missed for one reason or another – a sort of Tomb of the Unknown Drinking House.

The sign I've designed for a Zeppelin

pub is based on an incident that took place in Northampton caused by the anti-German scares that were about just before the First World War. It seems that a Zeppelin was seen over the town shining its lights onto the roofs of the houses of unsuspecting and sleeping inhabitants. The sign is based on a drawing from a local publication showing an impression of the reported incident. However, it seems that Mr. Basset-Lowke had launched a gas balloon from his Kingswell Street premises with a lamp attached which had drifted over the town causing the 'Anti-Hun' panic!

UNAMED Location Unknown.

There must have been hundreds of unnamed pubs in Northampton's past. Many of the beer-shops in the 19th cent never had names, or they weren't smart enough to get printed in the directories. Many changed name at the whim of a new owner, or because of some political or historic event. Some appeared and quickly melted away – businesses still do this today. In older times if the alehouse, inn or what-have-you didn't get a mention on some deed or other and that document didn't survive, we now have no knowledge of it. Much damage was done by the Great Fire of 1675, destroying not only many inns and taverns but also much of the town's documents. There will always be a host of pre-1675 pubs about which, without new discoveries, we will never know.

.oOo.

A Drinker's Lament.

When I was young in this town,
more years than I care to remember,
pubs and inns did abound
on every street and corner.

We carried on that war-time custom
of pub-to-pub crawl.
We trod the length of Bridge Street-
but we never drank in 'em all!

Each inn and tavern had its character
and so did all the bar-staff.
The beer tasted different from place to place
at a shilling for a half.

The Ram the Mitre and the Bell,
The Spotted Dog and Swan
fallen, have all these pubs,
into memory they've long gone.

But, oh! what memories we all have
of pubs and inns long past,
and recollections of those faces that,
peopled those old bars!

Thank God those old boys that we knew
didn't live to see what's done-
the knocking down or the tarting up
of good pubs one by one!

So now we're left, and so bereft
of the pubs we used to drink in!
The Signs have gone – the pubs have gone
and 'Theme Pubs' are the in thing!

So drink deep, and drink long
on ale that *claims* it's true,
and try to remember now and then
when pubs were real too!

J. A. Small 1993.

TARIFFS

In a couple of the old Directories, the Northampton Directory 1878 and Deacon's Directory 1890 there are price lists for the Phoenix Brewery and P. Phipps & Co. Respectively.
Here are a few examples:-

Phipps: No.10 Ale Extra Strong, Old. 2s..0d.
          No.4 Light Ale.   0s..10d.
          XX Porter.   1s..2d.
Phoenix: XX Households   1/-.
          NBC Imperial Stingo   2/-.
          E.D.S. Extra Stout.   1/6.

The prices seem cheap enough, but then you realise that they are for a *gallon* and it's delivered free! For those who are too young or have forgot the old money there was 240 pennies in a pound and 12 pennies in a shilling, 20 shillings to the pound. Prices such as, 1/4d meant one shilling and four pence, 36s equalled one pound and sixteen pence and could be written - £1..16s..0d. A new penny (1p) is equivalent to 2.4d. For example, the wage was in the boot and shoe trade around the 1890s; for a machine minder, was about £1 or 20/-, whilst a skilled man, such as a clicker would get about £1..10s..0d or 30/- (£1.50p).

NEW PUBS & CHANGES

The cut off date for pubs in this book is 1993 and the final draft has been written now, in 2010. In the almost seventeen years since I started to assemble the material into a book many new pubs have appeared (and disappeared!) and several old pubs have changed their names, sometimes more than once. This appendix is an attempt to keep track of some of them – it's not exhaustive because, frankly things move so fast these days I just haven't had the time or inclination to keep track of what in many cases are little more than short lived 'drinking barns'.

For the second edition I am revising the lists as of September 2017. I predicted that there would be a nostalgia reaction in the future and some silly names would revert and some new ones would have more thoughtful names. This has, to an extent, happened, the converted bank was the Rat & Parrot, but later became the Old Bank and Lloyds No.1 became the Eastgate more or less on the location of the East Gate of the Norman town, now sadly is a burger bar.

Although we've lost many pubs over the last few years and many have become drinking barns or gastro/winebar/bars there has been some good events. The Richardson Group opened the Charles

Bradlaugh in 1997, the Picturedrome in 1998 and reopened the Old White Hart in 2005. They also opened in 2005 The Church Restaurant at the bottom of Bridge Street. This was established around 1140 as a hospital (the forerunner of the modern pub, see intro.) and became a church in the late nineteenth century. This is the oldest secular building in the Town and it could be argued the oldest drinking house of all.

The Pomfret Arms has been re-furbished and re-opened by the Felce brothers (see entry) and they now have the Cotton End Brewery up and running and producing some fine real ales.

In 2011 Paul and Alyson Hepworth opened a completely new pub, The Olde England on the Kettering Road and later another pub (The Olde England 2) in Wellingborough; they now have yet another pub in this town, The Black Prince, alias The Racehorse on Abington Square which now houses J. Church brewery.

In 2008 Alaric Neville started with a brewery by reviving the Phipps Company and in 2015 the Phipps' Albion Brewery Bar opened in Kingswell Street.

In November 2016 Terry Steers and Adam Case (and Stella, the dog) opened the St. Giles' Ale House (no brewery as yet)!

No too bad, several good pubs serving quality real ales and three new breweries!

NAME CHANGES, NEW PUBS AND CLOSURES
"Errors & Omissions Excepted."
These lists, like the earlier ones are not complete due to, confusing opening and closures, name changes and the sometimes difficulty of identifying a true pub from some restaurant that serves beer.

One pub not listed is the Angel, (briefly called the Fat Cat) gutted by fire in 2012 it is said that it is to be rebuilt as it was – we'll see.
CLOSED
Some pubs have appeared since the first edition and are now gone. Others appear to be clubs now and some changed names before the end.
Barn Owl –closed.
Blarney Stone – Cobblers. – closed.

Broadmead – closed.
Bull & Butcher – club.
Castle – closed.
Clicker – closed.
Cricketers' Arms – closed.
Duke of Edinburgh – closed
Golden Lion – demolished.
Half-Way House – demolished.
Harbour Lights. – Bar Koda – Jacksons – Jolly Anker – club.
Lloyds No.1 – Eastgate – closed.
Hogshead – Bar Me – closed
King William IV, Kingsthorpe – closed.
Moon on the Square. – closed.
Morris Man – demolished.
Penny Whistle – downsized.
Prince of Wales – closed.
Shipman's – closed (for now?).
Silver Cornet – demolished.
Silver Horse – closed.
Sportsman's Arms – closed.
Victoria – closed.
Wedgewood – Butler's – closed.
Welcome Inn – closed.
White Horse, Kingsthorpe – closed.
Workhouse, Gold Street – Patriot. Closed.
Workhouse, Wellingborough Road – Bootleggers – closed.
NEW PUBS
Auctioneers.
Charles Bradlaugh.
Ecton Brook.
Five Ale Bar – Bar Serengeti.
Goose on Two Streets – Fox & Quill.
Lakeside.
Lighthouse (The).
Lloyds No.1 – Eastgate – closed.
Lord Byron.
Picturedrome.

Sir Pickering Phipps.

NAME CHANGES
If the change in is the main text,or it has closed it will not be here.
Bantam Cock – Danny Boys – Finnegan's Wake – Monkey's Head –
The Bantam.
Bear – Groggers Rest – Macgregors – Wolf on Sheep Street – Bear.
Belvedere – Baroque.
Bird-in-Hand. – Edge of Town.
Black Lion – Wig & Pen.
Britannia, Barrack Road. – Five Rivers.
Cock Hotel – The Cock.
Criterion – Boston Clipper – Boston.
Fagins – Mollys – O'Conners Bar. – Bar So.
Fiddler Maguire – Fiddlers.
Fish – Tommy Flynn – Market Tavern.
Five Bells (Old) – Frog & Fiddler.
Fox & Hounds – Dusty Fox – Fox & Hounds.
Hare & Hounds. . Hopping Hare.
Jolly Crispin – Cookoo's Nest.
King William IV, Bridge Street – Fitchet & Firkin – King Billy's –
King Billy Rock Bar.
Old House at Home – Old House.
Princess Royal – Cock & Bull – Jekyll & Hyde.
Racehorse – Black Prince.
Rat & Parrot – Old Bank.
Red House – Big Hand Mo's – Sevens.
Rifle Butt(s) – Hart of Duston.
T.P. Woods – Smithy's Palace. – Tabasco Jazz – Decadence – NBs –
The Pub With no Name.
Volunteer – O'Malley's – Punch & Judy – Volunteer.
Yates – Cordwainer.

SOURCES

BOOKS.

Cox. J.C. 1898 *The Records of the Borough of Northampton.* Northampton, The Borough of Northampton. (*"RBN* 1898" in text).
Rev. W. D. Sweeting (ed.) 1886-1891. *Northamptonshire Notes and Queries.* Northampton, John Taylor The Dryden Press (*"NN&Q"* in text, the author "**Taylor**").
All available Northampton Street Directories from 1791 until 1973.
Other books quoted from &c. are referred to in the text in *bold Italics*.

MAPS & PLANS.

Goad's Insurance Plans 1898-1954, copies at the Central Library (**Goad's Insurance** in text).
Ordnance Survey Plans, 1:500 1st Edition 1885, and 1:2500 various Editions 1985-1964, copies at the Central Library (*O/S* in text).
Old brewery estate department plans kept at Northamptonshire Record Office ("**NRO**" in text).
Schematic plan for the Great Election 1768, copy at the Central Library.

DOCUMENTS.

All relevant material held by Northamptonshire Record Office.
The local newspapers, both ancient and modern, especially the *Northampton Mercury* and the *Chronicle & Echo*.
Finally, one most important source of clues, information and stories - all the old boys (and girls) who over the years have regaled me with tales of the old pubs of Northampton Town.

PICTURE CREDITS

I would like to thank the following for the use of photographs and illustrations.
Northamptonshire Libraries and Information Service for the use of photograph of the Ram Hotel, drawing of the Cook's Arms and woodcut of Guy of Warwick in the Bearward Arms entry.
Northamptonshire Newspapers for the use of photographs of the Admiral Nelson, Plough hotel and Queen's Arms.

ABBREVIATIONS AND CONVENTIONS.
All quotations are in *italics* without quotation marks.
References to publications are in *italics and bold type*.
Directories usually have just the name of the Directory and the
year of publication e.g. "*Wright* 1884".
C&E = Chronicle & Echo.
'bhs' = Beer House Keeper (Wright's Directory 1884).
BVM = Blessed Virgin Mary.
N.B.C. = Northampton Brewery Company.
N.D.C. = Northampton Development Corporation.
NN&Q = Northamptonshire Notes and Queries.
N.R.O. = Northamptonshire Record Office.
O/S = Ordnance Survey.
RBN = Records of the Borough of Northampton.
'v' = victualler (Wright's Directory 1884).
VCH = Victorian County History.

FUTURE
As I mentioned at the beginning of this book under "Illustrations" I
would like this to be Volume One, this largely being documentary
information. Volume Two I would like to the edited material
supplied by *you*; your anecdotes, photographs documents or anything
relevant to Northampton's past pubs and those that ran them and used
them.
There is bound to be errors in a book like this and for these I
apologise and I would be grateful if people would let me know of any
they find.

Beer is proof that God loves us and wants us to be happy.
Benjamin Franklin 1706-1790.

He is a wise man who invented beer.
Plato.

.oOo.

NORTHAMPTON PUB MAP

This map was originally designed as a separate publication, but I felt that it would be useful to include it in the actual book. The original map covers a slightly larger area (A2) and can be still purchased if desired.

The map consists of eight sections, each with an overlap so one doesn't get lost and there is an extra one to cover the lower part of Bridge Street. Each of the nine sections has a small number towards the top of it. The map covers N-S from Regent Square to South Bridge and W-E the Railway station to St. Giles' Church.

The map is based on an original of 1891. A prison stood on the Mounts and the then recently opened Cattle Market (1873) was located south of Market Road, now called Victoria Promenade. Several streets have changed names since 1891. The signs I've used are the old familiar ones, the main entries in the text.

Pubs cover many topics and themes such as; Heraldry *(Eagle & Child)*, Trades *(Saddlers' Arms)*, Religion *(The Angel)*, Sports and Games *(Bicycle Tavern, Fox & Goose)*, Historical events *(American Banner)*, Politics *(Lord Palmerston)*, Famous Racehorses *(Bees Wing)*, and Locomotives *(Morning Star)*.

1	2	3	4
5	6	7	8
		9	

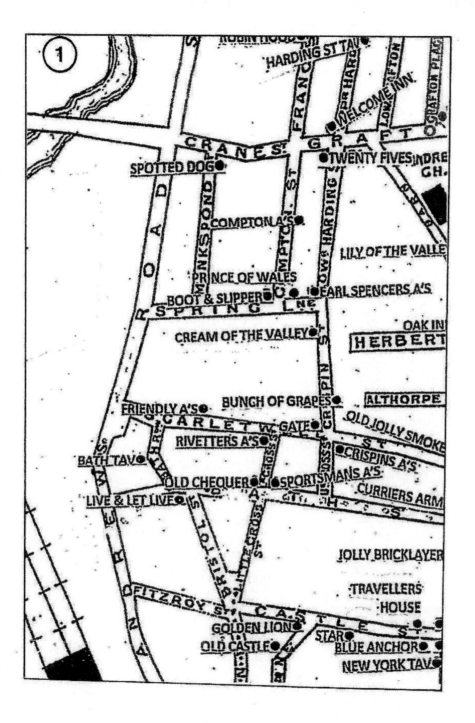

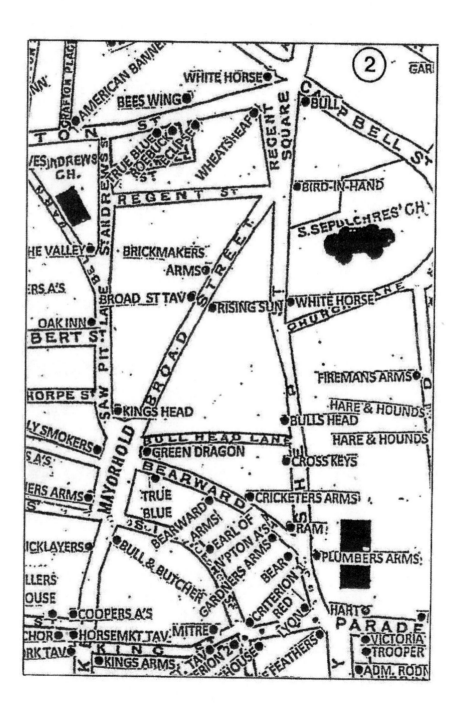

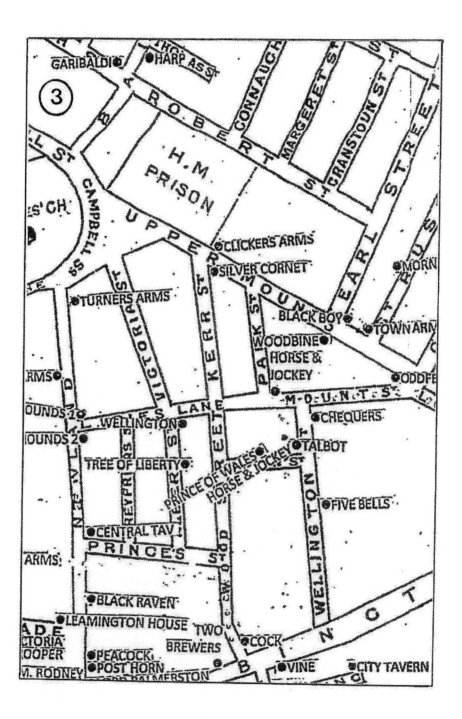

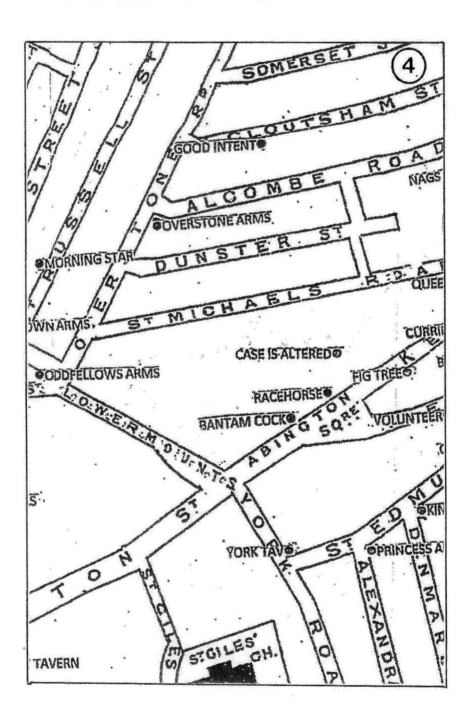

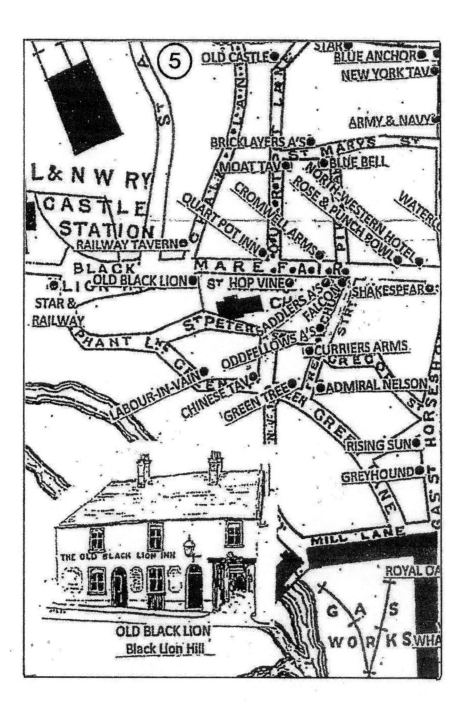

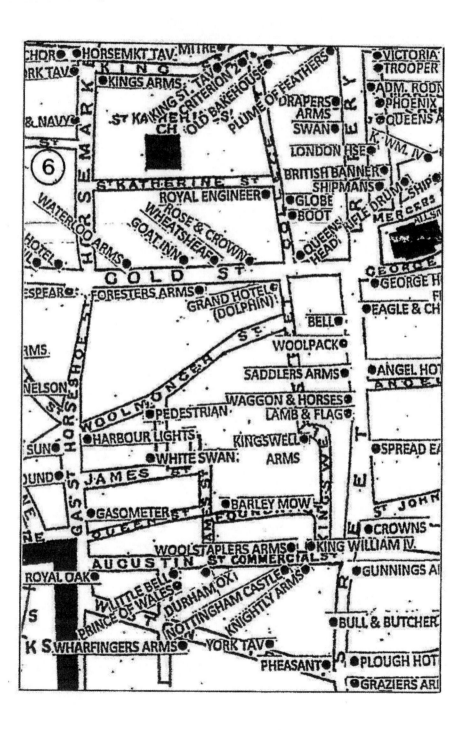

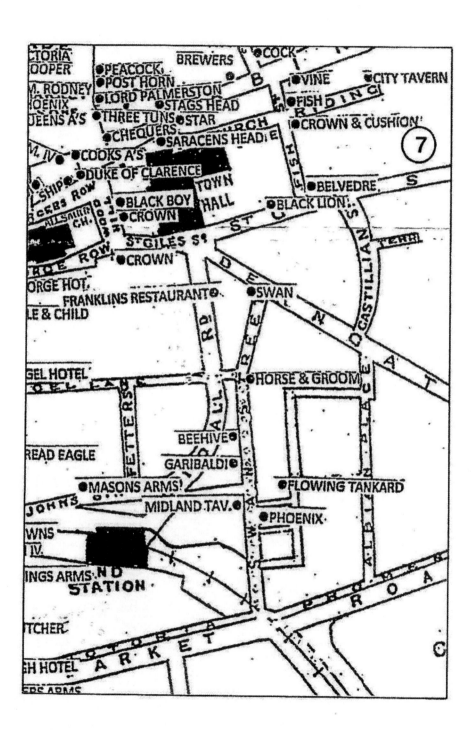

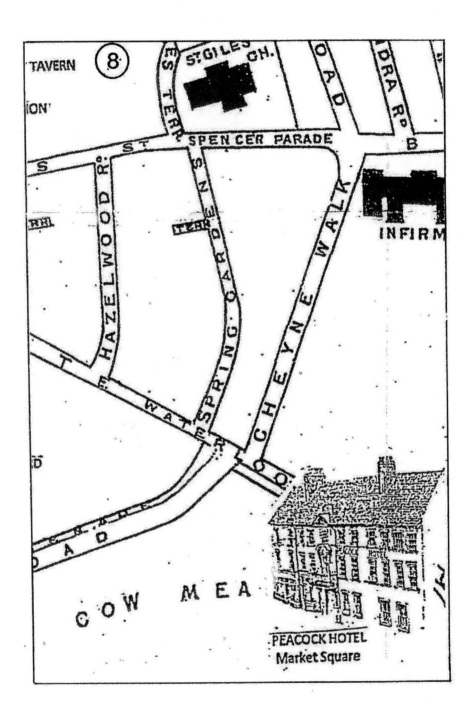

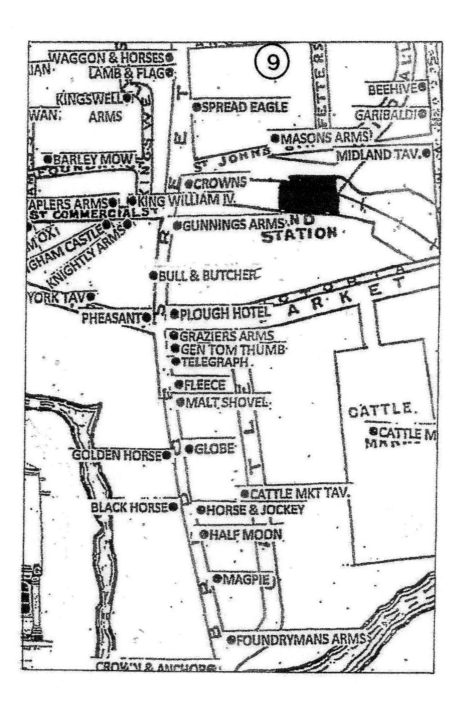